Katherine Wilson was born and raised in Washington, DC and graduated from Princeton University. She has lived in Italy for the past twenty years, working in television, film and theatre. Most recently, she acted in Giuseppe Tornatore's *The Best Offer* with Geoffrey Rush and Donald Sutherland. She lives in Rome with her husband and two children.

katherinewilsonwriter.com

Facebook.com/KatherineWilsonWriter

'A glorious memoir celebrating the holy trinity of Italian life: love, food and family. Her keen eye and sense of humor takes you through the winding streets of Naples at a clip, on a ride you hope will never end. If you love Italy, or the idea of it, you will love this book. And, if you ever plan to visit Naples, tuck this in your suitcase, it's the best primer I've ever read as a guide to this bustling, vibrant southern Italian port city'

Adriana Trigiani, *New York Times* bestselling author of *The Shoemaker's Wife*

'Deliciously entertaining'   *Sunday Mirror*

'This warm, witty biography made me yearn for (and eat) quite a lot of pasta'   *Red*

'You won't be able to put dowr
of titbits from Neapolitan cultu
you enjoyed: *Eat, Pray, Love* b

D1334246

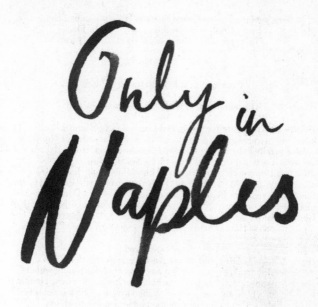

Only in Naples

Lessons in Food and Famiglia

KATHERINE WILSON

FLEET

2017

FLEET

First published in the United States in 2016 by Random House
First published in Great Britain in 2016 by Fleet
This paperback edition published in 2017 by Fleet

1 3 5 7 9 10 8 6 4 2

Copyright © 2016 by Katherine Wilson

A CIP catalogue record for this book
is available from the British Library.

ISBN 978-0-349-00632-1

Printed and bound in Great Britain by
Clays Ltd, St Ives plc

Papers used by Fleet are from well-managed forests
and other responsible sources.

Fleet
An imprint of
Little, Brown Book Group
Carmelite House
50 Victoria Embankment
London EC4Y 0DZ

An Hachette UK Company
www.hachette.co.uk

www.littlebrown.co.uk

For my parents, Edward and Bonnie Wilson,
and for my sister, Anna

INTRODUCTION

In Greek mythology, Sirens hang out on the rocky cliffs near Naples with their gorgeous curly hair, singing songs that entice sailors to the coast. They draw ships in with their voices, luring them to danger—to shipwreck, to death. No one hears their song and comes out alive.

Odysseus was desperate to hear it. The song was meant to be sweeter than anything in the world, and he wanted to be the only human being to experience it and live to tell the tale. So, with a mix of pride, curiosity, and smarts, he made a plan. He got earplugs for his crew and had them tie him to the mast. When his ship passed the Sirens, he screamed to his men to untie him, to change course and head toward land. They didn't, and he survived.

Afterward, I'm sure Odysseus was glad that his crew didn't listen, that his earplugged employees kept him safe. But I'm also sure that he wanted to go back. Not just to see and hear the Sirens, but to set foot on the magical land under the volcano that was called Neapolis, the New City.

And this was before pizza was even invented.

I did not arrive in Naples tied to a mast. I arrived on a packed Delta flight from Washington, D.C., in the fall of 1996. There were no Sirens, but I was sucked in and transformed all the same. My head was full of collegiate curiosity; my body was full of appetites that I didn't quite know what to do with.

Goethe said, "See Naples and die." I saw Naples and started to live.

Only in Naples

'A Pizza

When Salvatore sputtered up in his tiny red Fiat for our first meeting, he was over twenty minutes late. The car looked like a tin can and sounded like it was on its last legs. It spat a steady stream of exhaust, and I started to cough. Salvatore responded with two short honks of his horn and a big smile.

It was the first time I was meeting this guy, and he was twenty minutes late. What was *that*?

I was fresh out of college, and had arrived in Naples a few days earlier to start a three-month internship at the U.S. Consulate there. I was standing outside the entrance of the boarding school where I rented a room, wearing a boxy blue jacket with black trousers.

My internship wasn't as much a career move as it was a rite of passage—members of my family did an "experience abroad" during or after college. Big leather photo albums in my parents' attic in Washington show my father Waspy and smiling in Bordeaux in 1961; my mother all sueded out in Bologna in 1966. They had learned foreign languages, and they'd had the time of their lives. Now that it was my turn, where was I going to go?

Naples was not a logical destination. When I'd visited Italy on vacations as a kid, we avoided the city or passed through it as quickly as we could to get to Pompeii or Vesuvius. Naples was dirty and dangerous, we heard. My grandfather, whose parents were from Calabria, said that Neapolitans could steal your socks without taking your shoes off.

"You really should go to Tuscany," family friends had told me. "Have you seen Siena? Florence?"

The serene splendor of Tuscany would have been appropriate for an upper-class girl like me. It felt like what I was supposed to do, and I'd always been very good at doing what I was supposed to do. I spent my childhood overachieving at private schools, and in college I could have majored in Surpassing Expectations or Making Mommy and Daddy Proud. It was time for a change.

The American consul of Naples was a fellow alum of my parents' graduate school of international relations. I'd been seated next to him the previous spring at a fundraising dinner in Washington, and he asked me if I'd considered Naples for my experience abroad. He could arrange an unpaid internship in the political office of the Consulate if I was interested.

Naples?

I thought, Stolen socks and wallets, the Mafia, and corruption. I also thought, Pizza. I was intrigued.

I bounced the idea off people who asked what I was going to do after graduation. "I was thinking of going to Naples," I told them. That was when I got the Look. The Look was a wide-eyed, *beware* facial expression, accompanied by warnings of "It's filthy!" "It's dangerous!" and even "The good guys and the bad guys all look alike! There's no way to tell the difference!"

Aha, I thought. Sounds fascinating.

I now know that Naples is like New York City: you either

love it or you hate it. And if you love it, there's no use proselytizing. Those who hate it will not be converted. There is a chaotic, vibrant energy about Naples that forces you to let go and give in. If you fight it, judge it, or even hide from it, you might as well get out before you get your wallet snatched.

Lucky I hadn't gotten my wallet snatched waiting for this Salvatore guy, I thought, as he opened the creaking door of his car and got out to introduce himself. I mean, *twenty minutes?*

It had been Salvatore's mother, Raffaella Avallone, who had found me the room at the boarding school where I was staying. After working out the details of the internship, I had asked the consul's help with housing. He immediately passed the issue on to his wife, an Italian *signora* who hung out not only with diplomats but also Neapolitan society. She knew that the lady who got things done at benefit lunches, charity galas, and bridge tournaments was Raffaella Avallone. Plus, Raffaella had two kids this girl's age!

And so Raffaella learned that there was a young woman in need of a *sistemazione*, a setup. *Mi sono mossa subito* is the expression she would use. I got myself moving. She found me a place to stay and told her son Salvatore that there was an American girl whom he was to call and meet up with. "Salva?" she said. "Take her out. The poor girl knows no one here. And please, don't be late."

The next day I got a call from Salvatore. The telephone was a challenge, as my Italian was very basic and I could only communicate concepts like "I am hungry" and "I am American." Although I didn't understand most of what Salvatore said, I thought his laugh was adorable. Plus, I didn't know a soul in Naples. The night before, I'd gone out for dinner with two seventeen-year-old boys I had met on a bus. I wanted to be *in compagnia*. So I was glad that, if I had understood correctly, this

Salvatore was going to pick me up the next evening. Worst-case scenario, I figured, I could practice my Italian.

"You don't look American!" I thought I understood him to say after he introduced himself. Well, he didn't look typically Neapolitan, either. He was tall; not muscular, but long and narrow, with a thin torso that emptied into a little pool of tummy that hung over the button of his jeans. His skin was tanned, his lips full, his nose big and Roman. He was wearing a T-shirt that said MIAMI! in bubble letters.

I was expecting "Nice to meet you, sorry I'm late," but there was no apology, no niceties, no "What do you want to do?" There was, however, that adorable laugh again. It was a laugh on an inhale, which started at a high pitch and came down the scale to end at the note of his speaking voice. It was accompanied by a smile that showed lots of perfect white teeth.

He opened the passenger door, and the seat squeaked as I sat down. Salvatore seemed too big for this tiny car—his black hair stuck with static to the top. I noticed that his fingernails on the steering wheel were such perfect ovals that they could only have been shaped by a manicurist. He was a boy, not yet a man, who ate and lived well.

Salvatore's style of driving did not necessitate keeping his eyes on the road. He looked me in the eyes and tried out his horrific English, with no apologies for messing up his verb forms. How could a boy of twenty-three be so confident? I felt infantile, passive, silent. Try to say something in Italian! I told myself. Like, for example, Where are we going? You can't have *zero* control of the situation!

"*Dove andiamo?*"

"To my apartment. America! America! *Petrol-dollari!*" American oil dollars? Did he have some idea that I was super-rich from oil? I now know that thanks to the TV show *Dallas*, lots of Italians believe that if Americans have money, it's thanks to Texas oil. But in the car that first evening, I didn't know where this expression came from—only that Salvatore greatly enjoyed saying it. Over and over.

And then there was that laugh again.

"My" apartment, for a twenty-three-year-old Neapolitan, did not mean a dorm room or a flat with a roommate. It meant his *parents'* apartment. I had assumed that we would go to a pizzeria or that he would show me around the city. Instead he was bringing me home to Mamma and Papà.

The Avallones lived a short drive from my boardinghouse in Posillipo, the nicest residential area of Naples. Named Pausilypon by the Greeks—meaning "rest from toils"—the hill is the high end point of the promontory that juts out into the Bay of Naples. For thousands of years, before the area became part of the city, the Neapolitan upper classes would summer here in the villas that dot the coastline. Winding up the panoramic Via Posillipo, you can see the stone markers for Villa Elena, Villa Emma, Villa Margherita. Steps lead from these villas down to Marechiaro, the clear sea.

Although the city of Naples is one of the densest in Europe, Posillipo is airy and peaceful. The Avallones' building is opposite the entrance to the Virgiliano, a terraced park with views of the electric blue water and the islands of Capri, Ischia, and Procida, as well as the Amalfi coast. During the day, you can hear the squawks of seagulls; in the evening, the occasional buzz of a motorbike or distant fireworks over the ocean.

You think you're from Posillipo is a Neapolitan expression meaning you're a snooty ass, get off your high horse.

The Avallones' palazzo, which Salvatore's father had built in the 1960s, was set inland. It had twelve apartments, nine of which were owned by the family. The building had survived the massive 1980 earthquake unscathed (although Salvatore later told me he remembered leaving the soccer match he was watching on TV and running down steps that swayed and swelled like the ocean). The palazzo was theirs and it was built well, in a place of beauty and rest.

We pulled into an underground garage maze. It was unbelievable how many vehicles at how many different angles were parked in such a small space. They were nose to nose, side window to side window, bumper to bumper. I was confused: there was so much space outside! ("What," Salvatore would respond when I asked him about it later, "people don't steal cars where you come from?")

He parked the little Fiat between two other cars in one swinging, expert maneuver and led me to the elevator. I hadn't smelled the sea air. I smelled mildew and humidity and exhaust fumes.

We were silent in the tiny elevator that brought us to the third, and highest, floor. Salvatore opened the door to the Avallones' apartment with a bulky silver key and showed me in. "*Vieni, vieni,*" he said as he dumped the keys on an eighteenth-century chaise longue at the entrance to the living room. From the foyer, I peeked into the dark, elegant *salone*, where I could make out statues of gold cherubim and folds of heavy silk. Terracotta vases stood on pedestals.

I waited to see what would come next.

"*Mammmmma!*" he called. That resonant tenor voice that I had found so charming in the car was grating and nasal when he called his mamma. I was beginning to dread meeting his parents. It was hard enough to understand Italian and speak with someone my own age: the last thing I felt up for now was conversing with an imposing, formal, wealthy Neapolitan woman who was surely protective of her son. On her own turf! Also, I was ravenously hungry.

"*Mammmmmma! È pronto?*" (Is dinner ready? Wasn't he going to say that the American girl was here?) I heard the shuffling of bedroom slippers and in came a man whom I took to be Salvatore's father. About seventy, he was not a scary patriarch, but a gentle, distinguished man wearing a dark sweater and lots of cologne. We shook hands and he introduced himself as Nino. He spoke some English, thanks to the thirty years he had spent managing his family's luxury hotel.

"*Salvató, è pronto 'a magnà?*" Nino reverted to Neapolitan dialect to ask his son if dinner was ready, grabbing Salva's arm. He was as hungry as the rest of us.

I was led into the kitchen, where Raffaella was getting off the phone as she took the homemade pizza out of the oven and closed the refrigerator with her heel. It was all movement, all action, all graceful. She wasn't fat and stationary and stirring pasta sauce. She was gorgeous.

About five foot four and fit, Raffaella wore high-heeled boots and a pink oxford shirt. Her white jeans were tight and cinched at the waist with a rhinestone-studded leather belt. She was fully made up: lip liner melded into gloss, eyeliner smudged naturally into charcoal eye shadow. Her hair was short and blond, highlighted expertly. Despite the sparkles and heavy-handed makeup, her look was in no way trashy, only glamorous. I felt large and gawky in my blue blazer and baggy pants. My mother had called the outfit "slenderizing" in a spacious Washington dressing room, but next to this fifty-six-year-old in white jeans, I didn't feel slenderized. I felt like a silent American slug.

"*Ciao tesoro!* Honey, have a seat. I hope you like Neapolitan pizza! Nino, scoot your chair over."

When Raffaella moved, whiffs of Chanel perfume cut through the aroma of baked dough and basil. The *salone* of the apartment may have been opulent but the kitchen was minuscule. On the right side, a rectangular Formica table was built into the checkered tile wall and sat four people at most. The stove, oven, sink, and some (very limited) counter space were on the left. If more than two people were eating at the table, nobody could pass to get to the refrigerator at the back of the kitchen. Why would any family who clearly had money not build a bigger kitchen? I wondered.

As it turned out, extra space was reserved for the living room with its dining niche, where the Avallones ate when they had guests. The kitchen was for cooking and eating *in famiglia*. You can scooch around and bump into family, after all. Lean over them, step on them, feed and be fed by them. A lot of space isn't really necessary when you're with people you love.

There was no place at the table for Raffaella, but fortunately she wasn't planning on sitting. She was planning on doing at least eight other things, including making the American girl feel at home. At some point Salvatore's older sister, Benedetta, arrived, squeezed in, and introduced herself. She was twenty-six, three years older than Salvatore, and had intimidating turquoise eyes framed by thin Armani glasses. Her light brown hair was long and silky straight, and swished like that of the coolest girls in high school. Strangely (it was only 8:00 in the evening), she was wearing pajamas, decorated with pink and white teddy bears holding balloons, with a ruffle at the neck. *Mi piace star comoda*, she would tell me later. When I'm at home I like to be comfy. Her brother was wearing his comfy T-shirt and jeans and she was in her comfy PJs. Only their mother had spent time getting done up.

"*Benedetta lavora, capito? Ha iniziato a lavorare in banca,*"

Nino was telling me. His eyebrows were raised and he was grinning. He was clearly very proud of his daughter, and repeated several times that she was already working at the age of twenty-six. She works in a bank, already! This was very early for Naples, I inferred. She had finished university with top grades and in record time, and had been hired by the Banca di Roma in Naples to consult with clients about their investments. She had a *contratto a tempo indeterminato*—a no-end-in-sight contract, meaning that she could not be laid off *ever* and could retire at fifty-five. Life was good: she had hit the jackpot with her job and was planning on getting married the next summer.

"*Matrimonio! Matrimonio!* Wedding, do you know?" Nino was positively jolly. I interjected "*Veramente?*" (Really?) every once in a while and "*Mamma mia!*" to demonstrate my awe. So this slick, superconfident Salvatore was the brown-eyed little brother of the whiz kid with the turquoise eyes. That had to suck.

Raffaella, meanwhile, was saying something about a *multa* as she drizzled olive oil over the steaming pizza. Who had gotten this 50,000-lira parking ticket and who was going to schlep to the post office tomorrow to pay it? If I had known then that *multa* meant a parking ticket and that Salvatore was saying that he was nowhere *near* Via Toledo on that Tuesday at the end of June, and Benedetta was saying that her brother was the only one in the family who regularly *quadruple*-parked, I probably would have stopped saying *veramente* and *mamma mia* at regular intervals.

"Me? Absolutely impossible." Raffaella was now being accused by Benedetta, and she froze to make her case, the scalding pizza in an oven mitt suspended above Nino's head. Everyone seemed to have forgotten about me. Salva was going at it with his sister, Nino was looking around wondering when his pizza was going to appear, Raffaella was still talking about her whereabouts on that Tuesday at the end of June. I realized that this was just family business as usual.

Finally Raffaella placed the first slice of pizza on a plate and passed it over her husband's head to me. Salvatore's eyes, for the first time since we had arrived at his apartment, had settled on me.

What kind of a girl is she? How will she eat this pizza?

I understood immediately that it was important to everyone at the table that evening what I thought of the pizza. The pizza was hot, gooey, and thick—impossible to eat with my hands. So I picked up my knife and fork and tasted it. Objectively speaking, it was the best pizza I'd ever had. But my language skills were not yet sufficient to communicate that. So I said something like, "Pizza great yes thank you very much Salvatore family tomato pizza."

And then there was that laugh again.

I laughed too; it was a laughingly delicious pizza.

This was the first of many times that year that my eating would be a performance. The cacophony of voices would stop, silence would reign, and all eyes would focus on me as I dug in. I would feel enormous pressure as I twisted the spaghetti or cut into a pizza. (Will I flick a piece? Will I miss my mouth? Do I need to finish chewing before I begin the praise?) The question on everyone's mind would be, "What does the chick from the world's superpower think of *this*?" And I would satisfy them. *Mamma mia!* Phenomenal! *Buonissimo!* Never tasted anything like it!

And then I made a big faux pas, a *brutta figura*, as they say in Italian. I started eating the crust before the rest of my pizza was finished. Salvatore got up, came around to where I was wedged between Nino and Benedetta, leaned over me, and cut the rest for me in little pieces. He held my fork and knife in his beautiful manicured hands and I could smell his aftershave, his eyes keeping contact with me the whole time. He was so close!

"These pieces you must eat first," he told me, "not the crust! Always the crust last!" More words were coming at me so fast that it was difficult to understand. What I did get was just how invested he was in how my pizza was going to be consumed. I had potential. He just had to show me the ropes.

I managed to finish the pizza without dropping anything or further embarrassing myself. But some crumbs had fallen on my lap (my paper napkin was crumpled up in my tense, sweaty hand). Raffaella had spun around from the sink and was standing over me. She was silent, and still . . . and eyeing my lap. Before I knew it, she had plunged her hands—emerald ring, manicured nails—into my crotch. What the fuck is happening? I thought.

"*Briciole, briciole,*" she explained. I will never as long as I live forget the Italian word for crumbs, *bree-cho-lay.* There was no annoyance, just a job to be done before the crumbs got all over the apartment. Why would it constitute a problem that they were located in my private parts?

Raffaella started singing a song about a pizza with tomato. It had a "Funiculì, Funiculà" rhythm about it, and she twitched her hips as she sang it. *Conosci questa?* Do you know this one? she asked. Her voice was deep, rich, belting. Everyone else kept talking, mostly about practical matters. So many logistics tied the daily life of this family together, parents and kids in their midtwenties connected by the traffic ticket and when's the plumber coming to fix the leaking toilet? It seemed so strange to me that in the next room there were priceless artworks and vases. It felt like we were in an Italian American kitchen in Jersey City.

I didn't even know if I liked this guy Salvatore, I couldn't understand most of what was being said around me, but I felt that, without any ceremony, rites of passage, or coherent verbal communication, I fit in with this family. Without my fully understanding why, this felt like home.

Department of State

The U.S. Consulate in Naples is a big white square building on the waterfront of Mergellina, the port where motorboats leave for Capri and Ischia. It is surrounded by palm trees, and guarded by several open tanks where smiling Italian soldiers with Uzis keep an eye out for terrorists. In 1996, an enormous American flag and a photo of a very pink President Clinton welcomed visitors to U.S. territory.

My job at the Consulate was low stress, to say the least. I was working in the political office, and fortunately there wasn't much political tension between the United States and southern Italy in the late 1990s. Plus, I was unpaid, and the only intern at the Consulate. My co-workers were a mix of Italian locals with those sweet no-end-in-sight contracts, and U.S. foreign service employees, who were thrilled to be posted in a place like Naples, where they could relax and breathe easy before they got sent to Darfur. I usually came in around 9:30; the first cappuccino break started at about 10:15.

"Are you planning on taking the foreign service exam?" the Americans in the Consulate asked me. In truth, I didn't have any idea what I wanted to do career-wise. Both my parents had degrees in international studies, so I thought I might be interested in becoming a diplomat (or, in my less ambitious moments, becoming the ambassador to some small tropical country where I could throw really fun dinner parties with staff). But neither economics nor politics was my thing. What I loved to do was perform. Growing up, I studied acting at Washington's most important theaters and took private voice lessons with esteemed classical musicians. I participated in every monologue, poetry, and singing competition in the D.C. area. In college, I performed the leading role in nearly thirty plays. I combed bulletin boards for play tryouts, packed snacks for rehearsal breaks, and did homework during tech runs.

Onstage was where I was most myself.

But, according to my family, acting wasn't really a job. It was a great hobby, but I had to have a backup. I'd majored in cultural anthropology at college, which got me no closer to figuring out what profession to pursue—it just reassured me that I was open-minded, and wasn't it fascinating how Inuit women's rituals surrounding childbirth reflected their complex role in society?

My internship in Naples wouldn't give me answers, but it would give me a break before I returned to the States to figure out what I was going to do with myself.

My boss at the Consulate, an imposing, full-figured African American woman from Chicago, took me under her wing. She was smart, funny, spoke excellent Italian, and, I soon realized, had the best life I'd ever seen. In addition to the cappuccino breaks, our days were made up of two-hour lunches with Italian businessmen at yummy fish restaurants near the Consulate. Cynthia would talk most of the time, stopping only to dig into a plate of *calamari fritti*, and the handsome southern Italian magnates who hoped to win American support for some industrial enterprise would sit silently, not really knowing what to make of this Tina Turner with her loud laugh and the chubby little white girl who accompanied her.

My working day ended at 5:30 P.M., at which point I would walk the winding coastal road back to Posillipo. I didn't hear the whistles and catcalls of men on motorbikes—inevitable when a young woman is walking alone in Naples—because I was listening to early nineties rock on a cassette Walkman with fuzzy earphones.

I would get back to my dormitory just in time for dinner.

The Istituto Denza was a Catholic boys' boarding school that didn't have enough Catholic boys boarding to pay its bills. In fact, since it was September when I arrived in Naples and school started in mid-October, there were *no* Catholic boys boarding when I arrived.

The campus was lush, with pine and olive trees, magenta bougainvillea, and illuminated statues of the Madonna sitting at the intersections of the walkways. To keep it all up—the greenery, the soccer fields, the buildings—the Barnabite priests who ran the place decided to take in male university students from other parts of Italy who would pay the Denza for room and board. That wasn't enough. They were forced to take in (*ahimè!* horror of horrors!) female "guests."

Nobody explained this to me. A small, shuffling nun in white showed me to my room the first day with only a "*Buongiorno*" and a "*Prego*"—this way. The room had a single bed, desk, and two windows overlooking the tropical gardens. I could tell from the silence that there was nobody else in the building. Where were the other students in the dorm? I wondered. Was there a Meet the New American Girl social hour planned? Oh, and did they have any extra hangers for the closet?

"*Per cena,*" the nun remembered to tell me before she left, *about dinner . . .* and then she said a whole lot of words I didn't understand. I followed her arthritic hand as she motioned to the left, then to the right. Did she just say past the third Madonna and right at the second soccer field?

"*Grazie.*" I smiled. "*Grazie tante.*"

When it was dinnertime, I would follow my nose.

The *mensa,* or eating hall, of the campus was a good ten-minute walk from my building. Other than lizards skitting across the path and mosquitoes digging into my calves, there was no sign of life. A church bell gonged close by, and I hoped it meant *soup's on.*

I finally found the *mensa* (can you call a space with that divine a smell *cafeteria?*), a huge room with marble walls and floors, crystal chandeliers, and many empty tables for six. There was no line, so I got a tray and watched as a nun with an apron ladled out pasta with fried eggplant and tomato. She then handed me a miniature carafe of red wine. *Buon appetito, signorina.*

There were only two tables occupied that first night at the Denza—at one sat four visiting nuns; at the other, three young male college students. I stood with my tray deciding where to sit as they all watched. It was clear that there was a right answer for where I belonged, I just didn't know what it was.

I went with the guys. (Enough with gender division! *Basta,* already!) But as soon as I sat down I knew that it was the wrong choice. No one spoke.

Only a minute had passed when I heard female voices echoing throughout the dining hall. I turned to see that three smiling young women had just walked in the entrance. They were sisters, all with long black hair and almond eyes. They didn't rent a room at the Denza, I would learn, but came to have their meals there. Their parents lived in a small town in Calabria, on the toe of the Italian boot, and the girls had come to the big city to study. When they passed my table and said *"Ciao,"* I knew there was a God.

Maria Rosa and Francesca (and their little sister Isabella, who nodded and smiled and was the silent one of the Three Graces) had never met a foreigner. They had never traveled north of Naples, or tasted ketchup. They were full of questions: What did I do at the Consulate? Were all houses in America like the ones in *Dynasty*? Did American women switch their husbands as often as the characters on *The Young and the Restless*?

I held forth in my broken Italian about my homeland. It was a good thing I had a degree in cultural anthropology, because I was able to say things like *America, divorce, very easy!*; *Hospitals, very expensive!*; and *Too much guns.* My friends were enlightened, and I was no longer lonely.

Oreos

I am five feet three inches tall, and in September of 1996 I weighed 155 pounds. The Calabrese girls at the boarding school thought, That's what American food does to you. Salvatore thought, She likes to eat. What no one in Naples would have guessed is that I had binge-eating disorder. I loved food too much to become anorectic, felt disgusting puking it up, so what was left for me? BED: I would binge and then starve myself, avoiding food altogether for a few days or munching on celery sticks for nourishment. Be rational, rein in your appetites, my upper-class, East Coast upbringing had taught me. I tried. And then every once in a while I ate three boxes of Oreos in one sitting.

During my first six weeks in Naples, I stopped bingeing and lost twenty pounds. I did not go on a diet; in fact, I've never enjoyed food as much as I did then. What happened was in part a practical consequence of living in Italy, and at the same time something deeper.

Naples is an anti-binge city. In Neapolitan culture, mealtimes are sacred—food is freshly prepared and consumed *in compagnia*. There is no rushing, and you will hear the Neapolitan *Statte cuieto*—Keep your pants on—if you look anxious or pressed for time at the table. You eat when you are seated without distraction and preferably with a glass of wine. You eat when it is breakfast time, lunchtime, and dinnertime, period. *Punto e basta*.

Stopping in a little café after I finished work at the Consulate, I'd get an espresso, but I couldn't have gotten something substantial to eat even if I'd begged for it. Why would you want to eat at 5:30 P.M.? Pastries are put out fresh in the morning, and desserts are displayed after dinner. When food isn't processed and doesn't have preservatives, eating at random hours means that you eat food that is stale. And only crazy tourists do that.

Because everything I ate in Naples was fresh and full of flavor, at the end of meals I felt satisfied. There were no additives to make me crave more. For the first time in my life I could, along with the rest of the city, get up from the table and not think of my stomach until the next meal.

One evening at the Denza dining hall when I was waxing eloquent about American eating habits, Maria Rosa got a sad look on her face. The problem with your country, she said, is that you eat in a way that is *scombinato*. This means "disorganized" or "messy." I had told her about American college students ordering pizza at 3:00 A.M., and the look on her face—the empathy in those Sophia Loren eyes!—made me feel like I was confessing to heroin use.

The Italian expression for "eating disorder" is *disordine alimentare*, literally "disorganized, messy eating sickness." She had put her finger on it—I was a girl from the land of messy eaters who had an extreme messy eating sickness.

"*Non è vero?*" Don't you think? she continued, as I took in my messy eating diagnosis. "*Per esempio*, in America, people eat while walking. They dirty their hands with gooey sandwiches and then suck their fingers. And men in the United States get noodles in little cardboard boxes for dinner. They eat at their desk while they're working, right? *Che tristezza!* [What sadness, what a pity, what sorry lives they lead!] They're really not very good at organizing their meals, are they?"

Wait a second, was an Italian going on about American organizational skills? The flag-waver in me reared her head.

"It's not that they're not capable," I said, trying to keep my cool. "It's just that sometimes Americans eat well, like at a restaurant, and sometimes they grab a bite because they have more important things to do."

My Italian translation of "grab a bite" probably came across as "capture a mouthful." The second, more fundamental idea of "more important things to do" was met by stunned silence. Francesca mercifully changed the subject.

But it wasn't just about organizing my meals. The Italian girls my age all seemed to *live* in their bodies in a way that I didn't. I'd see them draped over a motorbike on the waterfront outside the Consulate. They'd hook their thumbs in each other's pockets, caress each other's hair, enjoy their own and each other's physicality. When it was time to get moving, they'd casually throw a leg over a *motorino*—three or four of them on one tiny little scooter—and unapologetically snake through a traffic jam. The word for what they are is *carnale*. The English word *carnal* is derogatory and has sexual connotations, but in Italian *carnale* is precious and sacred.

When my baby girl was born, ten years after my arrival in Naples, my father-in-law didn't call her *bellissima*, or splendid or adorable. He used the adjective that is beyond all compliments in Italy: he called her *carnale*. Of the flesh—wonderfully, squeezably of the flesh. After all, we are in a Catholic country, and the ultimate gift was the word made flesh. *La parola* became *carne*. In my Protestant background, I seem to have focused on the word part. Lots and lots of words. My relationship with the flesh took second place, my mind was given priority. And every once in a while my flesh demanded three boxes of Oreos in revolt.

After my first dinner at Salvatore's family apartment, there was a lot of kissing of cheeks as I said goodbye. I invariably dove for the wrong cheek (go toward the right first! Right first! I would chant to myself for weeks before it became instinct), and ended up bumping noses awkwardly with Benedetta. (For years, Benedetta's "cooler older sister" aura would cause me to drop things, ram into furniture, doubt my word choice. Whenever I got around the silky hair and turquoise eyes, my best bet was to find a couch and sit in silence.) Salva returned me to my dormitory and said, *"Ci sentiamo."* The literal translation would be "We'll hear each other," but the expression really means "Talk to you soon."

However, at that time, I thought it meant "Call me." So I said, "When?" and Salvatore said, *"Presto."* Soon. I took that to mean tomorrow. So while he was saying his goodbyes with a very noncommittal "Talk to you soon," I was receiving the command "Call me tomorrow." I didn't mind: I liked the idea of hearing his laugh again. I'd never met anyone so *happy*. I'd also never met anyone who smelled that good as he leaned over to cut my food.

So the next day I phoned him. We talked (listened? giggled?) for about five minutes. He called me Pagnottella, after a doughy muffin-like Neapolitan bread (which I didn't understand) and teased, "You like to eat, don't you?" (which I *did* understand). *Te piace mangiare.* He was referring to my chubbiness, and I'd met the guy only once. I should be offended, I thought. But strangely, I wasn't. It seemed that my appetite was endearing to him, possibly even attractive. There was nothing wrong with loving to eat and showing it.

And then he laughed again, followed by "*Ci sentiamo.*" I thought, now I need to buy another phone card so I can call him tomorrow.

When I called him the next day (I was a good girl, I always followed orders), he had his sister answer the phone and say he wasn't there. Years later, he told me that what he was thinking was that he'd never seen a girl so desperate for action.

Can a relationship, a life, be determined by a miscommunication? My moving to another continent, my becoming an Italian wife and mother: would it have happened if I had understood the meaning of *Ci sentiamo, Pagnottella*?

'O Sartù

Sartù di riso is a Neapolitan specialty that was invented by the chefs of the Bourbon king Ferdinand I of Naples at the beginning of the 1800s.

After the Greeks and Romans, Naples had been ruled by the Normans, French, Austrian Hapsburgs . . . you name the empire or dynasty, and it ruled Naples at some point. In 1735, Italy was still made up of city-states, and the Bourbon king Charles the Something of Spain (he was simultaneously Charles the First, Third, Fifth, and Seventh depending on which of his kingdoms you were talking about) conquered the Kingdom of Sicily and the Kingdom of Naples and joined them under his crown.

Naples under Bourbon rule was the place to be. In Paris, Jean-Jacques Rousseau wrote, "Do you want to know if there is a spark within you? Run, no, fly to Naples" to hear the masterpieces of Neapolitan composers at the San Carlo opera house. Mozart's dad brought him there on his Wolfgang Wows the World! tour of 1770 (on the trip, they also got some very swank silk outfits from Neapolitan tailors).

Insomma, if you could make it there, you could make it anywhere.

King Ferdinand I was the son of Charles. He was technically named Ferdinando Antonio Pasquale Giovanni Nepomuceno Serafino Gennaro Benedetto. Ferdy loved art, he loved music, and he also loved to eat.

Chefs were brought to his palace in the center of Naples directly from France, the seat of the Bourbon dynasty. They were supposedly the best chefs in the world. Pasta, fish, baked vegetables, elaborate cakes: they made sure that Ferdinand the First went to bed with a satisfied tummy. One day, the king asked his head chef, whom he called *'o monsù* (derived from the French *monsieur*), what was for lunch. He was told that rice was the first course.

"Rice?" King Ferdinand was furious. Rice was for the sick! Even today in Naples, there is an expression, *'O rriso d'o mese int'a 'o lietto stesa:* Eat rice and stay in bed for a month. Rice is considered insipid, insignificant, hospital food. It is even called a *sciaquapanza,* or tummy rinse.

"Please," the *monsù* insisted. "Enough pasta. We'll make the rice hearty! We'll add butter and cheese and . . ."

"Very well. I challenge you to prepare rice that I *like!*"

And so the Neapolitan *sartù di riso* was born. It is made with dense tomato *ragù,* pieces of egg, cheese, sausage, peas, and tiny fried meatballs or salami. Then it is baked in a buttered casserole dish.

The king was thrilled. Who knew? Rice could actually taste good and make for a decent meal.

It was a Saturday afternoon and I was in the Avallones' kitchen while Raffaella was cooking *sartù di riso,* one of Nino's favorite dishes. Salvatore had picked me up at the boarding school—always late, always smiling—and had deposited me in the kitchen with his mother while he finished studying in his room. He was in his third year at the University of Naples, studying law. In Italy, a university law degree is a combination of undergraduate and graduate studies, so after five or six years (or longer for some) "repeating" his books, he could take the bar and begin practicing as a lawyer.

He studied in his room all day, every day, and went every few months to take an exam. No listening to lectures, no comparing notes with fellow students, no interaction with professors. Just memorizing law texts in his boyhood room, which was adorned with teddy bears and third-grade soccer trophies. (I remember describing to Salva later that at Princeton we had precepts, small groups of students who were encouraged to express their opinions on the subject matter to the professor. Salva's reaction: Why would a professor care what a twenty-year-old *thought*?)

I had assumed that when Salvatore picked me up we would do something together. There had been chemistry, I thought, when he cut my pizza into little squares. On the phone the previous evening he had said not just *Ci sentiamo*, We'll hear each other, but *Ci vediamo*—We'll see each other!

And here I was in the tiny kitchen with Raffaella. Who was I for them? I certainly wasn't Salvatore's girlfriend, but I wasn't the Avallones' guest either. There was neither "have a seat in the *salone*, do you take milk or sugar?" nor "Salvatore, honey, why don't you come and show this girl a good time?" Maybe this was how it felt for brides in arranged marriages. Your future husband is busy somewhere, so in the meantime let's teach you how he likes his rice. Would an arranged marriage really be so bad, though, if my fiancé was someone who made me feel as happy and alive as Salva did? I wouldn't *have* to cook for him, after all. Or would I?

What I didn't realize was that I wasn't being judged, and I wasn't being primed. Raffaella's focus was on the *sartù*, and she was making it to satisfy my hunger as much as anyone else's.

Her dance was perfectly choreographed: she simultaneously stirred the *ragù*, fried the meatballs, sautéed the peas. I ducked and dodged. I was at times behind her, at times beside her. She had been to the gym, and wore New Balance sneakers and light green, fitted sweats. How was her makeup perfect after a workout? *"Non sudo,"* I don't sweat, she explained. Ah, that's convenient. The kitchen window was open and sea air was coming in. Look at the volcano! Raffaella pointed. When it's windy like this, you can see the towns surrounding the base of Vesuvius. Even the outlines of the houses. The wind sweeps away the mist and fog.

"Vieni, assaggia." Katherine, taste. Her wooden spoon was suddenly coming at me, full to overflowing with *ragù*, her hand cupped underneath to catch any spills. She stuck the whole huge spoon into my mouth, and I almost gagged on the wood. *"Com' è?"* How is it? I answered that it was *buonissimo*, and she dipped the same spoon back into the pot and tasted it herself.

"Hm."

I was told to cut the hard-boiled eggs into quarters. Raffaella laid the fried meatballs, spitting and sizzling, on freshly ironed dishrags. My Italian had improved enough to be able to ask, "How much egg? How many cheese? How many much peas?" Okay, my quantifying adjectives weren't perfect, but I got my point across. In response, she put her arm around my waist and whispered conspiratorially, *"Più ci metti più ci trovi!"*—the more you put in the more you get out. In other words: That analytical, precise, quantifying brain has no place in my kitchen, girl.

(Many years later, in my mother's kitchen in Bethesda, Maryland, I would find Raffaella staring at a ring of measuring spoons as if they were an archaeological find. "They're for measuring quantities," I explained. "In cooking?" she asked, bewildered. She then shook her head and laughed. *"Americani! Americani!"* Yes, we're a wild and crazy people.)

"Lella!" Nino was standing in the door of the kitchen calling his wife's nickname. He was pissed off. What had she done? I wondered. *"C'è una puzza terrificante!"* It stinks in here! Nino, I later learned, has an extremely sensitive sense of smell. He insists that his wife turn on the ventilation when she is cooking so that the smell of food doesn't waft into the rest of the apartment. *"Scusa, scusa!"* Sorry! she cheerfully replied, and turned on the hair dryer–sounding machine. Nino disappeared, still indignant.

Nino was fourteen years Raffaella's senior, and had spent most of their marriage managing the hotel that he and his brothers owned. He left early in the morning and came back late at night, Raffaella told me; it was the least she could do to care for him with a smile when he was at home. He was forced into early retirement because of an ugly family battle that nobody talked about, and now he was at home all the time. She made sure the ventilation was on when she was cooking, served him at the table, and accepted his negative comments about how the pasta was cooked with a smile or a wink and "I think you're right, Nino."

It bugged the hell out of me—she was cooking his favorite dish, for God's sake! But soon I realized that my irritation at Nino's outburst had no place in Raffaella's kitchen, either. "Ketrin!" she was yelling over the fan (the flat *a* and *th* of Katherine were too much of a challenge for most Italians), "make sure you add a little *ragù* first so the rice doesn't stick. . . ." I was forced to move on, to concentrate on the preparation of that rice.

The preparation became aerobic. Raffaella's biceps bulged as she stirred the dense *ragù* in with the rice. I was asked to lay out fresh dishrags (impossibly white) on the table, ousting the baby meatballs (they'd had themselves enough of a nap). I held the tiny balls in my fists until Raffaella offered me the pot with the rice and *ragù*. I plopped them in and she smeared the casserole dish with butter.

Salvatore emerged from his room smiling just as I was helping his mother pour the heavy mass into the pan. He came over and pinched my cheek. "Pagnottella! Did you learn how to make the *sartù*? There's going to be a test later. *Esame, esame!* Princeton!" He found himself delightful. I wasn't laughing. I was hot and hungry. And I really wanted to taste that *sartù*.

❖

My mother first put me on a diet when I was in kindergarten. I was never called fat: the words that were thrown around our household in reference to my weight were *chunky, heavy,* and *plump.* As a child, I was probably never more than eight pounds overweight. But for my mother, that was enough to call for drastic measures.

Bonnie Salango Wilson was born in Princeton, West Virginia, during the Second World War. Her father was a Presbyterian minister who was the son of Italian immigrants; they had come from Calabria at the beginning of the century. Although my great-grandparents were devout Catholics, they allowed a Presbyterian Sunday school to use their basement when my grandfather was a little boy. He thought the Sunday school was fun: Protestants were so child friendly! After college my grandfather enrolled in a Presbyterian seminary. His parents never worried about his conversion from Catholicism. It was enough that one of their eight children was a man of the cloth.

So my mother was born to an Italian American preacher in the South. Things weren't easy for a preacher's daughter in the 1950s—Bonnie was expected to be well behaved, accomplished, and, most of all, beautiful. And the definition of beautiful for my mother, a naturally curvy Italian-looking woman, did not leave any room at the seams. Beautiful meant skinny.

Bonnie Salango stopped eating breakfast and lunch in the early 1960s, and hasn't partaken in those daytime meals since. She has never weighed more than 120 pounds, and looks, still, like Elizabeth Taylor in her prime. My mother showed my sister and me the photo of her in a West Virginia local paper when she graduated as valedictorian from Georgetown's foreign service school. When I saw the picture, I didn't feel proud of her achievement. I felt proud of her thinness underneath that robe.

A "chunky" daughter was simply not going to cut it.

So it doesn't surprise me to hear that when I was reprimanded by my mother at the age of three for picking my nose and eating the boogers, my response was, "Why, Mommy, do they have too many calories?" In elementary school, my lunchtime "treat" was a Flintstones chewable vitamin. The teachers at Saint Patrick's were told that when cartons of milk were distributed to the class, Katherine should be given skim rather than whole. "Sweetheaaaaart," my mother would tell me in her Appalachian twang, "remember to always git the *blue*!"

"Mommy, why am I the only one that gets blue and everybody else gets red?"

She explained rationally and I understood rationally. So many extra calories, and for what? I trusted. I felt fine when the box appeared and I saw my blue carton buried in a sea of reds.

And then one day in first grade my best friend, Robin, skinny and blond and a whole-milk drinker until high school, insisted that I take a swig from her red carton. At once my world was shattered and new horizons appeared.

That first crunchy, steaming bite of *sartù* did the same thing to my twenty-one-year-old body that a swig of cold whole milk had done at Saint Patrick's Episcopal Day School in the fall of 1981. My carnal transformation was under way, and there was no going back.

Laundry

It was a morning at the end of September when I arrived at the Consulate with a great big Santa Claus sack of laundry slung over my back. I waved to the soldiers with Uzis, nodded to Clinton, and looked frantically for Cynthia.

My laundry had become an all-consuming preoccupation. I had no washing machine, there were no Laundromats in Naples, and when I took my sullied things to the *lavanderie* (dry cleaners), the women would take the bag and look inside. Shocked, scandalized, they would stare at me and say, *"Ma c'è roba intima!"* There are intimate robes!

What intimate robes? Where?

"You took your bras and underwear to the dry cleaners?" Cynthia asked me, horrified. "Oh, honey, no." She explained that in Naples *roba intima*—bras and underwear and even undershirts—are to be touched by no one but the owner. They are extremely, extremely private. Here I was traipsing around the city with my bag of dirty panties, shoving them in people's faces! How humiliating!

"But what am I supposed to do, Cynthia? I certainly can't

bring my intimate robes to Salva's apartment and ask Raffaella to put them in her washing machine!"

It hadn't occurred to me to do what any Neapolitan woman would have done: buy detergent and hand-wash my panties in the sink. I was raised by a woman who would never *handle* her intimates. She'd do what any respectable preacher's daughter from the South would do: she'd throw her stuff into the washing machine, and turn that temperature up as hot as it would go.

And so the political consul of the United States agreed to let me come over later that day with my unwieldy sack of soiled undergarments to use her enormous GE washing machine (the sack was enormous because my first solution to the no-washing-machine problem was of course just to buy *lots* of underwear). I counted the hours for the working day to end so that I could go to Cynthia's penthouse apartment overlooking the bay. I needed her words of wisdom as well as her washing machine.

"Let me explain," she began, after getting my panties spinning (anonymous in all that American space! How I love the Department of State!). She opened a monstrous bag of Doritos from the military base and set it on the coffee table between us. "There are some things you do *not* mention in Naples when it comes to hygiene and private parts. First of all, they *have* to think you bidet. At your own home, you give guests who ask to use the bathroom one hand towel and one separate bidet towel. When you are invited to someone else's home and you are given a separate bidet towel, *do not say,* 'No thanks, I don't need this.' That is an admission that you, as an American, do not bidet."

"But I don't bidet!"

"*They cannot know that.* They must think that you use the specific *detergente intimo*—intimate detergent, or pussy suds as I like to think of them. And that you dry yourself with the bidet towel afterward."

Her preemptive strike was too late. I remembered with horror that just days before, when Raffaella had handed me two towels when I went to the bathroom, I had actually said, cheerfully, "One's plenty! I'll use the same one for both hands!"

"But don't they understand that toilet paper, used correctly, can do the trick?" Or if not, I hoped, couldn't I be the one to enlighten them on the possibilities of what the Brits call the mighty loo roll?

"No." Cynthia had patience. Oh, did she have patience. "They find it revolting. Not cleaning yourself with a specific kind of soap after doing *cacca* puts you in the category of animals and Gypsies."

We munched on Doritos, and I told her more about Salva and the Avallones. I described how after dinner at the Denza, I would walk down the marble steps to the communal pay phone with a plastic phone card in my sweaty hand. My nerves would settle as soon as I heard his cheerful *"Eh, Pagnottella!"* In Salva's tone of voice, and in the honks of his horn as he picked me up in his little red Fiat to take me to eat his mother's food, I heard: *You are a woman, and you are beautiful, and you are full of healthy, human appetites.* I'd learned a lot of things growing up in America, but I'd missed that part. My whole body was starting to crave the way this guy made me feel.

As I began to fall for Salvatore, though, I worried about the negative preconceptions I had about Italian men. Weren't they all macho and didn't they all cheat on their girlfriends? Cynthia was single, but I'd seen her with several different handsome Neapolitans at events at the Consulate.

"Well, is he a nerd?" she asked.

I didn't know. He was Italian—how could I tell if he was a nerd or not? There weren't many cultural indicators I could read. How did he dress? Like an Italian. How did he express himself? Like an Italian. I couldn't use any linguistic or cultural markers to evaluate him.

"Because if you want to start something with an Italian, he *must* be a nerd. The others are slick and sleazy womanizers, and the nerds are handsome and charming anyway. Trust me."

"He lives with his parents and studies a lot," I offered.

"Good sign."

Soon, the washing machine beeped, and I thanked Cynthia.

As I was leaving, she put her hand on my shoulder and asked, "Are you really into him, honey?"

I wasn't sure exactly what I was falling for. Was I infatuated with him, or his family, or both? But I was starting to realize that maybe it wasn't so important to put a name on it so that I could put it away in a little category in my brain. Maybe I was being fed and loved and the rest would take care of itself. Luciano De Crescenzo, a Neapolitan philosopher, once said that if the Lord wanted to take everyone in Naples to heaven, all He would have to do is pull one line of laundry and the whole city would come with it, because all the buildings in Naples are connected by hanging wash.

My intimate robes had been spinning in an enormous American GE washing machine, but De Crescenzo's image of the laundry lines of Naples was a more accurate picture of the connections that were forming in my heart.

'O Ragù

Neapolitan *ragù* is so central to the culture and the base for so many recipes (including lasagna and *sartù*) that Eduardo De Filippo, a playwright and poet of Neapolitan dialect in the last century, wrote a poem about it. A husband tries to reason with his wife that what she has made is nothing close to his mother's recipe. The poem is a worshipful ode to *ragù*:

> 'O 'rraù
> 'O 'rraù ca me piace a me
> m'o ffaceva sulo mammà.
> A che m'aggio spusato a te
> ne parlammo pè ne parlà.
> Io nun songo difficultuso;
> ma lluvàmmel' 'a miezo st'uso
>
> Sì, va buono: cumme vuò tu.
> Mò ce avéssem'appiccecà?
> Tu che dice? Chest'è rraù?
> E io m'o mmagno pè m' 'o mangià . . .

M' 'a faja dicere na parola? . . .
Chesta è carne c' 'a pummarola.

Here goes with my translation (De Filippo is turning in his grave):

Oh ragù
the ragù *that I love*
was made only by Mommy.
Since I married you
we've talked about it, but the talk is just words.
We shall talk of it no more.

Whatever! You decide about the ragù.
I don't want a fight.
But tell me, you really think this is ragù?
I'll eat it just to fill my tummy . . .
but will you let me say just one last thing?
This is simply meat with tomatoes.

The key to cooking real Neapolitan *ragù* is to let it *pippiare*. This onomatopoeic verb in dialect refers to the *pi pi* sound of bubbles popping when the sauce is on a low flame for hours and hours. (Shouldn't I be doing something to it? *"Lascia stare!"* Raffaella told me. Leave it! Leave it! Why do you have to be doing?) Raffaella's mother, Nonna Clara, who had raised eight children in postwar Naples, used to cook her *ragù* for at least twelve hours. Any less and the sauce would be bright red. "You never want your *ragù* to be red, in Naples it must be closer to black and so dense that it's hard to stir," Raffaella told me. Stirring *ragù* for ten people in an earthenware pot for twelve hours: Nonna Clara must have had biceps to rival Rocky's.

I had been to the Avallones' numerous times for dinner. Thanks to the *ci sentiamo* mixup, Salvatore and I talked on the phone almost every day. There were no cellphones, and he lived at home, so I would inevitably talk to his mother first when I called—Beautiful weather, isn't it? How was the Consulate today, and what did you have for lunch? (Young Neapolitans dating could never *not* know each other's parents. An American mother might pass the phone like a baton, but in Naples that would be considered beyond rude. When Salva called my house in Washington months later and my mother said, "Hi! Just a second I'll get 'er," he asked me, *What have I done to your parents that they hate me so?*)

On the evening of my first *ragù*, rigatoni with *ragù*, to be precise, Salvatore had finished studying late. He walked into the kitchen wearing a Mickey Mouse sweatshirt. Even before he sat down at the table, his mother brought a wooden spoon overflowing with her dense *ragù* over to him, and he opened up. She cupped his chin with one hand and inserted the spoon with the other. *Imboccare* is the Italian verb, to spoon-feed.

I was floored by Salva's total lack of self-sufficiency and independence. And pride, for Christ's sake! He was twenty-three! When Raffaella saw me watching, disturbed, she did what she had to do. She used the same spoon to *imboccare* me.

Salvatore and I had swapped saliva but had yet to kiss.

Our plates of pasta that evening were so full of *ragù* that you couldn't see any white of the rigatoni. Raffaella mixed all of the pasta with all of the sauce, spooned it out in the dishes, and then put a whole ladle of *ragù* on top of each serving. "There needs to be enough sauce for the *scarpetta*," she explained. The *scarpetta* (literally, "little shoe") refers to the piece of bread that you use to sop up the sauce after finishing your pasta.

By the time Salva dropped me off at the gate of my boarding

school I'd forgotten my discomfort about the spoon-feeding. *Te piace il ragù, eh, Pagnottella?* he laughed. Yes, okay, fine, I loved the *ragù*, I told him. I also loved his smile, and the way he touched my cheek when he said "Pagnottella." Little Muffin-face.

It was time for him to say *Ci sentiamo* or *Ci vediamo* and speed off in his Fiat, but he didn't. He got out of the car and stood there. The air was moist, and smelled of magnolias and sweet fetid garbage. A motorbike buzzed by. I giggled to fill the silence.

Salva looked around awkwardly, everywhere but in my eyes. The moment was hesitant and charged and then his mouth was on mine. It was so sudden and forward that my only thought was, When did he get drunk? I've been with him all evening! No one could do that if he weren't drunk or on drugs! "Come on, Pagnottella, get in the car," he said. I did as I was told. Was this Salvatore? The guy I had been spoon-fed with an hour earlier? The one who tenderly cut my pizza into tiny pieces? Where were we going?

I was attracted to Salva and wanted to kiss him, but his behavior shocked me. I didn't have a lot of experience with American guys, but the ones I had "hooked up" with in college were gradual and tentative in their advances ... unless they were drunk. At Princeton in 1996, men were encouraged to ask, "Can I kiss you?" and not make a move until they had verbal consent. This guy went from zero to a hundred with no warning, and he was sober! There was no stepping back to see what my reaction was, no checking in with me about whether I liked it or not. What was he going to do next?

Salvatore parked the little tin-can car in a row of similar cars perched on the high promontory of Posillipo, where during the day we could have seen the sea and the islands of Nisida,

Procida, and Ischia. The car next to us had newspapers covering all the windows and windshield and was rocking slightly back and forth.

I later learned that coming to this spot to have sex in the car is a necessity for Neapolitan *ragazzi*, or young adults, who live in small apartments with their families and don't have any privacy. (The very word *privacy* does not exist in the Italian language, so the English word is used. It is pronounced with a rolled *r* and a long, languorous, luxurious *eye*.) There was even a man who stood behind a little table selling condoms, year-old newspapers, Kleenex, and Scotch tape. (It took me a while, but I eventually figured out the uses for all of these accoutrements.) I never figured out, however, why all these *ragazzi* chose a place with a gorgeous view. I guess a romantic context helped to set the mood, even if the women ended up staring at newsprint.

As I took in this 1996 Neapolitan equivalent of a 1950s American drive-in, Salvatore continued to kiss me. The pressure of his full lips and the smell of his cologne kept me in the moment, but the *ragù* breath took me back to his mother's kitchen. The cars were rocking around us, and his hands moved over me quickly, trying here and trying there. It was too much too fast. I moved his hands away. I even said no, semiforcefully.

Salvatore didn't push it, he just finished his kissing and said, "*Va bene!*" as if we had just finished a game of UNO and it was time to go home. He started up the car and drove me back to the Denza. When I stumbled out, vaguely nauseous and with unsteady legs, he called, "*Ciao, bella Pagnottella!*" out the window and sped off.

He didn't say "Listen to you tomorrow," and I was glad. I didn't know what to make of him now. How could I reconcile the sweet, dependent mama's boy with the silent groping man in the car? I needed to talk to some Italian women who weren't related to Salvatore. I needed to find out if this was normal behavior.

The next evening in the dining hall I waited anxiously for my Calabrese fairy godmothers. They would be shocked at how forward Salvatore was! If my Italian managed to sufficiently convey what had happened, they would surely commiserate with me. In the end, however, it was I who was in for a surprise.

I told them the story as best I could, leaving suspenseful pauses and playing up my role as unsuspecting victim. They ate their veal cutlets *con calma*, and with impeccable manners, nodding at the right times. When I finished, there was a long silence. Then Maria Rosa said, "And?"

"Yeah," Francesca added. "What did he do that was so awful?"

"He didn't even ask, or hesitate, or wonder if I wanted to be kissed! Or touched! He just kept going!" I answered. "His hands were everywhere! Do you think he might have been drunk?" I honestly believed that that was the only possible justification for his aggressive behavior.

"Of course not. He's a guy! What did you expect him to do?"

Now *I* was shocked. They interpreted it as completely normal male behavior! "So that's just what guys do here? They're that forward physically?"

"*No! Anzi!*" said Francesca, and gave me the gift of another Italian word that I will never forget as long as I live. *Anzi* means to the contrary, and is said with raised eyebrows and a decisive, descending, very long *a*. "Guys do much more! Let me get this straight: You've seen each other six or seven times, he's never even touched you before, and he didn't try to have sex?"

"That's accurate."

"Are you *sure* he's not gay?"

And so, in a sense, my relationship with Salvatore was saved by these two southern Italian women. They explained to me that here, a guy will keep going until he's stopped by the girl. Always, with no exceptions. And usually, the guy will be much pushier about it than Salvatore was. Use a slap when you need to, Maria Rosa told me. Offended? Why would a guy be offended by a slap? Never forget that men are needy and pathetic when it comes to sex. You have the power. Use it.

Bread and Wine

"Let's see if we can catch ourselves a mass," Raffaella told me one Sunday in October, using the Neapolitan verb *acchiappare*. I was confused since that's the same verb she would use for catching a fish or grabbing a crumb from someone's crotch. I knew she was a practicing Catholic, but I'd never heard of grabbing hold of a church service before it got away.

Masses in Naples are at all hours on Saturday and Sunday and there is at least one church on each street. Raffaella was perennially late, and never remembered which service started when. So catching ourselves a mass consisted of her packing me into her little blue Lancia (Nino drove a larger sedan) and speeding around the city looking for a church where the priest was starting *In the name of the Father, the Son, and the Holy Spirit* just as we arrived. She would triple-park and run in and out of the medieval churches (always making two signs of the cross, one on the way in and one on the way out) until she found a mass starting at the right time.

The Sunday morning service at Christ Memorial Presbyterian Church in Columbia, Maryland, started at 11:00, and we were never late.

"Giiiiirrrrrllllss! It's time for church!" my mother would wail, at least an hour before the service started. Our hair curled in ringlets, and our petticoats fitted under our dresses (my mother found us petticoats in 1980s suburban Washington), Anna and I would grab our sheet music and sing our last vocal warm-up. A quick *mee mee mee mee mee* up and down the scale to get rid of morning mucus.

Our grandfather (Mimi, we called him) was the preacher, and when he called us to the pulpit to perform, the congregation thought it was improvised. "Katherine, precious, why don't you come on up here and sing us somethin'?" he would ask, as if it had just occurred to him. Mimi was that good an actor. In fact, the performance was usually a song that we'd rehearsed hundreds of times, or a poem that we'd learned for a fourth-grade recitation contest that just happened to tie in perfectly with his "humdinger" of a sermon. We worked hard with him to get it *juuuuust right* for church on Sunday. The altar was a stage, and the congregation an audience of loving friends.

Anna and I went to an Episcopal elementary school, and my grandparents made sure we knew that "those folks might as well be Catholic." It wasn't a compliment. Catholic liturgy, Catholic dogma, and Catholic *rules* were something that my grandfather broke free of when he started going to that Presbyterian Sunday school in West Virginia in 1920. He wanted the freedom to emote, to be passionate—to *clap, gosh darn it*, when his granddaughter nailed "Für Elise" on the piano before the sermon.

Presbyterians aren't exactly freewheeling, though, and as my grandmother put it, "Your Mimi got himself in the wrong denomination. Shoulda been a Baptist." Now, *those* were people who knew how to take the stage.

For me, church was a perfectly rehearsed show. The big brown cross, American flag, and stained glass were the set, the hymns with their four-part harmony were the musical score, and my grandfather was the star. Reverend Salango's sermons were so moving that there was never a dry eye in the congregation, and his own handkerchief was always soaked with tears after the service (*Dang, I get myself worked up!* he'd tell us). My sister and I were the guest stars, and lived for the little pat on the shoulder that Mommy would give us in the pew to tell us we'd performed well.

I was thankful for the Reformation. I knew with deep conviction that Martin Luther and John Calvin would've loved hearing me perform *Les Mis*.

───────※───────

That first Sunday that I accompanied Raffaella, we sailed into the church of Santo Strato several minutes before mass was to begin. The church was built in the sixteenth century and had recently been repainted in garish Palm Beach colors. I wondered why they couldn't have chosen tones that were more *sobrio*, or subdued, as I followed Raffaella to the front of the church. (Even five hundred years ago, the Neapolitans chose similar hues, I later learned, when seeing the similarly bright frescoes of the churches in the center of town.) A statue of Mary, in an electric blue robe with her arms outstretched, rose above the altar. *Basta* with all that gray and washed-out blue, she seemed to say. We were near the beach, and the bright blue was a good color for her. All she needed was a few rhinestones and some chunky Armani sunglasses to be a true Neapolitan *signora*.

Santo Strato smelled of hairspray and incense. It was packed with women of all ages who were dressed and made up like they were going out on the town. Jeans were tight. Foundation was sponged on perfectly, with no caking or lines at the neck. And that eye makeup! Even seventy-year-olds knew how to smudge. Young women showed off their midriffs and new highlights and the older ones showed off their nips and tucks. Like Raffaella, the women sparkled and shimmered and made a lot of noise. Their voices had become deep and husky from calling sons and grandsons off the soccer field. "A *taaavola!*" they had yelled when it was time to eat, their cries filling not only apartments but the surrounding courtyards and piazzas.

In Naples, only the loud and persistent voices are heard. My little American voice peters out when interrupted; theirs get louder and more decisive. Often, when someone is interrupted in the middle of a story or it is clear that the listener has lost interest, the speaker will physically grab the listener's arm, look him or her in the eye with consternation, and start saying, "*Senti! Senti!*" ("Listen! Listen!") until she is sure that she's gotten their attention.

Many of the women in Santo Strato knew Raffaella, and there were hugs and kisses and very loud cries of "*Raffa!*" and "*Mirella bella!*" Raffaella's friends blatantly checked me out, top to bottom (eyes, boobs, waist, shoes) and then said, to her, Oh, she's American? She's so beautiful! Thanks, thanks, Raffaella answered. After being checked out, I was totally left out of the conversation. I caught the phrases "doe eyes" and "doesn't look American." One woman who had met me a few weeks before at the Avallones' said, "She's lost so much weight!"

Raffaella maintained physical contact with me always, her arm around my waist or our elbows linked square dance–style, as she talked about me to her friends. Was it protective? Proprietary? It felt awkward to hear these chic ladies talking about *me*—survivor of an eating disorder and wearer of a slightly frayed sweater that I had gotten at Filene's Basement in 1989.

Mary presided over it all, happy in her electric blue.

There was no hope of seeing a man in the congregation, in part because the Naples soccer team was playing the undefeated northern team, the Milan-based Inter. The men were not missed. In fact, I noticed that churchgoers in Naples were predominantly women. This was their realm, just as the stadium of San Paolo, where the Napoli soccer team was playing, was the realm of men. Boundaries were very clearly drawn, and few women tried to persuade their men to engage in activities together. Why on earth would women want men in church? Why on earth would men want women at the stadium?

"Nel nome del Padre, del Figlio e dello Spirito Santo," an amplified baritone voice cut through the racket, and I turned from a friend of Raffaella's who was caressing and examining my hair to see the priest, Father Giampietro. The flashy colors behind the altar made a perfect backdrop for Giampietro. He was a gorgeous thirty-five-year-old who wore cowboy boots (complete with spurs) under his robe, and had wavy hair, styled to perfection. One day while driving in central Naples, Salva and I saw him weaving through traffic on his motorbike.

"Giampietro!" Salva yelled out the window, teasing. "You're supposed to have a helmet! You're a priest!"

"But my hair!" the priest joked back. "It ruins my hair!" and he sped off around a curve to visit someone's dying grandmother.

That day, Giampietro's microphone whistled and popped. I wish, no, I pray, to DJ Mary that some talented sound technician might pay a visit to all the small churches in southern Italy. How much auditory distress could be resolved with a good sound check! Electronic amplification came on the scene several years ago, and if the truth were told, in most churches it is totally unnecessary, because they have cavernous spaces and domes that would make the acoustics ideal for even the least hellfire-and-brimstone of preachers. Giampietro was in no way hellfire-and-brimstone, mind you. But he was Italian, and his voice projected.

When amplification is used, nobody checks the volume level of the mikes and the piped-in music. And so, as Giampietro began his *Nel nome del Padre*, followed by the sign of the cross, his mike began popping and we heard a painful, high-pitched screech. Many of the women in the church were still talking. "I tried that risotto recipe you gave me but I wasn't sure if the *provola* cheese . . ."

Soon it was time for the responsive prayer. A young woman in jeans took Giampietro's place at the pulpet and instructed us in a monotone voice to repeat together *Vieni, Salvatore*, or Come, Savior, after she prayed for specific intentions. For the Church . . . *Vieni, Salvatore*; for the Christian family . . . *Vieni, Salvatore*; for the sick . . . I kept intoning with Raffaella and the rest of the congregation *Vieni, Salvatore*. Come, Salvatore.

I confess: my mind was on her son, not Mary's. It was blasphemy, I know! But, despite his physical forwardness, despite the miscommunications, despite the fact that I was seeing a lot more of his mother than of him, I realized that I was falling in love with him. I was falling for his long, tanned, graceful body. For the simple sincerity of his attraction to me, and for the smile that defied me to take myself or my problems too seriously.

Who knew? Maybe sitting next to his mother, saying "Come, Salvatore" together, was a sort of incantation and would do good things for our relationship.

As the Communion approached, recorded music began

playing, with a synthesizer beat that sounded like bad karaoke. Wasn't there supposed to be an atmosphere of mystery and serenity for Catholic Communion? This was supposed to be the *actual* body and blood of Christ, after all. I should have realized by then that in Italy, and particularly in Naples, anything is possible. Magic happens. The chaos and noise and colors give way suddenly, unexpectedly, to solemnity. How? The answer is always in the food.

Giampietro fed his girls.

Il corpo di Cristo, the Body of Christ, he was saying, and the ladies were lining up waiting for Giampietro to feed them their wafers. Most of them didn't put their palms out to receive the body of Christ, but opened up their mouths like little girls being fed their *mamma's ragù*. There was silence; the moment was sacred. This is the whole point of Communion, after all, being fed or *imboccati* in silence. Shut up and eat. The sleek sounds of a perfectly rehearsed Broadway show are not necessary.

When the Communion was finished and Giampietro once again made the sign of the cross, *Nel nome del Padre, del Figlio e dello Spirito Santo*, I could tell he had something else to add. Before he dismissed the women, before the cacophony of voices started up and recipes were rehashed, he paid homage to the absent men. He was, after all, a man and a diehard fan of the Napoli soccer team. *"Ricordatevi"*—Remember, he instructed— *"Forza Napoli!"* Let's go, Naples!

If my grandfather Mimi had been in charge, he'd have called me to the pulpit to knock 'em dead with an "'O Sole Mio" finale.

Insalata di Polipo

When Salvatore and I were together—in the Fiat, in front of the boarding school, in his room under a big Humpty Dumpty clock—his hands were all over me. *Basta!* I'd insist, swatting. (*They don't get offended*, Maria Rosa had told me. *Slap them if you need to.*) I was a good girl: I tried to be forceful and pretend I didn't like it. I never knew that romance could feel so much like play.

I started to call him *polipetto*—my little eight-tentacled octopus.

Octopuses (or octopi), I learned soon after, are solitary creatures. That's what makes them so hard to catch. They do not live in groups or schools, but can be found alone in a cave or holding on to the underside of a rock, camouflaged against the gray stone. Zio Toto, Raffaella's older brother, explained this to me on the feast day of Sant'Antonio, as Raffaella and her sister Pia prepared a massive meal. The highlight of the lunch was to be a six-pound octopus that Toto had caught the day before.

While no one in the family could be described as a shrinking violet, Zio Toto gets the Oscar for being the biggest *casinaro*.

In Naples, this word refers to someone who is constantly making *casino:* noise, mess, confusion. The word *casino* (cas-*ee*-no) is a different one from *casinò* (cas-ee-*no*), the site of slot machines and poker. Nonetheless, it helps to think of the noise of slot machines in Vegas to capture the feeling of being around a *casinaro.* Zio Toto, *casinaro* extraordinaire, makes a hell of a lot of racket.

He is also totally shameless. *Faccia tosta,* they would say, which is literally a tough face, meaning that he doesn't give a damn what anyone thinks of him. When he came to Washington for our wedding, he spent twenty minutes trying to persuade the ticket seller in the Washington metro to give him a discount. I should mention that he speaks absolutely no English, so it was all in pantomime. I did not offer to translate.

Zio Toto is missing a hand. He lost it in 1972, when he was setting up fireworks for New Year's Eve. In Naples, New Year's Eve is celebrated with explosives. On balconies, terraces, and in the streets, people set off their prized whistlers and bottle rockets until all hours. And every year on January 2, the newspaper of Naples publishes a list of the injured and sometimes the dead. Often they are children. The parents are people who would *never* feed their children mayonnaise or ketchup or let them out of the house without a hat and gloves in October because of the danger to their health. On New Year's Eve, however, they give little Guglielmo a leaping lizard to set off and tell him to have fun.

One would think that losing a hand might have interfered with Toto's octopus catching, particularly because he doesn't use nets, or rods, or underwater guns. (He did use dart guns for a brief while, before giving them up in favor of the visceral thrill of hand-to-tentacle combat.) But the loss of his hand didn't slow him down in the least. *"Che problema c'è?"* he says. What's the problem? He doesn't scuba-dive, so when he gets a glimpse of a *polipo*, he has to take a deep breath and plunge. His long gray hair trails behind him like a merman's as he dives for his prey.

Sometimes Toto hides behind a rock and throws a spearlike instrument into a cave where he suspects an octopus might be lurking. When the little bugger rolls out, Toto attacks. He keeps his left arm and stub close to his body and pumps his flippers to slice through the water to the *polipo*. With only his right hand, he grabs the octopus, squeezes and twists its head, sticks two fingers into its brain, and then pulls it up to shore. The octopus tries to position its tentacles on Toto's stump and pull him down to the depths. When Toto manages to bring an octopus up to the surface, he holds its tentacles and beats its head against a rock (with one hand, somehow managing not to let it slide out of his grip and go flying back into the sea).

Eight arms against one, and Toto is always the victor.

I am in the living room of the Avallones' apartment listening to Toto describe yesterday's slippery battle with the *polipo*. We are sitting on the silk couch, and he hasn't stopped grinning, or talking, for the last twenty minutes. I should be helping to prepare the meal: I am a woman, after all. The sea smell of the octopus overpowers the doughy scent of the spinach pie in the oven. I can hear the shuffling efficiency of Raffaella and her sister Pia in the kitchen, and know that any attempt at "help" would basically mean my getting in the way of their all-important preparation of the *polipo*. Giving my undivided attention to Zio Toto, I've decided, is my most useful contribution to the cause.

"Isn't it dangerous? I mean, the octopus could grab you and pull you down," I ask him.

"*Eeeeh*," he exhales, making a Neapolitan sound which is used to mean, What are you gonna do? That's life. I hear this often in places like the post office or bank, when I protest that they shouldn't be closing at 1:15 in the afternoon—it says on the door they're open until 1:30 and I have a bill to pay! "*Eeeeh,*" on the exhale. That's life.

Toto proudly rolls up the sleeve of his dress shirt. He unscrews his prosthetic hand so that I can get a better look at his war wounds. All the way down to his stub, there are reddish-brown hickeys. "*Quelli s'aggrappano, t'abbracciano.*" The little suckers grab on to you and hug you tight. Once, he tells me, he got badly bitten by a particularly aggressive *polipo* (one has to be careful not only of the suction cups but of the octopus's little hidden beak, too!).

The ritual for octopus preparation is this: after the battle, after the triumphant beating against the rock, Zio Toto, with long gray hair and Speedo dripping, delivers the octopus to his sisters, who stick it into a plastic bag. Back home in the kitchen, Raffaella pounds the creature again, this time on a cutting board with a meat tenderizer. Then, after she's cleaned him and removed his hard "beak," she holds his head above a pot of boiling water and dunks his tentacles three times. The tentacles curl up on contact with the water, creating an instant 1960s bob hairdo. There is a cork floating in the water—it makes the tentacles more tender. (Beating against a rock, dunked three times in boiling water with cork: Is this some kind of witchcraft?)

Lunch is ready, and I move to the dining table with the men. (Benedetta is at her fiancé's home, helping her future mother-in-law prepare and serve the Sant'Antonio lunch—there probably isn't one household in Naples that doesn't have an Antonio to celebrate.) Raffaella and her sister are buzzing, tasting, sprinkling things with last-minute salt or parsley or Parmesan. They begin serving. Young, able-bodied, and female, I guiltily wait to be served.

Raffaella has seven brothers and sisters. Their mother, Nonna Clara, cooked three-course lunches and dinners every day, washed sheets and blankets by hand, canned vegetables, and scrubbed floors. Her children, she used to say, *"non hanno voglia di far niente. Sono nati stanchi e vivono per riposare."* They don't do anything, they were born tired and live to rest. She called theirs a "rotten generation." Seeing Pia and Raffaella baking and serving, and hearing of Toto and his one-handed battle with the octopus, I wonder what Nonna Clara would have thought of my generation. Rotten? Not just moldy but positively in decay.

Toto is still describing yesterday's strategic strikes when Pia's thick fingers (how can fingers be so muscular?) set down in front of me a plate of *insalata di polipo*, octopus salad. I look at the little pieces of Toto's nemesis, mixed with garlic and olive oil and parsley, and feel that I know him. Poor little guy was just minding his own business in that cave when Toto's spear shot through! I put my sentiments aside and prepare to take a bite and exclaim to the table that it is the best *polipo* I've ever tasted.

When everyone has been served, Pia and Raffaella stop moving. They don't sit, they stand at attention behind the high backs of two gilded eighteenth-century dining room chairs. (There is an expression in Neapolitan dialect, *'A mamma stà assettata, 'o pate stà allerta e 'o figlio fuie.* If the mother sits down, the father gets worried and the kids run away. In other words, a mother sitting is an unnatural sight.) There is silence: Toto has stopped talking, plates have stopped clinking.

We all taste the octopus.

"È duro 'sto polipo."

It is Nino who has broken the silence. He speaks with his mouth full, exaggerating the movement of trying to cut through the chewy octopus with his overworked molars. Have I understood correctly? Has he just said that the octopus is tough, no good?

"*È buonissimo! È buonissimo!*" I start my performance immediately. It's fabulous! It's fabulous! Let's pretend Nino didn't say that!

I am completely ignored.

Salvatore seconds his father's statement. "*Ha ragione Papà.*" Daddy's right.

Boing boing boing go our molars, and I continue my praise. "*Mai assaggiato così buono.*" I've never tasted octopus salad that's so good, I say with the strongest, most authoritative voice I can muster. I swallow a huge chunk whole. My canines have not even punctured the flesh of the animal. I haven't lied—the truth is that I've never tasted octopus salad at all.

No one counters Nino and Salva: apparently, they're right. It isn't tender, it isn't tasty. The only question that remains is, whose fault is it?

After an excruciating silence, Pia declares, "Toto, this octopus you caught is really tough." Not the octopus that we cooked. The octopus that *you caught.* Fightin' words.

"Lella, did you perhaps forget to beat it?" Toto asks Raffaella nonchalantly. Since he is certain that his octopus was not by nature tough, the only question he has for his sister is where she went wrong. Raffaella was supposed to mash the octopus with a hammer before performing the dunking torture, Toto explains with authority, even though I suspect that he has never cooked an octopus. He knows each step in the process, and wants to make sure everyone remembers that.

"Forget?! Of course I didn't forget!" she yells over him. "It's the octopus, it wasn't tender at all." Clearly, the women did the absolute best they could with what they had to work with.

I was glad to stay at the table so I didn't have to watch the sisters wiping the octopus into the trash with oily paper towels. In the kitchen, they talked of the toughness of the octopus; at the table, the men lamented that when women get to a certain age, they don't care for cooking anymore. They forget to hammer the octopus, or they get lazy and figure no one will notice.

"You should have tasted Nonna Clara's octopus salad," Toto tells me. He closes his eyes and imagines it. Succulent, tender.

"Was it much better than this one?" I ask to humor him, knowing the answer.

"*Eeeeeh*" on the exhale is his only reply. What can you do? Life sucks when the preparation of something as important as a *polipo* must be left in the hands of women from a "rotten" generation.

Presenza

"What is that lady's role? What is she *doing*?" I asked Salva. We were watching a soccer program as we snuggled on the sofa, digesting a baked *gâteau di patate* that Raffaella had prepared with potatoes, breadcrumbs, mortadella, prosciutto, and mozzarella. I was happy to be resting my head on Salva's chest.

"*Presenza*. She is *presenza*," he explained.

Presenza can mean physical presence, or can refer to cutting a beautiful or handsome figure when used with *bella. Una bella presenza*. This lady was certainly beautiful, and most definitely present.

Surrounding the lady was a group of middle-aged men talking (all at the same time) about the formation of the Napoli soccer team. While the men were all seated in very comfortable armchairs, the *presenza* lady was perched on a stool. A high stool. Which was convenient, given that the camera did not zoom in on her face, as it had with the men, but panned up slowly from her spike heels to her long, strategically crossed legs. The camera hesitated hopefully at her short skirt, even changed angles to see if any more nude flesh could be witnessed. It then continued up, slowly (what's the rush?), to her generous cleavage and stopped, finally, on her face. The men, still arguing in the background, were oblivious to the fact that they were not being filmed. The cameraman, apparently, had eyes only for Roberta.

It was a shame, though, that no one had told her that she was being filmed in close-up. She was clearly bored to tears, following none of the conversation. Instead, Roberta was examining her split ends.

The cameraman, instead of moving on when he found her entirely unengaged, lingered on her. The audience could hear the men in the background arguing about the attributes of this or that goalkeeper, but could see only Roberta and her self-grooming. A few seconds of this had passed when I distinctly heard a whistle. It was someone from the crew trying to get Roberta's attention! On air! She looked up, searching for the camera, and started grinning. A vacant, plastic grin. Believe it or not, she was more interesting to watch when she was examining her split ends.

There is someone sexy, bored, and present like Roberta on nearly every sports program that airs on Italian television. Game and variety shows feature the more energetic *veline*, scantily clad young models who dance and prance. They are more than *presente*; in one game show, a sexy *velina* appears at regular intervals and performs a lap dance with one of the contestants. Everyone else on the show looks on as if it's a natural occurrence—no raised eyebrows or laughing there.

A high point of a *Who Wants to Be a Millionaire*–inspired show is the moment of the *scossa*, or the electric shock dance. A *velina* wearing a bikini a few sizes too small stands on a dance floor under a spotlight and jiggles her stuff. The challenge, the actress's fundamental conflict and the driving force of her artistic journey, as it were, is to keep the top of her bikini on as she jiggles without holding it up with her hands. Interestingly, when she fails at this and her boobs pop out, the camera does not move to something else. If she can't keep her stuff covered, the director apparently feels, that's her problem.

There is often a man in an animal suit (and remember, this is not a kids' program) who does a silly Smurf-like voice and spends a good bit of time trying to get his paws on the *velina*. He is very large and red and runs around the studio shouting something unintelligible (as always, everyone except the *velina* is talking at the same time). The host of the game show seems to find this hilarious. It's a marriage of Disney and porn: I mean, what else could you want from TV?

Former prime minister Silvio Berlusconi, as the world knows, takes great pride in his country's *veline*. News of his *bunga bunga* parties shocked the world. But they didn't shock many people in Naples. The fact that the prime minister invited *veline* (some not quite eighteen) to his villa in Sardegna, the fact that before extending his invitation he perused their photo shoots—these were simply measures that powerful men take to ensure that they have . . . stimulating dinner partners.

No, what shocked many Neapolitans was the jiggling. A boundary was crossed when they learned that Berlusconi sat, pants down, on an armchair as the *veline* jiggled their bare breasts in his face. It was choreographed by his chiefs of staff to ensure that one *velina* from every racial group *bunga bunga*–ed by and jiggled. In his face.

This wasn't a TV show, it was national news. And he was the head of the nation's government. Even for the forgiving Neapolitans, that was a bit much.

In 1998, Italians were fascinated by the Monica Lewinsky

scandal. They would ask me what I thought of my country's *brutta figura*. Specifically, they asked me, *"Per chi sei?"* Who are you for? I interpreted this to mean, are you behind the Democrats supporting Clinton or are you Republican and in favor of impeachment? I would answer as best I could that although the president had humiliated himself and his country, I felt that impeachment was too extreme a measure. . . . But no, they would interrupt, we meant are you for Monica or for Bill?

Wait a second. Him against her? That made no sense to me. Monica was not the protagonist but a supporting character. At the center was the president of the United States, who had abused his power and humiliated . . .

"Yes," Italians agreed. "Humiliation. He really could have chosen someone who was more beautiful."

The scandal here was not what he had done, but the fact that he had done it with someone whom they considered overweight and unattractive. So the one who got the respect was Monica. If she, without good looks, could seduce the president of the United States, it was she who deserved to be the star of the lurid *sceneggiata*, or show. The president of the world's superpower, with only one chick, and not even a pretty one at that? That girl must have something. If she were in Italy, they probably would have elected her president.

I know that a big concern of the Italian government at the moment is the continuing brain drain, or *fuga dei cervelli*, of intellectuals from Italy to northern Europe and the United States, particularly in the sciences. Parliament is working on grants and other incentives to keep young, talented researchers from leaving the country. I can't help but think, however, of what would happen if there were a *fuga dei culetti*, or a tits-and-ass drain, in which *veline* found work elsewhere and left the peninsula. Now, *that* would be a national crisis.

Given the context, I think the *belle presenze* on sports programs are one of the least offensive things on Italian TV. For one thing, there's no camera positioned *under* the lady's skirt. But, more important, the *veline* who appear on the soccer programs are, perhaps without even realizing it, so honest and transparent. Roberta is objectified and degraded, yes. But there is something very human underneath: an Italian woman, like so many others, who is just plain bored by men talking about soccer.

A Single Plate of Pasta

I was asked to leave the Denza to find alternative housing in the middle of October. The boarding boys had arrived, and apparently I was a menace. I had unknowingly broken all sorts of rules of the Catholic institution (bidets had nothing to do with it, but I can't help but wonder *if they had known . . .*). I had been seen walking with a student there, a young man. On another occasion I had been seen walking with a different young man. I had not always been wearing a jacket and scarf when I walked with these members of the opposite sex. I tried to explain to the priest who served as the dean of students that I had to walk across the campus to get from my room to the dining hall, and it was eighty degrees! Most of the students were men, how could I help it if we walked side by side for a few meters?

"Da noi non si fa così" was his reply. That's not the way we do things here.

I started looking for a room to rent close by. Since this "experience abroad" was footed by my parents' dollars (and in 1997, dollars went far—thousands of lire far), I had no trouble finding a nice room in an apartment in Posillipo. I saw a big fluorescent yellow AFFITA STANZA (room for rent) sign on a building near the Calabrese girls' flat when I visited them for coffee one day. It was perfect—I would be near them and the Avallones.

"Will you have to cook for yourself?" Maria Rosa asked, concerned, when I said I was leaving the Denza. She and her sisters knew that things could get messy for me when it came to eating. "I'll be fine," I told them.

Salva and his parents worried too. My new flatmates were two girls from Puglia who went home for weeks at a time and kept to themselves when they were in the apartment. No more dinner tray at the Denza, with its scrumptious *scaloppine*, little carafe of wine, and *Buon appetito, signorina:* I'd be left to my own devices at mealtimes.

Most of the time, I ended up at the Avallones'. "What have you planned for your dinner?" Raffaella or Salva would ask me on the weekends, when lunch was over and I suggested that it was time for me to go back to my apartment. If I didn't answer, with conviction, *"Pasta e fagioli!"* or *"Zuppa di ceci!"*—if I hesitated in any way, they would look at each other knowingly. Six hours later I would be sitting next to Benedetta with her teddy bear pajamas devouring Raffaella's lasagna.

It would have been unheard of for a Neapolitan girl to sleep in her boyfriend's room at his parents' house at the age of twenty-two. But the rules seemed to be different for an *americana*. The American women that Italians saw on TV may not have jiggled their stuff on prime-time game shows, but they certainly were promiscuous. In addition, I was from a culture where parents would send their daughter to live and work alone, on another continent, right after college! The Avallones would never have had the presumption to tell me what I was allowed and not allowed to do.

On holidays and weekends, I would find a cot prepared by Raffaella in Salva's room. I accepted the plan: If the Avallones weren't hung up on propriety, why should I be? (*"Non si fa così,"* I heard the housekeeper, a middle-aged woman from central Naples, mumble as she remade my cot one morning. Nunzia Gatti echoed the priest at the boarding school: that's not the way it's done. Apparently, my sleeping in Salva's room didn't bother the Avallones, but it certainly bothered their maid.)

"I'm renting a new place," I told Cynthia and my other co-workers at the Consulate. I was grown-up and independent, I wanted them to know. There were two months left of my internship and I didn't want to publicize the fact that I'd basically moved in with my new boyfriend's parents. Or that, when left alone, I didn't know how to eat.

I can do this, I would tell myself on the rare occasions that I cooked in my new apartment. The kitchen was tiny and attracted fruit flies. Hungry, I would open the refrigerator to find nothing. So I'd boil water for some spaghetti, open a can of tomatoes, and then open the refrigerator again, to find that there was still nothing. I learned that it wasn't a great idea to start cooking when I was starved, because that's when my mind embraced dubious mathematical calculations like: If Raffaella's *ragù* simmers over a very low flame for eight hours, it stands to reason that I can let my tomato sauce boil over an extremely *hot* flame for twenty minutes.

As a recovering binger, I had another problem: After years of all-or-nothing eating, it was really hard to know what a "normal" amount of food was when I cooked for myself. I would stare at the pack of spaghetti and wonder if I should boil two noodles or the whole thing. Any amount seemed too much or too little. I needed an Italian woman to sit me down, slow me down, keep me company, and show me what and how much to eat.

I felt that it was important for me to say *no, grazie* every once in a while to the baked gnocchi or *pizza fritta* that Raffaella was making at the Avallones'. I needed to affirm my independence, after all. But as I tasted the spaghetti that I prepared for myself, soupy and insipid, I had to wonder, who was I kidding?

Soft *Stracchino* Cheese Right
Out of the Fridge

I was in a flannel robe on the Avallones' living room sofa one evening watching a horrendously dubbed version of *Diff'rent Strokes* when I heard, "*Egoista! Sei un egoista!*"

Benedetta was screaming. Nino was booming. Salvatore and his mother were trying to make peace. All four of them were in Nino and Raffaella's bedroom with the door closed. *Egoista*, Benedetta was calling her father, and though I didn't know exactly what that word meant, I knew that it had to be something pretty bad.

The suffix *-ista* in Italian signals a vocation. So *autista* is a driver, *dentista* a dentist. My all-time favorite word in Italian is the term for the person at the beauty parlor who shampoos: *shampista*. I figured that *egoista* must be someone who was so into their ego that it became a profession (I now know it just means selfish).

Benedetta and Nino were fighting about her fiancé, Mauro. Benedetta had met Mauro only eight months before, and he had proposed almost immediately. Benedetta had had several

previous relationships, all of which had lasted for years. Raffaella told me that three of these boys had become part of the
family, and that when Benedetta had broken up with them (it
was always she who ended it, always the turquoise eyes), Raffaella had been heartbroken. "They were like sons! And I didn't
even get a chance to say goodbye!" When Benedetta dumped
Andrea, the last one, Raffaella made her promise that the next
man she brought home would be the one that she would marry.
It just wasn't fair to put Raffaella through that again.

Mauro was a short cardiologist who, unlike almost all of
Benedetta's previous boyfriends, did not hit it off with any member of the family. So for once the tables were turned: In the
bedroom it was Nino who was attacking, and Benedetta who
was defending her fiancé. The first time Mauro came over, I
later learned, he had opened the refrigerator, taken out a little
plastic container of soft *stracchino* cheese, found himself a fork,
and started eating. The refrigerator of his future in-laws! Without even asking! Where had this guy grown up?

He used the informal *tu* form for *you* with both Nino and
Raffaella. (In English there is only one form for *you*, but in Italian, there are two: the formal *lei* is used when you don't know
someone or you want to show respect, while the informal *tu*
shows chumminess. Or friendship. Or *dis*respect. I don't know!
I still don't know. I *do* know that you have to conjugate all your
second-person verbs based on where you think you stand with
someone. And often, the move from using *lei* to *tu* in a relationship is scarier than asking someone to the senior prom.)

The Avallones were not a formal family. They did not stand
on ceremony, and were far from judgmental. But really, this guy
pushed the limits. Salvatore explained part of the problem when
he told me that Mauro was a communist. Wow, I thought. Italian communists open the refrigerator without asking. They

have the balls to use the *tu* form with everyone. It was kind of refreshing to see someone who totally disregarded Neapolitan bourgeois social norms (which I was just starting to understand myself). *Insomma*, I liked the guy. He made me look good.

That is, I liked him until he embarked on an anti-American tirade one evening at dinner that ended with the phrases "capitalist imperialism" and "worse than fascism" and lots of spit on the table. Now I agreed with Nino. You do *not* open the refrigerator in someone else's apartment without asking.

While Raffaella kept her reservations about Mauro to herself, Nino did not. That evening everyone in the apartment building heard about Mauro taking his shoes off and filling the Avallones' apartment with the stench of his smelly feet (with Nino, it always came back to the *puzza*, the peeyew). Benedetta kept countering with *Egoista! Egoista!* I had never been party to such a row in someone else's home. Part of me was embarrassed and wanted to slip out without making a noise, and another part of me rejoiced in a stunning revelation: families other than mine—even happy, functional families—fought. They didn't just disagree, with respect and calm voices. Other families had it *out*.

I felt perfectly at home.

~~~~~~~ ☀ ~~~~~~~

"*Aaayyyed!* The ambassador's here!" My mother's West Virginia twang turned my father's two-letter name into one with three syllables, all diphthonged vowels. It was an early summer evening in the 1980s and my father was doing his laps in our pool. He swam with no bathing suit. "It slows me down," he would tell us.

Ed Wilson didn't like to be slowed down by anybody or anything.

My father grew up rich in Chicago. His grandfather, Thomas Wilson, was a captain of industry who had immigrated to the United States from London, Ontario, at the turn of the century. He worked his way up from cleaning manure in the Chicago stockyards to becoming president of the third largest meatpacking company in America. As president, he changed its name to Wilson and Co.

A lot of the canned meat that was unloaded by American GIs in the Bay of Naples and given to starving Neapolitans during World War II was Wilson. The hams baked by my maternal grandmother in a small West Virginia town in the fifties were Wilson.

My great-grandfather, instead of throwing away the cowhides and intestines of the animals, started producing footballs, baseballs, and tennis rackets: *We use every part of the pig but the squeal!* was the slogan. Wilson Sporting Goods was born. Thomas Wilson made the footballs that American kids played with and the hot dogs their parents grilled.

Little Ed was the first grandson, and he had everything he could ever want: his own horse, a chauffeur, tickets on luxury liners to Europe at the age of nine. After Princeton and Oxford, he got his PhD at Johns Hopkins University's School of Advanced International Studies in Washington, where he met my mother, at a reception for new students in 1967.

"He looked like a Kennedy, but fat," she told my sister and me.

When she became Mrs. Wilson, Bonnie Salango gave up her job at a Washington think tank to become a full-time wife and mother. My father was at the Department of Commerce, where he worked with the Bureau of East-West Trade to investigate market opportunities in Eastern Europe. My mother accompanied him to places like Bucharest and Sofia, and at home cooked Italian American meals for pudgy communists.

A *think tank*? I now wonder. A *government job*? The two of them could have taken their Bonnie and Ed show on the road; they could have fought it out in an Edward Albee play, or started a puppet theater for underprivileged toddlers. We would have been better off. But they both had advanced degrees, and they both shouldered lots of parental expectations. It was 1970, and they made "respectable" life choices.

I was embarrassed by my father, always. He couldn't get in a taxi without speaking some exotic foreign language with the driver; he couldn't be served at a restaurant without making sure the Czech waiter saw his imitation of Václav Havel. While the dads of our friends at the country club wore bermudas with little frogs or ducks on them, my father wore a tie that Romanian dictator Ceauşescu gave him ("I'm telling you, Bonnie, the guy likes me," he told my mom, who ignored him) with sheer white bell-bottoms. Ed Wilson needed to be at center stage—he had to be *noticed*. With his clothes and accessories (an obscure Central Asian medal of honor from the last century, an antique walking cane that he didn't need), my father begged to be asked, Where did that come from, Ed? Tell us the story.

My mother hated the way he dressed. She called his see-through pantwear *diaphanous*.

That particular evening, she had told my father that there was no time for him to swim, much less to swim bare-assed. My father paid her little mind, shouting as he dove in, "There is absolutely time, and I can't hear your screaming underwater! Ha!"

Splash.

Despite her anger and embarrassment, I think my mother

felt some genuine, if vindictive, joy when the Polish ambassador rang the doorbell and she escorted him outside to see my father freestyling in his altogether. I remember her crouching down with a grin at the end of the pool to catch her husband when he came up for a breath. "Your ambassador's here. Aren't ya gonna come say hi?"

Who knows, maybe this kind of vaudeville-meets-*Deliverance* was just what Polish-American relations during the cold war needed. For my sister and me, it was just the first act in the show that was dinner at the Wilsons'. Our job as daughters was to entertain and to look beautiful as we did it. After the meal, we might perform an Andrew Lloyd Webber duet or a dance routine to "Endless Love." Anna, just one year older than me, was blond and thin. She was more beautiful than me, played the piano better than me, danced better than me, and was cooler than me. I was not only overweight but severely near-sighted. I had tinted glasses (blue on the top and pink on the bottom—I thought they were *very* cool) and, my sister tells me, I smelled like peanut butter.

I could not compete with my Claudia Schiffer sister (no amount of lemon juice at the beach could get my hair so blond; no diet could make my thighs as skinny), so I excelled at school and played the clown at home. It was left to me to perform the postshow (that is, after-dinner) imitation of Ambassador Wisniewski, snorting as he tried to shell grilled shrimp with his Stalinesque fingers.

We were so unlike the families that we socialized with in suburban Washington. Our friends were always at peace with each other and with the world. Girls wore Laura Ashley, boys J. Crew. Everyone used soft, respectful voices in the dining room of our country club. In the midst of "Could you pass the salt, Chet?" and "How was field hockey practice, Ashley?" we were different: theatrical and argumentative and, I realize now, so very Neapolitan.

Gary Coleman was screwing up his face and saying, *"Che cavolo stai dicendo, Weelles?"* (translated literally, "What kind of cabbage you goin' on about, Willis?") when Salvatore came into the living room. He had been crying, and his eyelashes were stuck together with tears. He kneeled down and put his head on my lap. I could feel him taking huge post-sob breaths.

Salva was looking for solace on my big American thighs.

A door slammed. Plates clinked as Raffaella put things away in the kitchen. Nino and Benedetta silently licked their wounds.

In Salvatore's body, I could feel the depth of his love for his family. And as he held on to me tight, I felt like it wasn't just love for his family—it extended to me, too. Maybe this wasn't simply attraction or youthful infatuation on his part. Maybe it was something more.

When he looked up, I could see that his face was wet. His voice trembled as he explained, *"A mio padre non piace Mauro."* My father doesn't like Mauro. Salva flicked his hand under his chin in the Neapolitan gesture meaning nothing, zero, *niente.* The guy, his hand gesture said, had no chance.

English Lessons

My internship at the Consulate became part-time at the
end of October. We weren't exactly busy, so I asked
Cynthia if I could start teaching English in the afternoons to
earn some extra money. It didn't take much to convince the establishment, since I wasn't being paid.

The English-language schools I applied to in Naples had
names like the London Institute, Wall Street Academy, and
Cambridge Centre, and were located on the second or third
floor of crowded apartment buildings downtown. They were
made up of two classrooms at most, with cartoonish American
and British flags on the walls. I was hired immediately because
I was mother-tongue. The school I chose to start at paid 10,000
lire an hour (about five dollars), handed to me in cash by the
director at the end of each lesson. He spoke no English whatsoever.

Unbeknownst to the director of the language school, my
classes centered on two topics of conversation: What does everyone think of the United States? And, What does everyone think
of my relationship with Salvatore and our future?

Like many Americans, I was fascinated by what my students, most of whom had never been to the States, thought about my country. Could it be that I was homesick? In part, but it was more that slightly adolescent and narcissistic curiosity common to a lot of Americans: our great big national desire to know what they *really* think of us. I had my students write short essays. Here are some highlights:

"The Americans are a beautiful people because they are simple. They are always saying what they think. Not like Italian people."

"I think that United States is a big country full of people who lives in many different ways, trust in different gods, but they lives in a same place because they are like brothers and respect each other. Like blacks, chineses, European people."

"In America, all the streets are crowded by people of different races and colors (whites, blacks, yellows, reds) and this is beautiful."

"I'd like to go to the U.S. To learn how to be myself and, in spite of that, to be happy too. Not to make blood in my veins get water, to get alive."

"U.S. is the place where all things leave before spreading all over."

"If I will have time in America I'd like to ski in Colorado, in Aspen of course, running like hell on my skis with big black sunglasses and a crazy long hat. After this will I get a little tired? Yes, maybe. And then? Iowa!!!!!! I would go there for two months, getting fuel for myself, relaxing on the green, kidding with the dolls. I'd like to rent a big factory [I think he meant farm, *fattoria* in Italian] and sleep alone a very long time."

After we'd pulled apart their perceptions, and misconceptions, of my homeland, we would move on to grammar.

The question of the day might be: *Do you-all* (plural of *you*, each student can give his or her opinion) *really think Salva loves me?* Or, let's try the third person present interrogative of *love: Does he love me enough to move away from Naples and his parents?* As their English got better, I challenged them to dissect my emotional state. *Am I in love with Salvatore, or with Naples in general?* Or even, *Am I simply in love with his mother and what she cooks?*

Because I enjoyed teaching and sharing the beauty of my mother tongue, it was extremely frustrating for me that Salvatore seemed to have no desire whatsoever to improve his English. We were spending a lot of time together, and I was an English teacher, so wouldn't it have been natural for him to use the opportunity to better his language skills? Did I really have to be subjected to his singing, to the tune of John Denver's "Take Me Home, Country Roads," "Hoven road, in the sun. To the place I rerun! *West Virginia!* [with gusto, he knew that part!] Sunshine Momma, run to road, in the song . . ."?

I understand that when you grow up listening to songs with lyrics in a language that you don't understand, you focus on the melody and the rhythm. A nonsense approximation of the words is just fine. But shouldn't it make him just a tad self-conscious that there was a native English speaker listening? Not in the least.

When I would correct his grammar, for instance by noting, "Salva, the first person of the verb *to come* is 'come.' No *s, capisci?* I come," he would respond with his version of Boy George: "*Cumma cumma cumma cumma comeleon, you giva go, you giva go* . . ." There was no hope. Years later, I would have to leave this teaching job to my bilingual and easily embarrassed children.

At the same time Salva refused to learn English, I was getting more fluent in both spoken Italian and in the parallel language of hand gestures, which is necessary for survival in Naples. Americans use hand gestures too, but they employ them in a completely different way. Except for a few precise ones ("Tsk, tsk" with the carrot-peeling movement of two index fingers; curling up one index finger to mean *Come here*), American hand gestures are large, sweeping, and general. And they vary from person to person. In Naples, they are so specific that there is even a dictionary of *gesti*, complete with pictures of someone's hand and the description of the movement. As a foreigner, you must learn this language just as you learn the verbs or adjectives of the spoken language.

When I first arrived in Naples, I would ask the doorman at the boarding school if there was any mail for me, and he would respond without a sound, looking me straight in the eye. He held, however, his thumb and index finger in the form of a pistol and shook his thumb almost imperceptibly from side to side. My response would be to look him in the eye and ask again, is there any mail for me? Once again, he would do the jiggling-thumb-gun thing, and jut out his lower lip just to make things clear. *Oh, grazie*, thank you! I would say, and wink, thinking I had just engaged in some profound covert communication but still having absolutely no idea whether I had any mail or not. I later learned that that hand gesture means *niente*, nothing, and can also be expressed with a click of the tongue and a hand flicking under the chin.

Watch out, that guy is trying to cheat you is expressed by pulling down the lower eyelid of one eye with the index finger. *Let's eat* is all the fingertips of one hand together doing a pecking motion toward the mouth, while *pasta* is the index and middle finger doing a twisting motion simulating a fork gathering up spaghetti. These are just a few of many, but my all-time favorite is the gesture that means someone has died. It is (get this!) the index and middle fingers of the right hand straightened upward together, representing the soul of the deceased, doing a circular, Slinky-like motion up to the sky. The other fingers are closed in a fist. Along with the hand gesture, a quick (rather cheerful, strangely enough) whistle is emitted. This is apparently the sound of the soul of the deceased going to heaven. Just a hop, skip, and a jump! You will hear people in Naples (where to say someone is *morto*, or dead, is considered rather bad taste) describing how Aunt Maria (as soon as the name is uttered, there goes the soul up to heaven with a whistle so we remember she's dead!) made the best frittata. . . .

As for my spoken Italian, the language I was learning was Neapolitan dialect. Not *dialetto stretto*, or pure dialect, but Italian with a marked Neapolitan accent and with many expressions that are unique (I now know) to Naples. The idea of having a down-home southern accent in Italian did not bother me, because I think in some visceral way it took me back to my mother's Appalachian twang. It's a different language, I know, but I swear that the feel of it, the pull-up-a-chair-honey-soup's-on of it, is the same. Ham hocks and beans in southern West Virginia or fried pizza dough smothered in tomato and mozzarella in the countryside surrounding Napoli. Tight Italian soccer shirts and gel in the hair or oversize basketball jerseys and Walmart. The cultures in many ways are polar opposites. But when you're called to the table by Mama, or Mamma, in that way, in a way that goes straight to your innards . . . you could just as well be in Bluefield, West Virginia, or Secondigliano, Provincia di Napoli.

An analogous situation might be an Italian girl, a bit shy, pretty in an old-fashioned way, who has come to the United States to learn English. "Oh, you're from Italy! Whereabouts?" She responds with a smile, "I's from Rome but learned myself English in Memphis." That was the sort of impression I gave, linguistically. In Naples, I learned that any and every verb could be reflexive. I ate myself a plate of pasta, I watched myself a film. My vowels were long and lazy, especially the *a* (in Naples, it lasts so long that you don't know if the speaker is going to get around to finishing the word). My *s* sounded like *sh*. "To have" was for me the Neapolitan *tenere* (which is more like "got myself") instead of the Italian *avere*. "*Tengo na famma 'e pazze*," I would say, meaning that I was very, very hungry. Or, literally, "I got myself a crazy hunger."

It was the night before I left home for Princeton University. My father, uncle, and grandfather were all die-hard Princeton alumni. They went to reunions every year with orange top hats, they sang the college anthem "Old Nassau" at family dinners, their response when they found out that someone had gone to another Ivy League school was, "What a shame, he seemed like such a nice man." Throughout my childhood I thought my father's legal name was Edward Wilson '63.

So everyone was ecstatic when I was admitted to Old Nassau and decided to go. I was supposed to be ecstatic, too. I was supposed to be "*so* psyched." My mother was supposed to be relieved and proud and ready to enjoy her husband's company in a peaceful empty nest. We both pretended that we couldn't wait. I was going to be Katherine Wilson '96! There were auditions for *Kiss Me, Kate* with the Princeton University Players that very fall! In the checkout line of Bed Bath & Beyond, pulling the biggest suitcases down from the attic, attaching that luggage thing on top of the station wagon, we talked about how "cool" it was going to be.

And then the night before leaving I went upstairs to brush my teeth and set my alarm for the next day. My mother came to my room with an excuse, did you pack your toothbrush or something, and I gave her the opening of a very quiet, very contained, "Mommy, I don't want to go."

"*Sweetheaaaart*," she bawled, "it's just the worrrst thang thit ever happened to me! My baaayybyyy girl!"

In Naples they say, *'E figlie so' ppiezze 'e core*. Your children are little pieces of your heart. But to feel what that expression means, you need to imagine Dolly Parton saying it. No, actually, you need to imagine Dolly singing it. Because this dialect, like that of the American South, lays bare so much suffering and so much love that it does to the body what good country music does—it goes straight from the ears to the gut.

Melanzane a Funghetto

The Avallones' apartment smelled like a geriatric ward. Ben-Gay stung my nostrils as I walked into Salvatore's room to find Nunzia Gatti massaging his bare shoulders and neck. Salva was sitting at his desk; Nunzia was behind him. I was appalled.

The desk where Salva "repeated" his studies faced two French doors through which he could see the Bay of Naples and Vesuvius. *"Dunque,"* he was repeating, *"la legge canonica del Settecento prevedeva . . ."* Eighteenth-century canonical law foresaw the enforcement . . . I could not believe my eyes, or my ears, or my nostrils. Had Salva really asked the Avallones' housekeeper of twenty years to massage him with Ben-Gay? Was he really studying his law texts while she did it?

I said nothing. No one noticed me standing there.

"Grazie, Nunzia," Salva thanked her when the massage was finished, and she went to wash the Ben-Gay off her hands and to return to chopping eggplants in little cubes to fry. She was making *melanzane a funghetto*, following strict instructions from Raffaella. (Nunzia, born and raised in central Naples,

surely knew how to prepare *melanzane a funghetto* when she came to work for the Avallones. But Raffaella had to make sure that the recipe was exactly the same as hers, and so one morning twenty years ago Nunzia followed Raffaella around like a little duckling as she prepared the *melanzane*, learning from scratch.)

"*Oh, ciao, Ketrin!*" she said cheerfully as she passed me on her way out.

Nunzia came in the mornings to do simple cooking and heavy cleaning in the apartment. What are *le pulizie grosse*? I asked Salva when he described Nunzia's responsibilities, translating the expression in my mind as the Big Cleanings. I saw that Raffaella did a lot of cleaning herself: she swept, dusted, even got up on a ladder to wipe the windows down with old *Mattino* newspapers. So why did they need a housekeeper? "The big cleaning," it turns out, meant keeping things clean in the Neapolitan sense of the word. For this she needed Nunzia Gatti.

In Italy, one's apartment must be spotless. Outside, many Italians think nothing of throwing their cigarettes on the ground or otherwise littering in full view of other people. It is shocking to witness the contrast between the filthy streets of Naples and the shiny, disinfected, pine-smelling cleanliness of Neapolitan apartments. A home should not be superficially clean, or *pulita per la suocera*. (This expression, meaning *mother-in-law clean*, is used in a highly pejorative way and refers to something that is clean for show. An apartment that would pass the test of a five-minute visit from a mother-in-law. Dusted, clothes hung up, no dishes in the sink.) No, one's apartment must be *Italian* clean. Toothpicks getting the crud out of the molding. No dust in the rungs and rivets of the radiator. Outside, *Chi se ne frega!* Who cares! is the mentality, it's not my house.

Many Americans, on the other hand, would not be caught dead throwing a dirty Kleenex on the ground at the park but think nothing of leaving their houses in a state that would have an Italian mother dialing up social services. An Italian grandmother told me of an American mother she knew in Rome in the 1960s who was so much fun! So positive! So kind! *But that apartment.* No one could understand how the woman could live, let alone raise a family, in such a pigsty. *Mio Dio.* Beds unmade and clothes on chairs. Those poor children!

Nunzia Gatti was around sixty and square-shaped. She spoke almost exclusively dialect, and used a *third* form of *you*—the most respectful, feudal form, *voi*, which exists only in Neapolitan—with every member of the family except me. When we first met, I was uncomfortable with the idea of using the familiar form with her while she "Madam'd" me, so I did what I often do: I used the formal *lei* with her, sprinkling it with a few *tus* so I didn't seem too uptight. Pretty soon we were *tu*-ing without saying anything about it. Nobody, including me, would dare say, Let's use *tu* with each other from here on in, whatta you say?

Nunzia, coming from a different social stratum, was a sort of foreigner in this household just as I was. She took it upon herself to warn me in hushed tones about the dangers of getting too involved with a Neapolitan upper-class boy, a *signorino.* "*Vieni qua*"—she would beckon me with her index finger to follow her to the balcony where she was beating the rugs with a long wooden rug-beater—"*Sai come si dice a Napoli?*" You know what we say in Naples? "*Mogli e buoi dai paesi tuoi!*" Wives and cows from your hometown. She didn't mean, as I first thought, that I should be careful of buying a cow or a wife that wasn't from Washington. The idea was that Salva and I would never work as a couple: relationships only work if the husband and wife come from the same place and the same socioeconomic background. "Oh yes," I would reply with a polite smile, "I understand."

I was uncomfortable with Nunzia and with the culture of servitude that made it okay for Salva to ask her to rub Ben-Gay on his neck. It was so servile, so lewd! When I exploded at Salva, wanting an explanation for it, he was confused. "It's no big deal! She works here and my neck was hurting. Your family has a housekeeper too!"

Doris Belen Hernandez moved to Washington from Honduras in 1984. She was hired by my parents to clean our house several times a week and was responsible for vacuuming, ironing, and making the beds. She called my parents, Bonnie and Ed, "Mrs. Bony and Mr. Head." My mother cleaned up frantically before Doris arrived, worried that she would "just have too much to do, poor Doris!" My mother, the *signora* of the house, would "give orders" that started with "Doris, do you think if it's not too much trouble that you could try to maybe . . ." and ended with "That is, if you have time!" When she needed to be sure Doris was coming on a certain day, she would say, "You're not thinking of coming by on Tuesday, are you?"

Raised poor, my mother was uncomfortable with the idea of hiring "help." She liked to pretend that Doris came because she felt like it, or because she happened to be in the neighborhood.

Doris was not a workaholic. She watched soap operas in our family room. She chatted with her friends on the phone. Our house was large enough that when she cleaned, nobody saw or heard her. We would see the beds made, notice that we were out of potato chips and leftovers, and think, "Oh, Doris must have come."

When we did cross paths, Doris was entertaining. Her English left much to be desired, but this didn't stop her from doing some fantastic imitations of all of us. My father huffing and puffing as he tried to tie his shoelaces for a tennis match, belching and saying "Goddammit!" (with a Spanish accent). "Kaaaaatherine, you're not gonna wayar that are ya?" with tragically scrunched up eyebrows was my mother: Bluefield, West Virginia, by way of Tegucigalpa.

Doris was irreverent and entertaining, and in the Wilson family, that was enough.

"A housekeeper, yes, but I certainly would never ask her to massage—"

"But it's okay to ask her to clean the toilets?" Salva was honestly clueless about the difference.

"Where I come from, you pay a masseuse to massage and a cleaner to clean!"

With a high-and-mighty slam of the door, I went to find Nunzia to hear more reasons why I shouldn't fall into the trap of marrying a *signorino* like Salva.

An Italian friend of mine told me about a recent trip she had taken to the States. "You Americans," she sighed, "some of you have estates as big as Italian villages but no one to pour your coffee in the morning."

"That's not true," I countered. "If you're famous you do."

Raffaella's relationship with Nunzia took me a while to get a handle on. Raffaella gave orders using the familiar *you*, and I got a grammar lesson in the imperative familiar. *"Metti le lenzuola sopra ad asciugare!"* Hang the sheets upstairs to dry! *"Non usare quella scopa in casa!"* Don't use that broom indoors! Raffaella's assertive tone missed that of Cinderella's stepsisters by only a smidgeon, and was quite frankly petrifying to me. When Nunzia made a mistake in her simple cooking tasks, Raffaella didn't call to her from the other room but looked her in the eyes and asked, "*Ma perchè?*"—But why?

Raffaella referred to Nunzia as a *brava donna*, a good woman, faint praise that in Naples basically means "not a thief." It's too bad, though, she told me once, that Nunzia doesn't know how to cook or clean.

To test Nunzia, Raffaella would play tricks on her. One day she took a big piece of *pizza di scarola*, a focaccia-like bread stuffed with escarole, olives, and pine nuts, and put it in the refrigerator, knowing that it was Nunzia's favorite. When Nunzia left, she checked the size of the slice. "Watch this!" she told me mischievously the next day when all three of us were in the kitchen.

"Nunzia, where is the *pizza di scarola* that was in the fridge yesterday?" Raffaella feigned nonchalance, but was seriously enjoying this.

"It's still there, ma'am, in the fridge."

"No, I mean the other half. Somebody ate it."

Silence.

"Who was it?"

"Actually, it was me, ma'am."

"*Aaah, ho capito, ho capito.*" I see. Raffaella looked at me and winked, joyous in her victory.

Nunzia, I assumed, resented her high-maintenance boss. When Raffaella left the room, she rolled her eyes and even flicked the back of her hand in the Neapolitan gesture signifying someone who is *pesante*, or heavy, hard to take.

After episodes like this, it surprised me when I found out that Nunzia came to Raffaella sometimes to get her shots. She had some kind of thyroid problem and had to get shots every month. Since Raffaella was known for her skill in administering shots, Nunzia stood in her employer's marble bathroom and rolled down her thick pantyhose. Raffaella returned from whatever fancy reception she was attending to plunge the needle in her maid's pudgy backside. Dressed in a Chanel suit and balanced on three-inch heels, Raffaella would hold an ice pack for at least five minutes to Nunzia's butt—*"Non ti muovere!"* Don't move! There was that familiar imperative again!—before packing her in the Lancia to give her a ride home.

Pasta e Fagioli

Many of the students in the English school where I taught were college guys in their twenties. *"Teeeacher, we go out later, you come?"* they would suggest in class. Nobody was asking me for a date—it was a group. Sometimes I went. I enjoyed them, especially a smart, unattractive guy named Gianmarco who really liked talking about me, and America.

One afternoon after class, Gianmarco told me that he and some of his high school friends (both young men and young women, *ragazzi* and *ragazze*) were going to Abruzzo to ski over the weekend—did I want to come?

I'd never been to Abruzzo! Skiing was fun!

I asked Salva midweek what his plans were for the weekend. "Plans" can be translated as *progetti* in Italian. Projects. "Do you have plans?" translates roughly as "Any projects up your sleeve?" Often, in Naples, projects are not scheduled more than one day in advance, which can make an American go bonkers (*How do we know we'll be alive?* Salva asks me when I want to book plane tickets a few months in advance).

"Nope. No projects this weekend," he told me.

"I'm thinking of going to Abruzzo," I ventured. "Do you mind?"

His voice was clipped when he answered. "Do whatever you want. *Sei adulta e vaccinata*." You're a grown-up who's had her vaccinations, an expression meaning you're free to choose for yourself.

He had an exam coming up, so chances were he'd be spending most of the weekend with his *Code of Canon Law* book. I wasn't interested in any of the men I'd be traveling with, so I had a clear conscience. I bought some heavy sweaters with little snowflakes on them and packed a suitcase for the trip.

Much of the Abruzzo region is made up of little towns named after rocks: Roccaraso, Rocca di Mezzo, Rocca Pia. They are nestled in the Apennine Mountains, which cut through the center of the Italian boot. We were headed for Roccaraso, where Gianmarco's parents, like the Avallones and many other Neapolitan families, had a little apartment. Zio Toto, I would later learn, goes skiing there every winter. (But the plastic hand? I asked Salva. "Oh, he duct-tapes it to his ski pole. You've gotta avoid him on ski lifts, because if the tape gets wet and starts to come off, he asks the person next to him on the *seggiovia* to re-attach it.")

Roccaraso is an hour-and-a-half drive from Naples. In the car with Gianmarco and his friends, I noticed castles and fortresses from the Middle Ages zooming by. Gianmarco was definitely nerdy, and not very cute, and still he drove like a maniac. I was riding shotgun. In the backseat two guys and two girls were packed in, and it became apparent as we flew over the mountain roads that they were paired off. The "group of friends" wasn't an amorphous gang hanging out: there were exactly three couples, and the two couples in the backseat were sucking face by the time we reached L'Aquila. This would be a long weekend.

Roccaraso was bombed beyond recognition during World War II ("by the Americans!" one of Gianmarco's friends in the backseat exclaimed, and I decided to keep quiet), so there is nothing medieval about it. The buildings are from the 1960s and are brown and rectangular, with Swiss-like wooden balconies. We parked on the main street and piled out.

I remarked on the silence, the peace, the mountain splendor. "Just wait," Gianmarco said. "Wait till the rest of Naples gets here."

The first cold weekends of the year, the period surrounding New Year's Eve, and the week of Carnevale in February are the periods of the Neapolitan Descent, he explained to me. At these times, the town becomes the site of Neapolitans *in trasferta* (a sports term referring to a team that is playing an away game but that is also used to describe a group that goes somewhere en masse). No serene, tranquil Abruzzese atmosphere then—it's more like an eighth-grade field trip. Naples *in trasferta* is chaos, noise, laughter. Pushing and shoving. Women in full-length furs (which they wear exclusively in Roccaraso; Naples is too warm) doing what they call "laps" down the main street to be seen.

I didn't know Neapolitans were big skiers. Given the way they drove, I was starting to get skeptical about going down the mountain with them. My fears were justified.

After a breakfast of croissants and cappuccinos in his little gingerbread-house apartment the next morning, Gianmarco and his dark-skinned, black-haired guy friends got done up in high-tech Spyder ski attire. The women had hairbands that matched the buckles on their ski boots. They all looked like expert downhill racers who'd just come off the pages of a ski magazine.

I wasn't an expert skier. I took after my mother.

Before they were married, Bonnie Salango made Ed Wilson believe that she loved the outdoors. Sports were very important for my father, and he told my mother he could never marry a woman who didn't enjoy tennis, skiing, and swimming as much as he did. "Oh, I ski," she told him, batting her eyelashes. "We can go *after* we're married."

Their first and last "after-we're-married" ski trip was to Aspen, Colorado. My father didn't think it necessary to verify that his wife could make it down the mountain on her skis. He took her to the top of the highest slope, and after spraying to a parallel stop, noticed that she hadn't managed to get off the chairlift. As he slalomed down (in an enormous Siberian wolf hat that would be a source of embarrassment throughout my skiing career), he looked up to see Bonnie riding the lift back down the other side.

"*Bonnie! What in God's name are you doing?*" he screamed.

"*Ayyyed, ya never told me to get off!*"

She went up again, and this time managed to dismount. My father led her to a black-diamond slope. When she saw how steep it was, she calmly took off her skis and pushed them down the mountain. Then she sat on her waterproofed butt and slid down to the base.

"Shouldn't someone help that woman?" a gentleman asked my father.

"Oh, I think she'll be just fine."

My mother never skied again, but my sister and I went to Aspen every year with our father. Anna looked like Suzy Chapstick coming down the mountain, while my lavender ski pants were always too tight around the thighs and my glasses fogged up under my goggles. I never saw any reason to give up the snowplow, which was why my father and sister gave me the nickname Plow.

Despite their professional appearance, Gianmarco and his friends had never given up the snowplow either. They pizzapied straight down the mountain at perilous speeds, snapping photos of each other with their cameras as they went.

It was terrifying. People were coming at me from all directions. It seemed that no one slalomed—they were all on straight daredevil trajectories, from young kids to elegant white-suited *signore*. And their speed didn't stop them from having loud conversations from opposite sides of the slope. They argued about which *rifugio*, or restaurant on the mountain, had the best grilled meats, or the best *scamorza* cheese. Let's meet at the Aremogna at two! No, the Pizzalto restaurant has better *bruschette*!

As if this weren't stressful enough for a nonexpert skier, the "lines" for the chairlifts were great masses of pushing people who had trouble keeping their balance on skis.

"Can you please get your skis off mine?"

"But he's pushing me!"

"She butted. I was after that lady in the white hat."

"I did not! I was here first!"

Katherine, you're going to have to use your poles to push ahead, Gianmarco told me gently when he saw that I'd been standing in the same spot for ten minutes. I could *not* push my skis onto someone else's, butting in line and risking a colossal fall at the same time. "Don't worry, I'll meet you at the *rifugio*," I told him.

The cuisine in this part of Abruzzo is meat- and cheese-based. You won't find quite as much butter and cream as in the Alps, and virtually nothing is fried. It is, however, fatty: sausages and lamb chops, grilled *scamorza* cheese, and salami that is to die for. The pasta specialties are *cazzarielli e fagioli*, a gnocchi-like pasta with beans (and sausage, in case you haven't gotten your caloric intake for the day), pasta with truffles, and in the summer, pastas with every kind of mushroom you can imagine. You don't see brightly colored vegetables in this mountain village, and fruit is expensive and hard to come by.

We sat at a long wooden table in the sun. I soon realized that this was not about refueling: we wouldn't be grabbing a burger or bowl of chili before we hit the slopes again. This was a *destination*. The skiing had been a fun mode of transportation to get us here, and now we could unbuckle our boots and dig into a heavenly *antipasto*, *primo*, and *secondo*, accompanied by deep red Montepulciano d'Abruzzo wine. We started with a platter of fresh ham, *salame*, and cheeses, followed by steaming *cazzarielli e fagioli* on plastic plates. When the grilled lamb chops and sausages came out, I worried that I'd have to roll down the mountain (or at least slide like my mother had in Aspen).

"It's normal to feel large in Roccaraso," one of the girls in our group reassured me. "*Qui, si lievita.*" You get bigger here. The word comes from *lievito*, or yeast. You expand like pizza dough. Maybe that's because of all the sausage and cheese and infrequent trips to the bathroom, I offered. No, the young woman told me with authority. "It's all the oxygen. You will find that in Roccaraso you are hungry and sleepy." (I declined to note that most places in the world have this effect on me.) I would later hear people in Naples talking about going to Roccaraso to *pigliarme nu poco 'e ossiggeno* or "get myself some oxygen."

The *ragazza* finished off the last bone of the little Abruzzese lamb and pulled a foldable aluminum tanning mirror out of her backpack. She held it up to her face to augment the sun's rays as she digested. "This place is so good for your health," she told me. "The best Italian wet nurses were from Abruzzo. Rich *signore* from Rome or Naples or Milan would handpick women from these mountains to nurse their babies. Their milk was rich, fatty, and yellow: the best. Abruzzese food is good for you, Ketrin."

After that lunch on the ski slope in Roccaraso, I felt confident that I could land a job as an Abruzzese wet nurse, no questions asked.

***

I got back to Naples oxygenated. Gianmarco hadn't tried anything with me, which had been an increasing concern with all the couples smooching around us. I couldn't wait to see Salva and tell him about the skiing and the fabulous meals in Roccaraso.

But he didn't want to see me. He gave monosyllabic answers on the phone, and didn't invite me over. Alone in my little apartment, I wondered what I'd done that was so awful.

"You *what?*" Maria Rosa asked me when I went to get her advice. "You spent a weekend in Roccaraso with another guy?"

"It wasn't a guy! It was a group!"

"Even worse! So American women *are* loose like the ones on *The Young and the Restless.*"

"But I did nothing wrong! I touched no one, I kissed no one. . . ."

She thought for a moment, and then said, "Go immediately and apologize to Salvatore if you want to continue the relationship. Tell him that you did not *touch* any other man. That you had a major lapse of judgment, but you've come to your senses."

I did. I repeated the script that she had written for me (with the same intonation of the Catholic prayer of confession *mea culpa, mea culpa, mea maxima culpa*: through my fault, through my fault, through my most grievous fault). After hearing my apology, Salva said, "I just have one question. *Stiamo insieme?*" Are we together? He held eye contact with me. This was something he cared a lot about.

"*Certo,*" I said. Of course.

"Because maybe in your country you can have lots of guys at the same time and it's okay with all of them. But Ketrin? It's not okay with me. *Siamo una sola cosa, adesso.*" We are one thing now, you and I.

That sounded good to me.

Rococò Cookies and Eggnog

As I walked the Via San Gregorio Armeno with Raffaella on December 10, 1996, my mind worked up a list of things that were surely not sold on the street in first-century Bethlehem:

1. sausages
2. swordfish
3. watermelons
4. pizza
5. spaghetti
6. mussels

"There was no pizza in Palestine!" I exclaimed to Raffaella when my mental list was complete. "There was no spaghetti. People didn't sell fish near the manger on a cold December night!"

Raffaella had brought me to this famous street in the center of Naples because it's been the home of the Neapolitan Christmas tradition of the *presepe,* or Nativity scene, since the seven-

teenth century. Artisans display their handiwork on both sides of
the tiny alley from the beginning of November until January 6,
but traditionally Neapolitans go between the Immacolata, December 8, and Christmas Eve. On December 10, San Gregorio
was one great pushing pack of humanity.

"Ketrin, look at that one! It has a moving water mill." She
pulled me through the crowd to look at the crèche close up. It
had not only running water, but twinkling lights and a pizza
oven that lit up from the inside. A three-centimeter-tall baker
with realistic stubble used a long wooden baking paddle to slide
a pizza in and out of the oven. It was extraordinary.

But I was not to be stopped. History was history. Jesus's birth
was Jesus's birth. "How could washerwomen be washing petticoats in a river? Petticoats near the manger? Raffaella?" My future mother-in-law was fingering tiny terra-cotta shepherds. She
had put her glasses on to examine the quality of the workmanship. "There was no river near the manger. There were no petticoats. There were no washerwomen!"

"Which of these shepherds do you like better?"

We were here today because one of the Avallones' shepherds had emerged this year from its tissue paper packaging
with one leg missing. The two shepherds that she now held up
for me to see were different only in that one had blue seventeenth-
century breeches, the other green.

"*Blu! Quello blu.*" I wanted to get back to the Truth.

I was intent on convincing Raffaella that even though I
wasn't Neapolitan, I knew about Jesus's birth and the manger
and the no-crib-for-His-bed. It was important to me because I
had heard a lot of negative press about the way my culture ex-
ports its commercial, capitalist Christmas traditions. Christmas
trees and Santa Claus (along with Halloween) are recent im-
ports in Naples. In Italy, the *presepe* is the symbol of Christmas,

the *Befana* witch is the one who brings gifts, Carnevale is when kids dress up. Why, many Italians feel, must we be subjected to other cultures' *usanze*, or traditions? A tree gets needles all over the floor, and ghosts and goblins scare little kids. Not to mention a big fat man who drives a sleigh and eats your food.

When I was in elementary school, I had an arts-and-crafts project every year at Christmas. With red and green felt, white school glue, and beads that never stuck where you wanted them to (how I hated arts and crafts!), I would make a frame for that year's school picture. With much sticky difficulty, I would slide in the passport-size photo of myself as, for example, a toothless second-grader and present it to my parents as a Christmas tree ornament.

Thanks to these ornaments, the Wilson family Christmas tree documents every stage of my youth, and that of my sister, Anna. Believe it or not, these artifacts have defied every law of Christmas ornament degeneration and are in a perfect felty state, right up to senior year of high school. (At a certain point, we must have stopped doing the crafts, so I'm sure Santa Claus took over.)

Because we need dark recesses to hide our awkward phases and long, exposed branches for the photos where we look pretty, the Wilsons always look for a tree that is scraggly and asymmetrical. No fluffy, well-proportioned firs for us. One shadowy crevice in the back of our tree is the assigned slot for Katherine with Permanent Teeth Before Braces. Another low, hidden area in the rear is home to Anna's I'll Only Wear Fluorescent Pink phase. In the front, one can find the Anna with Ringlets zone, next to the Katherine After Her No-Brownie-or-Anything-Else-Brown Diet section. On protruding, well-lit branches in the foreground, Anna and Katherine are quite serious and beautiful (mouths closed); in the backstage holes, we are giggling kids letting our teeth and pounds show.

One summer on the boardwalk of Nice, I won a stuffed monkey in one of those twenty-five-cent carnival games. He had red shorts and big boxing gloves, and a wide-eyed expression that said, "Bring it *on!*" When we got home, we all agreed that the angel that crowned our Christmas tree had had her day in the sun: it was time for a new cast. The monkey now sits in the place of honor, daring anyone to mess with us or our ugly-ass tree.

That December, instead of decorating our family fir, I helped Salvatore, Raffaella, and Nino set up the Avallones' *presepe*. (Benedetta was with her future husband's family now almost all the time.) Raffaella told me that Neapolitan tradition dictates that the father, the paterfamilias, is responsible for the crèche. *La mamma* is responsible for baking cinnamon *rococò* cookies and making sure everyone is warm and well-fed as they position the figures. There was a look of disgust on Raffaella's face when I asked about eggnog (Milk? Eggs? Alcohol? Together? *La prego no!*), about tea (who ever heard of tea in Naples?), or about cider (big mugs of hot liquid? Why don't you just make chicken broth if you're cold and hungry?). Fine! I gave up. There would be no warm liquids consumed.

"Nino!" she belted to her husband, even though he was sitting right next to her. When there was tradition to uphold, her voice got deeper and louder. Proclamatory. "It's time for you to set up the *presepe!*" He didn't move, just nodded. Raffaella proceeded to unwrap the base, a great slab of wood supporting mountains and caves made of cork. As the three of us watched, munching *rococò* cookies, she used a little eyedropper to make sure the water flowed down the mountain properly. "Nino!" she bellowed when she had finished fixing the *presepe* plumbing. "Now it's time for the *personaggi*!"

Salvatore and Nino and I started unwrapping the figures. We gently peeled open the tissue paper and held up each character for Raffaella to see. *"Il macellaio!"* The butcher! Raffaella called his name like he was an old friend who had unexpectedly turned up after a long absence. She told Nino that the butcher goes on the left side of the highest mountain. *"Il pizzaiolo!"* Salva was cradling the pizza man, awakened after a year of hibernation. To the right, on the second tier, said Raffaella.

Each had his own specific place on the stage. All of them, that is, except the solitary little men in breeches that I kept unwrapping. "Who's this?" I asked, and Raffaella explained that it was a shepherd. The shepherds were to be scattered randomly alongside their tiny sheep across the mountains. "So I can put it anywhere?" I asked. "Yes! Anywhere except in the Nativity cave." I positioned my shepherd next to a little hill of dried branches, at which point Raffaella picked him up and placed him somewhere else.

Then, when Nino unwrapped the shepherd missing a leg, something beautiful happened. *"Poverino!"* Poor little guy! "He lost his leg!" They were all really, honestly upset. Could Salva truly have that much empathy for a tiny terra-cotta figure? We were in Naples: of course he could.

The shepherd was passed around. This is the funeral, I thought, this is the ritual, and then they're going to throw him away. My family said goodbye to our angel, too, before she and her wings got recycled. But no! Raffaella had the solution. "We'll just have to pretend he's sleeping." She positioned the one-legged man behind a tree, laying him down on the moss so that his missing leg wasn't visible. When Raffaella and I went to San Gregorio Armeno two days later, it was not to replace the shepherd but to add one more standing witness to the crowd.

That gimpy shepherd partially hidden by the tree now lives in what my family would call the Land of Katherine's Disastrous Haircuts. He's not perfect, but like the pizza man or a dweeby fourth-grader, he's part of the Christmas scene.

Capitone

One figure was not positioned in the manger scene the day the *presepe* was set up: baby Jesus. Traditionally, the father puts baby Jesus in the crib after midnight on Christmas Eve. Nino's moment with the minuscule porcelain baby was to be after dinner, after mass, but before that big Nordic guy swooped in (the kids all up, the kids waiting, the kids liking this import as much as that fabulous trick-or-treat idea!). The *Befana* witch would have her moment on January 6, the day of Epiphany—no reason you couldn't have both her and Santa bring gifts, the Avallones felt. The more the merrier.

Raffaella hosted sixteen people for Christmas Eve dinner. She included all of her future son-in-law Mauro's family, and Benedetta wanted to be sure that everything was perfect— a *bella figura*—the fancy set of plates and crystal, place cards in silver holders, even little favor bags for the kids. She wore something shimmery and red, and made up her turquoise eyes so that they shot out at you even more than usual.

She left the preparation of the fish to her mother.

The fishmongers in Naples are open all night long the three

days before Christmas. *Le mamme,* wanting to make sure that the fish they get for Christmas Eve dinner is the freshest, set their alarms for 3:00 and 4:00 A.M. They want to get to the fish as the fishermen bring it in, before anyone else has a chance to claim it. The clams must be squirting. The eels must be fat and splashing. The sea bass must have eyes that "sparkle."

"*Nessuno mi fa scema.*" Nobody can make a fool out of me, Raffaella said as she stuffed a wad of cash in her sexy lace push-up bra. It was 5:00 A.M. on December 24, and Raffaella was going down to the Piazza Mercato fish market. "They put eye-drops in the fish's eyes to make them look bright. They put food coloring on the gills to make them look rosy. But I don't fall for that." Nonna Clara was the expert at looking a fish in the eye to see whether it'd been "made up," and she taught her daughter well. The message for Neapolitan women is clear: Go ahead, make yourselves up. Make your eyes look glamorous. But be damn sure that your bass is as natural as the girl next door.

When Raffaella returned from the market hours later, she looked and smelled as if she'd been on a fishing vessel on the open sea for days. She held three plastic bags, one of which was moving in a very disturbing sci-fi way. In it was the *capitone.*

If you look up "eel" in an English-Italian dictionary, you will find *anguilla.* But an *anguilla* is smaller and skinnier than a *capitone,* and is eaten on Christmas only if a family is too poor to buy the thick, powerful, splashing *capitone.* "At my place, we eat *capitone* at Christmas" is a Neapolitan expression meaning, Don't be thinking we're low-class.

When the fishmonger cuts off the head of the eel, it continues to writhe, and the man with his tough rubber gloves has to use serious muscles to keep the bugger on the chopping block. It is really entertaining when the *capitone* escapes and a chase ensues. (When I was having trouble years later keeping my toddlers in check, Raffaella invoked this image, telling me it's normal. Toddlers are like eels, you grab 'em from one end and they slip away from the other.) Raffaella's eel was chopped into four chunks, and still continued to thrash in the plastic bag.

The second bag held the clams. The first course of Christmas Eve dinner is *spaghetti a vongole*. Usually, the name of a pasta with fish includes the preposition *con* meaning "with." Linguine with shrimp. *Paccheri* with swordfish. But there is no spaghetti *with* clams because the two become one. A translation might be "clammed spaghetti." Neapolitans would say *"si sposono,"* they get married. The spaghetti bride and her clammy husband are an organic, inevitable match.

The third plastic bag held our fresh, bright-eyed beauty, the sea bass. She was to be baked whole, flanked by potatoes, for the main course. In addition, there would be the *insalata di rinforzo*, the strength salad. It is made to pump up anyone who might be gaunt and feeble, and features boiled cauliflower, olives, and carrots. There would also be fried codfish, sautéed escarole, and desserts, desserts, and more desserts.

At eight o'clock on Christmas Eve, I found my place card (*Ketrin* printed with a gold marker) and settled in for what would be a three-hour meal. The eel kept reappearing in various incarnations (the thing was five feet long, after all) including pickled *capitone*, fried *capitone*, and *capitone* in tomato sauce. It nauseated me. It was oily and black. It nauseated other people too, but that didn't stop them from eating it.

"I don't like eel. I've never liked it. But I'll have a piece for tradition's sake," Nino told us, and a few cousins followed suit. Same thing with the cauliflower salad. "I'm stuffed! Plus it grosses me out. Could you pass me some? *Giusto pe' tradizione.*" The conversation centered on recipes: how someone's grandmother prepared her *insalata di rinforzo*; who liked fried cod-fish and who preferred it baked.

Benedetta's future in-laws spoke knowledgeably about traditional recipes, which surprised me. "His mother left grilled chicken breasts in the refrigerator for him. She never cooked," Raffaella had confided to me about Mauro. Horror of horrors. "Benedetta and I are educating his palate."

When it was time for mass, we had difficulty standing we were so stuffed. The children were bouncing off the walls with excitement—just two more hours until Santa comes!—when we packed into cars smelling of perfume and rarely worn wool coats. Men dozed through the service. The hymn *"Tu Scendi dalle Stelle,"* "You Come Down from the Stars," was sung entirely by the soprano section of the congregation.

We returned home at 1:00 A.M. for the ritual of Nino putting baby Jesus in his crib. "Nino!" Raffaella called her husband to attention, his coat and hat still on. *"Il presepe!"* She handed him the tiny baby in tissue paper and pointed to the *presepe*, just in case he'd forgotten what his job was. This was the responsibility of the paterfamilias. And the real head of the family could relax in the knowledge that there was no chance of a blunder: there was only one place that baby could go.

Pizzetta, Cappuccino, and Orange Juice

My internship at the Consulate ended at Christmas. On my last day there, we had to evacuate the building because a mysterious package that looked like a bomb was found on Cynthia's desk. Nobody knew who had brought it or what was inside. So we all hung out at a café across the street and I was able to say my goodbyes *con calma*. After a few hours, we were notified that it was safe to enter the Consulate. The kind soldiers with Uzis informed us that the package was an elaborate *presepe*, complete with running water, that had been given as a surprise gift to the political consul.

"You gotta love this place," Cynthia said when we hugged goodbye.

My internship was over, but no part of me wanted to go home. There would be time later to figure out my future—for now, I was still interested in figuring out Naples, and seeing where this relationship with Salvatore was headed. Life was organized in semesters, I thought, so I told my parents that I wanted to make this "experience abroad" two semesters rather than one. I planned on going back to America at the beginning of June.

To earn extra money, I took on teaching jobs at other English schools. When I wasn't in class I rode buses and walked the streets. I missed theater, and what I found on the streets of Naples satisfied my craving.

The first dramatic performances of my life were the "lullabies" that my mother sang to my sister and me. They were lullabies that weren't soft or tender. She had no intention of putting us to sleep: we were her audience.

Vocally, Bonnie Wilson was not a soprano but a tenor. With her diaphragm working overtime, she sang Gershwin's "Summertime," sounding something like Luciano Pavarotti singing *Nessun Dorma.* Her version invoked the insomnia and anxiety in *Turandot* rather than the sweaty, lazy days of summer on a southern plantation.

Lyrics	Bonnie Wilson's Subtext
Summertime, *An' the livin' is easy*	The livin' will never be easy! There will be shows to put on! Exams to pass! Swim races to win!
Fish are jumpin'	Who the hell cares what's jumpin'?
An' the cotton is high	I've never gotten high, and neither will you.
Oh yo' daddy's rich	Your father and his family were rich but

not rich enough. He
spends too much money,
and soon what he had
will be all gone. You
should worry about that
when you're older, if
you have the time.

An' yo' mamma's good lookin'   Well, yes.

So hush little baby   If you keep quiet I can
finish these last notes

Don' yo' cry   with a flourish.

Vocal energy reminiscent of my mother's singing can be heard at any fruit and vegetable market in central Naples. Men wail, almost tragically, *"Pomodori due euro al chilo!"* Tomatoes, two euros a kilo!

"What are those guys going on about?" my sister asked me, years later, when she came to visit. "Are they mourning? Are they imploring? Are they passing kidney stones?"

"No," I answered, "they are simply stating the price of their tomatoes. With the intention of being heard."

My childhood had taught me that the best thing is to perform; the next best is to be in the audience. I didn't have to look far to witness theatrics in Naples. It became a kind of sport for me to go into a coffee shop, or bar, in the afternoon and order three things that are not, that should never be, consumed together. For example, a small pizza, a cappuccino, and an orange juice. A huge no-no for a multitude of reasons. First, cappuccinos are generally not ordered after eleven in the morning. Second, orange juice can never be consumed alongside anything with milk in it because of acidity. Third, pizzas should be ordered with a soda, beer, or water. Absolutely not coffee or anything warm, or for heaven's sake anything with milk.

So the response of the barista will be, first, incredulity and shock, followed by something akin to missionary zeal. *"Insieme?"* Together? *"La prego no!"* Please, I beg you, no! His eyes pleading, his voice plaintive, with his performance he will try to persuade me to change my mind.

The best performances to be found in Naples are on the sidewalks, in buses, and in coffee bars. I have witnessed arguments, love scenes, even tragic dialogues that rival anything seen on the stages of the Teatro San Carlo or the Bellini. There was a standoff on the 140 bus that runs from Posillipo to Piazza Garibaldi in the spring of 1997, for example. The initial disagreement was over a fart that a middle-aged man presumably expelled in the packed bus. The gentleman didn't have a seat, and stood nonchalantly holding the rubber loops hanging from the roof. An elderly lady sitting near him, holding her nose with a handkerchief, started in. She told the Bangladeshi housekeeper sitting next to her, "It's just rude. We all have to breathe this air." She glared at the man.

"Signora, I agree." The lady behind her declared her allegiance, and now it was just a matter of time before the whole bus, or at least the native Italian speakers, chose sides and put their two cents in. Interestingly, the accused continued to feign nonchalance until the argument got heated. Then he shut everyone up with his bellowing voice and *"Ma come fate a sapere? A sapere tutto?"* But how do you know? How is it that you think you know everything?

This kind of scene makes you want to miss your bus stop and keep riding until the curtain comes down.

I found another very simple way to witness the performance

art that is Neapolitan speech: to ask directions. The rhetoric, the art of saying so little in such a spellbinding way, reminds me of that great rhetorician Jesse Jackson reciting *Green Eggs and Ham* on *Saturday Night Live* twenty years ago. Such a sense of rhythm, such skill at creating dramatic tension. He will not let your mind wander; he will not let you miss one syllable. Nor will he let you *not* care about his green eggs and ham. It makes no difference whatsoever that the words he is reciting are Seussian nonsense.

And so it was with a gentleman, a well-dressed-in-his-Sunday-best Neapolitan gentleman, whom I asked for directions. He was out for a stroll, walking slowly (toes splayed out in that typical way of Neapolitan men) and obviously with no destination in mind. I was a young woman who was also on her own and obviously foreign. These two factors, combined with an innate southern Italian sense of hospitality and the desire to perform, made this man want more than anything else to be of help. But unfortunately, he did not know where Via Noce was. Instead of saying, I'm sorry I don't know, he began a monologue which could have had a score, it was so musical.

"Via Noce, Via Noce." He paused. At this point, I knew that he had no clue where the street was, otherwise his hands would already be in motion. They would be outlining my trajectory, *a destra a sinistra*, right and left with his hand curling up and then a big smile and his arms straight ahead when he came to *diritto*! *Sempre diritto*! Straight on down!

But he did not know.

"I have grown up in this area, *signorina*. Not too far from here, and I can assure you that this Via Noce, this Via Noce of which you speak, it is not, and I repeat, not, a cross street of Via Toledo. That it is not."

This was the introduction, and it was performed solemnly,

with no hand movements and a somber facial expression. His voice was level. After a pause, it was time to move on to the central piece of the monologue. He became more animated, and took his hands out of his pockets.

"It could be farther up this direction"—his eyebrows were raised in the hypothetical, one arm straightened to the right. "Or indeed it could be in this direction"—his arm straightened to the left, maintaining eye contact with me always. He paused. Oh, there were so many possibilities of where this street could be, given the fact that he did not know! "Because I, to my dismay, do not possess this particular piece of knowledge, I must be truthful. Truthful to you, and truthful to myself." Again, he paused for dramatic effect. He was a man of integrity, he wanted me to understand. The pauses were timed so that the drama was heightened, the tension not dissipated.

"The truth is this," he said, and I understood we'd come to the conclusion. "If I knew, it would be my great pleasure to impart this knowledge to you, a person who does not know, and would like to know, the location of Via Noce. And with this, I wish you a good day, *signorina*." He spun around and walked away. With a flourish.

Fresh Eggs

"*Sai chi era esigente? Nonna Clara.*" The one who was really *esigente*, or hard to please, was Nonna Clara. To hear Raffaella talk of someone *else* being particular in her tastes was ironic. I had told her that I didn't envy her *salumiere*, the owner of the food shop where she buys her cold cuts, bread, and cheese, after she had spent fifteen minutes complaining about the thick and tough prosciutto ham he had sold her the day before. "Like this!" One eye became a slit as she held her thumb and forefinger to show just how thick he had cut it. "You think that's thin? You call that thin?"

A line of customers waited patiently as Raffaella and Signor Buono, the *salumiere*, hashed it out. It was a matter of trust. "To trust is good, not to trust is better," is an oft-repeated Neapolitan expression. Remember, a mother tells her child, it is always better *not* to trust.

Neapolitan parents want to prepare their children for the real world, where cheating and lying are the norm. The worst thing is to raise a child who is *baccalà* (as dumb as a piece of cod), or *addurmùto* (like a zombie). There is no end to the pejorative terms for a person who is naïve and trusting. My favorite is probably *dorme cu 'a zizza mmocca*—he's still sleeping with his mommy's tit in his mouth. The opposite is the highest compliment that you can receive in Naples: to be considered *scetàto*, awake. It's better than being smart. It means that no one can cheat you, you know what's up.

In Mr. Buono's shop, it was fundamental for him to regain Raffaella's trust after the prosciutto episode. The other *signore* could wait.

"I'm easy," she repeated later. Easy? But what about the prosciutto? I asked. "Well, the truth must be spoken. It's in the interest of the *salumiere*. It would be terrible for him if he continued to sell prosciutto like that and no one told him about it!" So she was actually helping him, while at the same time showing him and the other ladies in line that she is *scetàta*, she knows what's up. She's no baby sleeping with a tit in her mouth, or a German tourist who will eat whatever you sell her. "I'm not a difficult customer. Nonna Clara was a difficult customer. It was a nightmare to shop with her. Thank goodness the *ovaiolo* would come to the house."

When Raffaella was growing up, the egg man would come to her home once a week with a basket of eggs and fresh cheeses from the countryside. Nonna Clara would not merely greet the *ovaiolo*, give him money, and take her eggs and cheeses. Oh no. She would invite him in, take his jacket, and they would *buongiorno, buongiorno* each other. She would offer him a glass of water, he would refuse. (Not coffee? Why not coffee? I asked Raffaella. Coffee is for people who are in *confidenza*, she explained. People with whom you share your shit.) They would then sit in two armchairs facing each other in the living room.

It was the moment of reckoning.

Nonna Clara would position herself next to a lamp and remove the lampshade. Then she would take each egg from the basket, one by one, and hold it up to the lightbulb. This way, she could see if the egg was fresh. If there was a shadow, it meant that the yolk had detached from the white and had formed a space next to the shell. That was a sign that the egg was at least three days old.

And so, with eight children, a tiny apartment, and three meals to cook (not to mention the cleaning and ironing), Nonna Clara inspected each egg. When an egg passed the test, she would put it in her basket with *"Chisto mm'o piglio io"*—I'm gonna get me this one. When she saw the suspect shadow, she looked the *ovaiolo* in the eye and told him, *"Chisto t'o magne tu."* You eat this one yourself. Then she would hand it back to him, adding, *"È bbrutto comme 'a faccia toia."* That one's ugly as your face.

When she finished, she would ask after his family and animals, and wish him a pleasant week.

When I heard these stories about Nonna Clara, or when Raffaella told me that she had just been to the De Cecco pasta plant to complain that one pack of *bucatini* was not up to snuff (What about the cost of gas? The two hours of her time?), I understood why I got so stressed when I went food shopping in Naples.

My mother did not have any sort of relationship with any human being at the suburban Safeway where we shopped when I was growing up. Her relationship was with the mammoth grocery cart that she plowed down the aisles of the supermarket. At the wheel of her cart, Bonnie Wilson transformed into a Formula One racing pilot. She would issue an angry "Dang!" at her vehicle when it veered in the wrong direction. She would pat the cold metal with appreciation and let out a satisfied breath as she positioned me, my sister, or her enormous black leather purse on the plastic seat.

Theirs was a relationship built on trust. At the Safeway, not to trust was okay, to trust was better.

Into her much-loved cart, my mother would hurl cereal boxes with cartoon characters (which had been tempting American kids like us since the early 1960s), plastic bags of frozen strawberries, easy-to-open bottles of Heinz ketchup. We bought food with preservatives. We bought food that came in shiny packages. My mother, efficient and American, had us in and out of that joint in time for swim practice or dress rehearsal with food that would last us for weeks.

And so, on the rare occasions when I would go food shopping alone in Naples (I almost never ate at my apartment, but every once in a while bought ham or cheese to have in stock), I didn't know how to contend with the *salumiere* behind the counter. The man would ask me how much prosciutto I wanted and what kind. I was not allowed to see or touch, and I had to look the man in the eye and answer.

"San Daniele or Rovagnati?" At least there was a multiple choice option, so I could simply repeat the last word that he had said. As for the quantity, I would say, "One hundred grams," which would certainly be too much or too little. It should have mattered to me—it seemed to matter even to the man who was selling me the ham.

"Stop should-ing on yourself!" my sister often reminds me. That first winter in Naples, I stopped should-ing and started schlepping once a month to the big American-style Italian supermarket, Conad. There I could throw prepackaged things in my grocery cart like Frisbees, things that were well marketed and had those easy-tear corners. At Conad I was a confident consumer. There, thank the Lord, I didn't have to listen to my weak voice making it painfully clear that I wasn't quite sure how I liked my food.

Impepata di Cozze

Winter in Naples is short and wet. By April, it seemed that summer had arrived. Air-conditioning and roll-on antiperspirant became inextricably linked to my nostalgia for and love of my homeland.

I arrived at the hospital of Fatebenefratelli, or the Hospital of the Do-Good Brothers, on a stiflingly hot morning in early spring. I had come to assist Raffaella, currently a patient in the women's ward on the fourth floor. Dressed in a Duke T-shirt and running shorts, sweating as I pressed the call button for the elevator, I noticed a statue of San Giovanni di Dio, arms outstretched, greeting patients and visitors and welcoming them to Fatebenefratelli. San Giovanni's expression was serene, and the statue was exquisite. But why wasn't the elevator coming?

When I was informed that the elevator was out of service, I tried not to think about the what-ifs, about stretchers or emergencies and the inherent logistical problems of a hospital with six floors and no elevator. I told myself to let go of those images of sterile, high-tech institutions where a Visa gold card can get you places. Here at Fatebenefratelli nobody is interested in your

credit cards or whether you have insurance or what kind. Your
health is in the hands of fate. And San Giovanni. And of the
modern-day do-good brothers and their do-good sisters.

Raffaella and Nino had both contracted salmonella at an
elegant wedding several days earlier. When many of the guests
started getting sick the day after the wedding, everyone thought
of the mussels and clams and other seafood that had been
served. In Naples, pasta with shellfish is a staple: there would be
no Christmas Eve without *spaghetti a vongole*. Children of four
are served *impepata di cozze*, or sautéed mussels, parents disappointed only that they can't give their poor little Ciro a glass of
white Vesuviano wine to help wash it down. Because shellfish is
eaten so often and because hygiene is not always optimal, hepa-
titis happens.

A Neapolitan friend of ours was violently ill and hospital-
ized after eating *spaghetti a vongole*. When he recovered, I
asked him if he would give up shellfish for the rest of his life. He
looked at me as if I had lost my marbles. "The rest of my life?"
he asked, incredulous. "My doctor told me I should avoid mussels and clams for a week or so, but I don't know if I can hold
out! My mother has found a new *pescivendolo* [fishmonger] who
swears by his mussels."

Surprisingly, the results of the investigation about who ate
what at the wedding reception (which wasn't easy, given that the
dinner lasted four hours and included about forty dishes) indi-
cated that the culprit was a mayonnaise that was served with
shrimp. On a hot day, the caterer had left the mayonnaise (made
with raw eggs) outside for too long, and many of the wedding
guests contracted salmonella.

When I heard this, my heart immediately went out to the
bride's parents. In Naples, where a wedding is what you eat and
the good impression (or *bella figura*) that you make with your

friends is directly related to the quality of the pasta and the suc-
culence of the mozzarella, this was social annihilation. That
family has always liked to skimp on what they serve, people
started to whisper. The caterer must have been cheap.

Thank sweet Jesus that the newlyweds were vomiting on
the other side of the world, at some resort in Thailand.

So this is how we ended up at the hospital of the do-gooders.
I climbed the steps to the *reparto femminile* on the fourth floor
with trepidation. When I entered the women's ward, however, I
was struck by its unexpected beauty. Because the hospital is located on the promontory of Posillipo, there are breathtaking
views of the sea out the huge open windows. It is stunning, particularly at dusk, when the fuchsias and violets of the sunset over
Vesuvius are as intense as a screensaver. Fatebenefratelli hospital has nothing of the whites and greens of rational science and
sterile medicine. It's all fluorescent pinks and blues and bright
red blood on white scrubs.

The sounds that you hear are not the beep-beep-beeps of
monitors but the constant howl of wind and the screams of patients. Here, you can feel the wind on your face inside, and
smell the evidence of doctors and nurses smoking under the
RESPECT YOUR PATIENTS, DON'T SMOKE sign. Here you are in
close contact with human frailty, with human suffering, right in
the midst of nature's beauty and terror. Smells, sounds, and colors are all larger than life.

At Fatebenefratelli, you can see in every direction how
Mother Nature really pulled out all the stops in this city. The
drama of a volcano would have been enough. But Madre Na-
tura added the sea, the cliffs, the islands of Capri and Ischia.
The little island of Nisida, which houses an Alcatraz-like prison.
I could only imagine the intensity of watching a loved one per-
ish in such a setting.

Fortunately, Raffaella's condition was not so critical. None-theless, I was in no way relaxed. As the saying goes in Naples, when you're sick, one of the most dangerous places you can be is at a hospital. And here we come to one of the biggest contra-dictions in Neapolitan culture. If you ask an Italian about the United States, he or she will often point to health care as the greatest contradiction in our democracy. All are equal in Amer-ica, right? But a hospital will treat you only if you have insur-ance, or a credit card, or both. This is a hugely simplified way of seeing things, and only partly true, but that's the perception. If you are hurt, or sick, and poor, you are alone.

Here in Naples, there is another kind of contradiction when it comes to health. It is a city where if you fall, or faint, or feel sick as you're walking down the street, you will not have merely one Good Samaritan to help you out. You will have a crowd vying over who has the honor of taking care of you, even of tak-ing you to their home if need be. They will argue over who is most qualified, who lives the closest, who best understands your predicament. I once fainted on a bus in Naples, and apparently after some heated discussion among the other passengers, it was decided that the bus would abandon its normal route and take me and a kind middle-aged lady who had been elected my pro-tector directly to the hospital of the Incurabili, which was the closest. (Yes, there is a hospital of the Incurables.)

The contradiction is this: After such a touching show of love and generosity toward a fellow human in need, you arrive at a hospital where the doctors are smoking in the halls. Where the generator has been broken for a year and nobody has both-ered to fix it (so, if there's a power outage, none of the machines will work). If you have had a heart attack, you risk dying in the waiting room because the diagnosis was performed so perfunc-torily. Or maybe a nurse got a call on her cellphone and forgot about you. *Insomma*, a hospital where unless you have some loving, smart, pushy relatives to take up your cause, you might be better off never setting foot.

Raffaella shared a room with three other women, all of whom had pretty stable conditions. As I entered, I was surprised to see that she had managed to brush her hair and put on makeup. Another surprise was the unmistakable aroma of Neapolitan coffee. I knew that Raffaella hadn't eaten for three days, and coffee was off-limits. "Who had coffee?" I asked, and the four women's eyes darted guiltily to one another. I felt like a kindergarten teacher. One of the patients had pulled her IV drip with her down four flights of stairs to the hospital bar to sneak a little glass juice bottle full of sweet black *caffè* back up to her roommates while the nurses were chatting and smoking cigarettes. I didn't know who the guilty party was, but I saw that the mood of these ladies was sky-high. They were giggling. "Who had coffee?" I repeated.

There was an eighty-year-old patient called Nonna, or Grandma, by her roommates. Her dry, brittle lips were rimmed with black, the black of the syrupy nectar that is Neapolitan coffee. Her lack of teeth and her heavy dialect made it hard for me to understand what she was saying, but whatever it was ended with the gesture of lifting the handle of a little cup of espresso, and with the words *tazzulella 'e caffè* (l'il ol' cuppa coffee). It was so tender the way she said it, and the coffee had obviously done such wonders in improving the ladies' mood, that I decided not to tell the nurses.

It was rare to find a chair to sit in in Raffaella's room. During visiting hours, Neapolitan hospitals are swamped by relatives. It's a lovely thing to see. If you arrive ten minutes before visiting time begins, you find the reception area crowded with families, elbowing each other so that they can be the first out of the gate when the receptionist comes to announce that visiting hours have begun. They are chomping at the bit. It seems that they are not here because they are prey to guilt, or because some sibling forced them to do their "duty." They are here because it is clearly the only place for them to be now, a few days after Aunt Patrizia has broken her hip. They are here to hold her hand, to massage her back, and, most important, to make damn sure that the doctors and nurses don't fuck up.

In the States, if you have a relative in the hospital, you might stop by to see how they are doing, perhaps bring a book or flowers. Here, you come with your job cut out for you. You are responsible for the complicated, time-consuming, and ultimately exhausting job of checking on the doctors and nurses. This means making sure they know that your mother is taking blood pressure medicine. That she is allergic to certain antibiotics. Has this information been communicated, often and to the right people? If you're not sure, you must follow the relevant doctor around (you certainly can't worry if you're bothering him, this is your mother's health we're talking about) and remind the nurses, emphatically and at regular intervals.

I was sitting by Raffaella's bed when a nurse dropped a little white pill on her tray. "Take this," she commanded. If I had been Raffaella, I probably would've taken it. The nurse was very firm, after all. But fortunately, Raffaella grew up in this city and learned early on not to blindly follow orders issued by someone in a position of authority.

"This isn't mine. I think it's Flora's heart medication. She usually takes it at around this time. Hey"—she motioned to Flora's niece, who was reading a magazine next to her aunt's bed—"can you go and find out who this is really for?" The girl set out to find the nurse. This sixteen-year-old surely knew the results of her aunt's last blood tests, which medicines she was to take and when, and which doctor to get furious at when her *zia* was not being tended to correctly. If she was here at visiting hours, it meant that her family had prepped her well.

When it was time for lunch, four completely different menus were prepared and brought in for the four patients. A soft potato dish for Nonna, who didn't have many teeth, a simple pasta for Raffaella, with her stomach problems. Relatives closely examined what had been prepared, and of course complained. They were angry. The food was not fresh enough, the pasta overcooked. To me, it looked and smelled divine. There were cloth napkins and real silverware, a little glass dish of freshly grated Parmesan cheese to put on the steaming pasta. Nothing was prepackaged. It did not even vaguely resemble hospital fare from my homeland. But complaining was the thing to do, and if I said it actually looked good, I would have been laughed at. People would pity Raffaella, who had that clueless American girl to look after her: she might as well not be in the hospital, she'd be better off at home.

I had to show my stuff. I had to be forceful. I had to reassure Raffaella that I was doing my job of *stare dietro*, checking up on the hospital staff.

I put on my best angry face and took the plate of pasta into the hall, searching for the least-scary-looking nurse. When I found her, I tried my hand at the role of protective Neapolitan relative. "This pasta is overcooked! And reheated! It's inedible!" (Meanwhile, I hadn't eaten in hours and was seriously considering taking it into a private corner and scarfing it down.) The nurse issued a rebuttal, which I paid no attention to, so proud was I of my irate outburst. I took the pasta back to Raffaella, who was in turn reading the riot act to another nurse because Nonna's potato dish was also inedible—"*sanno di niente*"—they taste like nothing. "My fish tastes like a bedroom slipper!" a middle-aged roommate added to the discussion. Oh, man, what energy it all took. I was exhausted just watching them. This team of women, patients and relatives together, could have taken over a small country.

A continuous struggle, conflict and argument and distrust. Passivity was not allowed. Although the medical care left much to be desired at Fatebenefratelli, on a psychological level the combat did these patients good. From the outside, I saw that it had the same effect as that hit of clandestine coffee. To live in Naples is to be on your toes, to have a thousand eyes, to stand up and fight for yourself and your loved ones. When you cannot or do not do this, it is a bad sign. It might even mean that you're too sick to risk going to the hospital.

Casatiello

The day after Easter is called Pasquetta, or Little Easter, in Italy. In Naples it is also called Fatta Pasqua, or Easter's-Done Day. If there is one day in the liturgical calendar that is a challenge for Christians, it is Easter Monday, Easter's-Done Day.

I had spent Holy Week catching a mass with Raffaella almost every day. I didn't miss the wooden crosses and perfect harmonies of the Protestant church services I grew up with— I loved the smell of incense and the sound of Giampietro's boots clicking on the marble floors; the dripping wax and Chanel perfume, the cleavage and ringing microphones. Holy Week in Neapolitan churches was that and more. It was also a crescendo of anticipation, of pregnant waiting. There was the palpable sense that something huge was about to happen.

For Catholics and Protestants alike, Easter Sunday is the culmination of that waiting. Out come the fancy clothes and bonnets, the chocolate for the kids and the explosion of orchids. The choir singing Hallelujah, the trumpets announcing the joy of Easter. Pump up the karaoke, He is risen! The tomb is empty!

RRRRrring! goes the alarm clock on Monday morning. Wait, didn't we sing "He is risen!" yesterday? Hallelujah and all that stuff? What do you mean there are lunches to be packed, traffic to battle, life in all its banality to attend to? What a buzz kill.

When I was in high school, my Monday-after-Easter depression was due primarily to a Cadbury Creme Egg hangover. I would wake up on Monday morning in that lethargic, flatulent, morning-after-the-binge state. I would have to zip jeans that were too tight and make it through AP English, trying to get my mind on Elizabethan poetry and out of the rut of "Did I eat four or five chocolate eggs before lunch and six or seven after?" and then "How can I manage to eat only celery until next weekend?"

This is all to say that the day after Easter should be a holiday everywhere for Christians, like it is in Naples. A day to let it sink in: the chocolate, the music, the impossible fact that He died for me and rose again. *Insomma*, give us a moment to digest it all and figure out how we're going to live our lives.

On Pasquetta in Naples, families traditionally do a *gita fuori porta*, a trip outside the city. Usually people take a picnic lunch to the countryside, or a frittata to the beach. When Raffaella was a little girl, she and her family would go to the mountains near Avellino, where her maternal grandparents were from. On the morning of Little Easter, she and her brothers and sisters would come downstairs (wishing each other Happy Easter's-Done Day!) to find eight round *casatiello* rolls on the kitchen table. The *casatiello* is a dense bread made with black pepper, *salame*, lard, bacon, and cheese (provolone, Parmesan, pecorino, *più ci metti più ci trovi!*) and crowned by a hard-boiled egg.

Nonna Clara would make one *casatiello*, of varying size, for each of her eight children. Rosaria, the oldest, would have a roll as big as a tire, while little Nunzio's would be no bigger than a bagel. The kids would start shouting immediately, *"Chist' è mio! Non toccare!"* This one's mine! Don't touch it!

They would wrap their *casatielli* in cloth and hide them under their shirts for the picnic. You knew which one was yours, could recognize it a mile away. You had to protect it. That was your day-after-Easter lunch.

"How did Nonna Clara bake eight rolls, plus two enormous ones for Mamma and Papà, in a nineteen-fifties Neapolitan oven? Was she up all night?" I asked Raffaella.

"What oven? We didn't have an oven!"

Che problema c'è? With the help of her older daughters, Nonna Clara would take the ten *casatielli* to the communal oven, which was located down two sets of stone steps from their apartment on the Vomero hill. The *forno* served the whole neighborhood, and there was always a line. When it was her turn, she'd give a couple of lire to the baker and wait for her babies to brown. She wouldn't leave the spot, staying watchful for the hour and a half it took to cook them. You never knew when other people might come and claim your *casatielli* as their own.

"How could she recognize which were hers?" I asked Raffaella.

Raffaella laughed and shook her head. What questions! "Ketrin, how does a mother know which child is hers?"

Raffaella made me a *casatiello* that first Easter Monday I was in Naples. We had decided to go to Caserta, a town near Naples and home to a palace that rivals Versailles (which few people visit, most go to Caserta for the mozzarella), and were planning on having a picnic at the palace gardens. I had eaten, and eaten, and eaten on Easter Sunday. Try the goat with roasted potatoes, Ketrin. The *ricotta salata* and *salame* is the traditional Easter appetizer—how can you not eat it? Taste these two *pastiera* cheesecakes and tell us which one is better, Zia Pia's or Zia Maria's. We need your vote.

So there I was, once again, on Easter's-Done morning, feeling flatulent and sluggish. I should skip lunch, my brain said, or at most find some celery in Caserta. But there was my very own *casatiello* on the counter. It was waiting to be wrapped lovingly. No brothers and sisters were vying for it, Salva and Benedetta had their own and were satisfied. I had no choice.

In 1751, when the Bourbon king Charles commissioned his architect to design the royal palace in Caserta, Luigi Vanvitelli presented him with a model of the building and gardens. It was so beautiful that it filled the king with an emotion "fit to tear his heart from his breast." And this was a guy who grew up in the Royal Palace of Madrid—he knew magnificence when he saw it. The Reggia di Caserta is truly breathtaking. The palace has twelve hundred rooms and the park and gardens extend for nearly two miles. It is considered an architectural masterpiece.

It was hot that year on Pasquetta, and we followed Raffaella to a spot near one of the baroque fountains. She rolled out a blanket and set up the drinks and plates. We took out our *casatielli*. Mine was a little smaller than Salva's, a little bigger than Benedetta's. We compared, and then we dug in.

Sitting on a soft 1970s blanket with the Avallones, I ate it all. I ate the bacon, the lard, the hard-boiled egg. When I'd finished, satisfied (aah, this *casatiello* is not too big, not too small, but juuuuust right!), I rested my head on Salva's lap. Raffaella was carving a juicy melon and talking about where she could find electricity to plug in the hotplate for the little espresso maker she'd brought. Benedetta was spreading coconut sun lotion on her arms. Nino was reading the paper.

I was realizing that I was no longer B.E.D.-ridden.

In all my years of bingeing, it wasn't the actual binge that was the problem. It was the punishment afterward. I had a healthy appetite, and sometimes I ate too much, but I was human. I got hungry again. On depressing, mundane, life-back-to-normal Pasquetta my body needed to be fed just as it did on the sunny, sacred morning of Easter. Even the day *after* the celebration, after the chocolate and the lamb, or the *pastiera* and the ricotta. I realized in Caserta that if I punished and denied myself on Easter's-Done Day, as I had for the last decade, then maybe I was continuing to miss the whole point of Easter itself: The sacrifice was *Jesus's* body, not mine. To us, He said, "Take and eat. This is my body." He didn't say, Take and eat my body . . . and then feel guilty about it and don't eat anything for a while. He said, *Buon appetito, signorina.* Enjoy.

Gelato alla Nocciola

$\mathcal{B}$enedetta's wedding was planned for the end of June in Positano (Nino's objections to Mauro notwithstanding) and the spring was a flurry of wedding preparations. I was part of it all. I went with Raffaella and Benedetta to choose the wedding dress, put in my two cents as to which *bomboniera* was the prettiest. (The *bomboniera* is a little souvenir given at Italian weddings. It is usually silver and small and collects dust in people's apartments for years afterward.) We all went to a huge clothing store near Pompeii to choose the suits for Nino and Salva. Or rather, for Raffaella to choose the suits for Nino and Salva. She pinched and straightened and stuck her fingers all over their bodies. They stood stock-still while she manhandled them, although Salva sent me air kisses across the room. I was asked whether I liked the wider or narrower pinstripe, the Armani or the Ferré, and I did eenie meenie miny moe silently in my mind.

I could not believe that they were about to spend 1,500,000 lire (nearly $1,000 at the time) on a suit. But I realized later, for a well-to-do Neapolitan family, this was borderline thrifty.

Raffaella was a highly talented costumer, and Salva and his father both looked dashing. "You really like the Ferré?" Salva asked me in the car on the way home. We kissed in the backseat, and then he asked, "Now I want to see what you're going to wear, Pagnottella!"

My stomach lurched. We'd never explicitly talked about when I was leaving, but I assumed that he knew I wasn't going to be here at the end of June. Who ever heard of a semester that finished at the *end* of June? "*Vediamo,*" I said. We'll see.

From that moment on, everything that happened would trigger tears. I was leaving soon and Salva hadn't even realized that this was the end. The next Saturday I called him, bawling. I loved him and I loved this crazy place and I loved his family, but I certainly couldn't leave my country and move to Naples at the age of twenty-two! Salva sped over to pick me up, asking, What's wrong?

When I couldn't answer in any intelligible way, he said how about *gelato alla nocciola*? His suggestion made me cry even harder. How could I stay here for a man who thought that all of my pain could be alleviated by buying me an ice cream? When my answer was even more tears, Salva took off for Ciro, the best *gelateria* in Naples, and triple-parked. He bought an enormous cone of *nocciola* and got extra Kleenex. With one hand he dried my tears and with the other fed me the ice cream.

It was just what I needed. Once again, I needed to shut my brain off and be fed.

We drove around the city all afternoon, the elephant in the Fiat being my departure and our future together. Finally, I told Salva that we had to talk. He parked in a piazza in central Naples. "About what?" he asked. "About us. About next year," I explained.

"Okay, then, talk," he said. "*Parla.*" (Salva still does this when I say we need to talk. He says, Okay. Talk. It is the one word which makes me, normally a chatterbox, totally tongue-tied.)

"Well, I was thinking . . . I like you . . . I would probably miss you. . . ." As I stammered on, Salva's eyes were not looking at me but out the window at another car that had parked nearby. I had no idea at the time, but Salva realized that they were planning a *scippo*, a robbery. He knew that we had to get out of that spot as quickly as possible if we wanted to keep our wallets, our watches, and our car.

I was telling Salva that maybe I could see about doing a master's in Italy—my parents had both studied at Johns Hopkins University's School of Advanced International Studies, and there was a program in Bologna, a five-hour train ride from Naples. I didn't love political science or economics, but I liked the idea of staying in Italy the following year to see where this relationship was headed. International relations might be an interesting field after all. . . .

But Salva wasn't listening to a word I said. He wasn't even looking at me. He was focused on those guys in the car next to ours.

"*Va bene, va bene.*" Okay, he said, and started the car. He drove off so fast that I thought maybe he was angry that I wasn't staying in Naples the next year. But after a minute or so, he looked at me and smiled. We still had our wallets, we still had our car, and, although I didn't know it at the time, we had a future without an ocean between us. There was much to smile about.

Pasta al Forno

꩜f Neapolitans are the world's experts at dramatizing the mundane, they are also experts at what they call *sdrammatizzare*: to dedramatize, to undramatize. The *s* at the beginning of a verb makes it the opposite, so *sdrammatizzare* is to suck the tragedy from something and spit it out with a great big smile.

Naples is a city whose history has been marked by occupations, invasions, poverty, and tragedy. Unemployment hovers around 13 percent. The *camorra*, the Neapolitan Mafia, holds business and industry hostage and causes endless violence. Soiled maxi pads and stinking diapers crown the mountains of trash that line the streets. (Naples has the highest garbage collection tax of any city in Italy. Garbage isn't collected, and the money ends up in the hands of the *camorra*.)

How to explain the cheerfulness of Neapolitans? It goes much deeper than great food, great weather, let's enjoy the *dolce vita*! The *dolce vita* is not so *dolce* when people live in poverty, the air reeks of refuse, and corruption and injustice are commonplace. The smiles and songs on the lips of Neapolitans can in large part be explained by the art of *sdrammatizzazione*. They manage to take the drama out of situations that are truly dramatic—when there is tragedy, or suffering, or, quite simply, when the stakes are high.

I had been accepted into the master's program in International Relations at SAIS Bologna, which meant that I would return to Washington for a summer of intensive economics courses. Although I would be coming back to Italy in the fall, I knew that it would be a different Italy. I would be a graduate student in the North. My "year abroad" was over, and this crazy, chaotic, colorful chapter of my life was coming to an end.

Gelato or no *gelato*, I was miserable.

Raffaella organized a going-away party for me the night before my departure. She set out Coke and Orange Fanta and plastic cups. (It was a party for twenty-two-year-olds—if anyone felt like wine or beer they could ask for it, right?) She baked a *pasta al forno*, which she knew was my favorite: a pasta casserole chock-full of bacon, béchamel, and no fewer than four different kinds of cheese. Covered with breadcrumbs, it came out of the oven golden brown and crispy on top. Of course, she also prepared about six other dishes for the party, but it was the *pasta al forno* that I smelled when she opened the door for me that evening.

I told myself that I would hold it together. Enough with the tears! I had been crying most of the day. But when I looked in her eyes, I couldn't.

I started sobbing. *Drammatico*, no? Raffaella's reaction was anything but. It was the amazing, unexpected art of *sdrammatizzare*. Did she cry? Did she Oh-I-understand-honey? Did she even hug me? No, she slapped me across the face. Not so it hurt, just so I would come off it. I was so shocked that I did come off it. Her own eyes were glistening, but her voice was forceful and, yes, cheerful. "*Ué ué!*" (which is like "Hey you!"). "The *pasta al forno* is almost ready, come and see how crispy you want it on the outside. . . ."

I was forced out of my sadness, slapped out of my own personal drama. I followed Raffaella into the kitchen to help (read: watch, dodge, and whimper).

Salvatore came in and said, "*Ciao, vita mia!*" He had given up calling me Pagnottella, Little Muffin, and was now using the Neapolitan expression "my life." I mean, please! Couldn't he have chosen a term of endearment like *sweetie pie* or even *darling*? "My life" sent me back into my drama once again, and the tears started flowing. My tears started Salva crying too: no macho stiff-upper-lipping for him. We were hugging, he was repeating "*Vita mia!*" and we were pathetic. We were also physically in the way of the *pasta al forno*. Something had to be done.

Another slap would have been difficult for Raffaella, as she still had her oven mitts on. So she slapped us with her words.

"*Ué ué! Vogliamo finí?*" Y'all want to come off it now? She was smiling. She was cheerful. She was a master in the art of *sdrammatizzazione*.

As a parent, Salvatore has drawn on his mother's lessons. There are no sobbing "*vita mia*" moments when one of our children cries. Before I manage to Oh-honey them, before I arrive with my furrowed eyebrows and I-understand-your-pain-let-me-feel-it-with-you, he's there. He's there with his finger outstretched and a smile on his face. He's touching their tears. "Mamma Ketrin! Let's taste these tears to see if you put enough salt in the water when you were making this little one." He always tastes them. Not for pretend—he really tastes them. And guess what? The amount of salt always happens to be just right.

Caffè Macchiato

When I arrived back in the States in June of 1997, I missed Salvatore, I missed the Avallone family, and I missed Naples. On top of it all, I desperately missed Neapolitan coffee.

I should mention that in both suburban Maryland and downtown Naples, coffee is essential to my being, and staying, human. And the sounds that are linked to the experience of coffee consumption trigger in me a drug addict's vein-jumping response. In the United States, there is the squeaky Styrofoam sound of "to go." There is Billie Holiday singing in a Starbucks, a background to the barista's (or Starbucksista's) efficient assembly-line voice calling out, "Venti chai" or "Skim soy latte" (isn't life complicated enough as it is? I wonder). There are people standing in line who are not talking.

In Italy, the sound of coffee in a bar is clinking porcelain. It is cacophony, racket, loud voices arguing and laughing over the *ssssshhhh* of the espresso machine. These sounds, a prelude to the hit of that syrupy black nectar that is called *caffè*, remind me that everything is possible. I can fight the good fight.

I think the fundamental difference between the experiences of coffee in the United States and coffee in Italy comes down to the concept of "to go." In America, coffee is taken to go because there's a lot of liquid to be consumed. It accompanies you as you go about your morning. There is comfort in the feel of large quantities of lava-hot liquid under your fingers, of knowing that this coffee will be with you for hours. Your big hot cup of American coffee or latte or macchiato or whatever else Starbucks has decided to name it, will be held close, cuddled and nursed. Your very own grown-up sippy cup, thanks to that marvelous plastic mouthpiece (a *beccuccio*, or little beak, they would call it in Italian), which enables you to sip without spilling or scalding your mouth. Sipped and dripped. American coffee is sippy and drippy. It is like the saline bags that are linked to an intravenous drip: the level of fluid in your bloodstream never drops below a certain level.

Italian espresso, on the other hand, is a hit. A fast, intense bang to your veins. It is a one-gulp switch of the wrist that wakes and revs you up in an instant. For this reason, Italian coffee to go makes no sense. Or rather, it makes sense only when you can't make it to the bar and the uniformed barman brings it to your office on a tray, in a porcelain cup (you'll bring it back, you're trusted, they've got plenty of them). You can get your one-gulp hit somewhere other than the bar as long as it's close by and the whole endeavor is performed quickly.

Many Italians, particularly in Naples, ask me with a big smile whether I prefer American or Italian coffee. Their faces tell me they know the answer, they know the only possible answer. They are fishing for a great big national compliment. No one can say that Italians are not patriotic—I mean, really, who cares whether you're a superpower if your coffee is bad? Most Italians (and particularly Neapolitans) find coffee in America terrible. I have heard it called *brodaglia*, or bad broth, and *acqua sporca*, dirty water. Many find even the idea of it, particularly coffee poured from a pot (reheated! *Ahimè!*) disgusting.

With a revolted but curious look on her face, Benedetta picked my brain about American "dirty water": "I've seen in movies and on TV those big cups that sit all day on American desks. What do you call them? *Moogs?* They can't really be filled with coffee, can they?"

"Mugs, and usually, yes, they are."

"All that liquid is coffee?"

"Yes."

"Doesn't it get cold?"

"Eventually, yes."

"And Americans drink it anyway? When it's getting cold?"

"Yes."

And then the crux of the matter. "You don't actually like that dirty water that they call coffee in America, do you?"

"I do."

Truthfully, I don't mind the taste of a Venti, I enjoy the relaxing experience of Billie Holiday singing in a Starbucks. People waiting in a line. A straight line, in which you know your position. It's not that no order exists in Naples when it comes to ordering a coffee, it's just that the "line" is a very amorphous formation. To an American, it may seem that people are crowded around the cash register trying to elbow each other to be first. Some people are, and do, but often people do know their place in Italian "lines"—they are simply not physically standing one in front of another. They remember who has entered before and after them: the order is an unspoken reality. They feel no need to re-create this order physically, because, after all, we all know that the lady with the white hair is after the young guy with the leather jacket and before the man with the beard, right?

So the person behind the cash register, seeing three or more people standing shoulder to shoulder, asks, *"Chi c'era?"*—Who's next? I, not remembering who came in when, sure only that I've been in that spot an awfully long time and am in dire need of caffeine, do not say, as I should, *"Io!"* (Me!) and order. I look at the people on either side of me, and trust. If no one is in too much of a rush, one of them will point graciously at me and say, *"La signorina."* Ahhh, it's nice when that happens. Authorized, I order my hit. What stress.

So when I went to Starbucks that first summer home, it was so relaxing that I sometimes felt like maybe I didn't even *need* a hit. But I would often go with a friend, to talk over coffee. To talk while drinking. Yes, we Americans multitask! And talking while drinking means that you need liquid, large quantities of it. So I would order a Venti, a drip drip drip sip sip sip into veins that were used to the sudden rush of the godly nectar that was my espresso. The Venti tasted good, though. As long as I didn't think of it as *caffè.*

Burgers and Fries

"*Fidarsi è bene, non fidarsi è meglio*," Raffaella reminded me on the phone when I called from Washington. Again the trust thing: to trust is good, not to trust is better.

Raffaella was using the expression not in reference to a person, however, but in reference to hamburgers. I had said that I was missing Italy but enjoying American hamburgers. "Better not to trust hamburgers?" I asked.

"When you eat at restaurants, you don't know what they put in the food." She worried about me like I was her daughter, and she doubted my judgment. Now that I was far away, she realized that I was naïve, a babe in the woods. I needed her protection. For all she knew, I was living on the edge, performing daredevil maneuvers like ordering meat in restaurants where I didn't know the owner. American restaurants where I didn't know *anyone* in the establishment! How could I be sure that the meat was decent?

"*Mi raccomando*," she said, using a term that means, Watch out! Heed my advice! And keep me in your mind! all at once. "When Salva arrives in Washington, you two can cook at home."

Salvatore had started planning his trip to the United States as soon as I left Naples. We missed each other and he wanted to see America. "Yes!" I said, "Come visit! We can see Washington and New York! I'll introduce you to American food courts!" I was thrilled.

He bought his tickets. "*Allora*, I arrive on July fifteenth and leave on August thirtieth," he told me over the phone. Wait, I thought. Did he just say a month and a half? I couldn't wait to see him, of course, but I was taken aback. A month and a half under my parents' roof?

Words like *visit* and *vacation* are tricky. You think they can be easily translated from one language to another, from one culture to another. *Una vacanza* is a vacation, right? *Visitare* is to visit someone. But for a Naples university student, *vacanza* meant, apparently, between one and two months. The translation in American English would more accurately be a "summer internship" or an "experience abroad." It could even be translated as "taking up an alternative residence."

In my family, anything that lasted over two weeks was the stuff of résumés and college admissions. Vacations, on the other hand, were no longer than two weeks and usually meant a cruise. Our Wilson grandfather traditionally took our family on vacation every other year, alternating with my father's brother's family. My mother and aunt planned these vacations, which meant that while our friends from Washington went to Hilton Head or Cape Cod, we went on a cruise in Southeast Asia or the Galápagos.

My mother couldn't admit that we cruised because it was a fun thing to do, and because our grandfather was paying for it. She would come up with creative reasons for why it was "impor-

TanT'" (with the pronunciation of the two *ts* very marked when it came to talking about spending money on oneself) that the children *understand the differences* between Asia and America. Or that they *experience firsthand* the ecosystem of the Galápagos.

Anna and I pretended that we were Captain Stubing's daughters from *The Love Boat*. We relished the fact that there was no argument between our parents over where to have dinner, no battles over the price of entrées. A cruise director could direct the show that was our family, and we could be kids in between the ports of call.

<hr />

Salvatore arrived in America with gel in his hair, wearing a checked dress shirt tucked into beige pants. He was carrying a man-purse and pulling a suitcase packed with gifts for every member of my family. Raffaella had bought an Armani scarf for my mother, a Marinella tie for my father (a brand that is worn by Berlusconi and sold only in Naples), a necklace for my sister, and a number of other gifts that she instructed Salva to give to "aunts, uncles, godmothers . . . whomever you think appropriate."

For me, she had packed Neapolitan *taralli* crackers, made with lard, pepper, and nuts.

My parents were standing in front of the ornate columns of their big suburban house when I pulled up with Salvatore after getting him at the airport. They seemed to be on unusually good behavior. My father welcomed him with *"Benvenuto!"* and my mother smiled. Who were these people?

We showed Salva into our modern, gray kitchen. I thought he would be taken aback by the size of the room and the fact that it looked out over our pool and extensive lawn. But he seemed unimpressed. He started fumbling around in his suitcase to find the wrapped gifts, and handed them to my parents, saying, "For you." I'd never heard his accent so thick, or so adorable. He was sweating, even with the freezing American air-con.

"This will go great with my Bali pants, *grazie mille*," my father said.

My mother spun around the Formica island trying on her scarf in different ways, and cooed, "*Gentilissimo grazie grazie Salvatore!*" She'd gotten a *Parlo Italiano* audiotape and was listening to it every day in her car so that she could outdo my father linguistically when Salva arrived.

He blushed and laughed. I'd never seen him blush. I'd never seen him at a loss for words.

"I didn't know what form of *you* to use with your parents," he told me later, "I wanted to show them respect!"

I reassured him that there was only one form of *you* in English, and that they would happily answer to Bonnie and Ed (or Bony and Head). He relaxed and started to enjoy the antics of what he considered a "typical American family." (*Typical American fathers do not swim nude*, I had to remind Salva when we got back to Italy. *They do not make loud animal noises in elegant French restaurants; they also do not buy live lobsters at Whole Foods so they can swim with them and then boil them for dinner.*)

My mother planned three weeks of travel for the four of us. While a Neapolitan *mammà* would have spent time organizing and preparing typical dishes for my boyfriend to taste, Bonnie Wilson was compiling a folder with maps, brochures, and tickets for the Show Salva the U.S.A. tour. We hit New York and Los Angeles, Boston and San Diego. My mother organized the strategic strikes with great efficiency: Who knew if Salva was ever going to come back to America? We had to get as much in as possible.

At the end of the trip, she booked us tiny, internal cabins

(we certainly couldn't afford a porthole!) on a Carnival cruise going to the Caribbean. If Salva was ever going to really fit in with the Wilsons, he had to know how to cruise.

Salvatore's English was improving, but he had begun to develop his linguistic trademark of adding one incorrect letter to English words. (Years later, at our son's Catholic school, the teachers were *nunts*; my best friend Leo from college was *Lero*.) What we took to the Caribbean was a *cruiser*. My parents and I regularly corrected him with a loud *crooooozz* in unison over the racket of steel drums or announcements about muster stations. Salva snapped his fingers to the beat of the reggae, ignoring us.

My father's clothing choice and loud voice fit in, and Salva ditched the Armani suits his mother had packed after the first day and pulled out his T-shirts with bubble letters. We rocked the cocktail bar and the karaoke lounge. When he got back to Italy, Salva told his friends how much fun the cruiser had been. It was a shame, though, that we hadn't really stopped at any ports of call.

"What do you mean?" I asked him. "We went to the Cayman Islands, Cozumel—"

"But the ship only stopped for a few hours. We didn't *visit* those places." There was that verb again, *visitare*. For Americans like us, cruising was a way to *get in* lots of places in a short time. We *did* Grand Cayman, Cozumel, Belize . . . in just one week. What more could you want? But for the Neapolitan in Salva, we might as well not have gone. When you dock at 9:00 and leave at 4:00, you don't even have time to taste the island's typical dish.

Our cruise ended in Miami, where a Princeton classmate of my father's had a house that he wasn't using. It was a sprawling estate in South Beach, and on our arrival, a handsome young *maggiordomo* showed my parents and me to our bedrooms in the main house. Salvatore, he told us, would be staying in the guesthouse, a separate structure across the lawn. It was a young man's dream come true, complete with a Jacuzzi and beers in the refrigerator. A bachelor pad! I thought Salva would be thrilled.

During the afternoon he seemed to be. He asked me to take pictures of him to show his friends in Naples: in front of the house, relaxing in the hot tub, reclining on a lounge chair. But after dinner, when we kissed good night before going our separate ways, I sensed that something was wrong. "Is this the only key?" he kept asking. "*Solo questo?* You just turn it once like that?"

Hollywood has conditioned the world to think that an isolated house in America is inevitably going to be a site of violent crime. Plus, Gianni Versace had been killed just a few weeks before in Miami, and newspapers were still covering the story. My father thought it very funny to tell Salva that Versace's murderer was a serial killer ready for more Italian blood.

I was preparing for bed when I heard a tentative knock at the door.

I opened it to find Salva in pajamas printed with flying soccer balls. "*Mi sono cagato sotto,*" he whispered. I got scared, shit-in-my-pants scared. He crawled into the single bed with me. "It was so quiet. And those wooden doors wouldn't keep out a fly."

Back in Washington, Salvatore and I went against his mother's advice and trusted—we ate out. We consumed burgers at restaurants. We drank bottles of ketchup. We got free refills. Salva was awed by straight lines of customers, by waiters who told you their name, by eighteen-wheel trucks. We hopped from enormous thing to enormous thing, from shopping malls to supermarkets to sports complexes. Having grown up in Naples, he had never seen spaces like these.

At one point, I feigned interest in joining a Gold's Gym in Rockville, Maryland, so that we could get a full tour. The trainer shook our hands, and smiled with a lot of very white, very American teeth, telling us that his name was Gary.

"Why is he telling us his name?" Salva whispered to me in Italian. "What does he want from us?"

"*Tranquillo, tranquillo,*" I reassured him. "He's just going to show us around."

Salvatore marveled at the high-tech equipment and the spacious changing rooms. When we finished the tour, Gary invited us into his office to discuss prices for membership and various personal training programs. What are you most interested in? he asked us. Cardio? Weight lifting? I was about to answer (Salva's English was still shaky, and I wanted to get out of there as quickly as possible to introduce him to the great American phenomenon of fudge at another food court) when my boyfriend spoke up.

"She needs . . . how to say . . . the leg part . . . here?" He turned to me and pointed to his thigh. "*Ketrin, come si dice* coscia?" How do you say *thigh*?

Silence. I did not translate. I would not translate.

I had a vague sense of where this was going.

But Salva would not be stopped. Nor would he let the language barrier get in his way. Oh no, this was too important. "Do you have some machine for *thees*?" Now he pointed at my thigh. "To make more slimmer?"

Now, I should mention that I have a character flaw the Italians call *permalosità*. *Permalosa* is the word that is used to describe someone who is thin-skinned, who takes everything personally. Like, for example, me. Watch what you say around Katherine, she's *permalosa*. Oversensitive, easily offended. I readily admit that I have never, and will never, like sentences that start with "Don't take this personally, but . . ." I don't like them and I don't like the creature who utters them. If you know that I may take it personally, that I probably *will* take it personally, just keep your mouth shut, no? I am highly *permalosa*. And, like many young Anglo-Saxon women, nowhere is this more the case than when it comes to body image.

So, if I weren't *permalosa*, I might have seen this episode as an example of my boyfriend's encouragement, of his desire to lovingly nudge me and my thighs toward self-improvement. But since my ego and hence insecurity were about as enormous as that Gold's Gym, I asked the personal trainer if there were any machines that would make my boyfriend's biceps look like they'd lifted something heavier than a fork. There was confusion and fear in the eyes of that trainer as he quickly dispatched us, handing over a brochure and telling us to call if we needed any more information.

Bologna

The typical dish of Bologna is *tortellini in brodo*. Traditional Bolognese sauce (which is not anything like Neapolitan *ragù*—it has almost no tomato in it, in fact) is eaten with ta-gliatelle or fettuccine, while the meat-filled tortellini must be swimming in broth. At hardcore restaurants in Bologna, they will refuse to serve you *tortellini al Bolognese*. Only *in brodo*.

At restaurants in Naples, pasta doesn't swim. Get a soup.

When I arrived in Bologna to begin my year at SAIS, Salva-tore and I decided that we would see each other every other weekend. He came north bearing Styrofoam care packages from his mother, which he would toss on my desk before un-dressing me. The *parmigiana di melanzane*, mozzarella, and *pasta al forno* could wait.

"She told me it's all for you," he would say, after we had got-ten our fill of each other and were hungry for food. "Mamma made me promise not to eat it. I get it all the time and you don't. She said you're *sciupata*." *Sciupata* is the Neapolitan word for scrawny, but it also means pale and generally unhealthy. It's what one becomes when one doesn't have a *mamma* in the kitchen. When, for example, one pursues a master's degree in a city where the pasta is swimming in broth.

My fellow students, my fellow *sciupati*, were from all over the world. They were smart, sophisticated, global. They were twentysomethings who could write cover letters in three languages to attach to their impressive résumés. They hopped continents frequently, had work experience in places like Burma, and most already emailed in 1997.

Meanwhile, Salvatore stayed in Naples, memorizing by heart three-hundred-page law texts in his room of teddy bears and elementary school soccer trophies. We both purchased cellphones as big as small toaster ovens and talked in the evenings. My head was full of kinked supply curves and what was happening in Bosnia, while he would tell me what wonderful things he had had for dinner. "And what did you eat, my *pagnottella*?"

I refused to answer him. Word would get out.

In the United States that summer, Salvatore had been enthralled by what was, in 1997, a consumer culture that was much more advanced than that of Italy. Although he was challenged by verbs like *to be* and *to go*, he immediately learned expressions like *reward points*, *preferred customer*, and *supersaver*. What intellectual energy he had left after eight hours of rote memorization of his law texts he used to redeem coupons to get a 20 percent discount on bath soap (yes, on another continent), or to write letters to places like Walmart (with my linguistic consultation) that went something like this:

Dear Sir/Madam,

I would like the new Bonus Club Membership. Please. Thank you.

Salvatore Avallone
Via G. Pascoli, 4B
Napoli, Italia

In economics class, I learned that southern Italy was the Appalachia of the EU. Unable to withstand regional shocks and bounce back with labor mobility, it was a place where market capitalism was turned upside down. How did young Neapolitans do that and manage to get away with it? By living at home until they're thirty, by working in the black market, by ignoring the rules and being so very *grounded*. Neapolitans turned the global system on its head in one *gesto*, like a flick of the spatula when frying a frittata.

The young people I knew in Naples didn't seem the least bit interested in being mobile, flexible, independent, global. *No, grazie*, they seemed to say. We're just fine here, with our extended family, smelling things simmering in a pot for hours. But we do like that supersaver discount idea; do we qualify?

Every other Friday afternoon, I would get the Eurostar to Naples, to soft sheets and deep red *ragù* and the world of sensory satisfaction and emotional connection. Five hours passed quickly. Medieval Bologna, Renaissance Florence, the aqueducts outside Rome. (They always made me remember the signs on the Beltway pointing to Washington, the unquestioned seat of the Empire in 1997.) When I saw the sea at Gaeta, I knew that Naples was near and I was coming home.

Pulling into the Napoli Centrale train station, I could see the laundry (intimate robes, pajamas, and all) on the lines that connected the buildings to each other. *"Pronto, Mamma?"* Cellphones would start ringing as we neared the station, loudly, all at the same time. From middle-aged businessmen to young girls in university up north, everyone got a call from their *mamma*. Their conversations were the same, no matter the age or gender: Yes, the train is on time, that sounds good for lunch, but did you get the mozzarella? *Sì, sì, see you soon, love you, Mamma*.

My to-do list in Bologna:

Write a paper on the Warsaw pact
Exercise
Read econ chapters
Figure out a job in which I can earn money and have fun
Destroy the judging mother in my head
Become famous
Take calcium pills

My to-do list in Napoli:

Make sure when cooking crustaceans only to use sprigs,
    not the flowers, of parsley
When going back to bed for afternoon nap, put full
    pajamas on (no half-assed siesta)
Tell Nino to get extra ricotta for me
Bring full array of eye shadow
Kiss Salva on the soft spot behind his earlobe
DON'T EAT CRUST OF PIZZA FIRST

Tonino Reale

The SAIS master's program includes a year in Bologna and a year in Washington. It was understood that after my year in Bologna, I would go back to the hum of central air-conditioning, to "Have a nice day!" and a linear career path. As my fellow students organized their summer internships and their upcoming semesters in D.C., I started buying bags of chocolate amaretto cookies. I discovered Bolognese binge food.

It wasn't just that I missed Naples and the Avallones (although it would have greatly helped to have been spoon-fed some of Raffaella's lasagna on a regular basis at that point). Once again, I was hungry for the stage. Although I'd performed my way through high school and college, I had never acted professionally. It was time for me to work in theater as a grown-up: I wanted to take a risk and see if I could make a living doing something I loved.

When I told my mother that I'd decided not to finish the program in Washington, she reminded me that I wouldn't have an advanced degree: all I'd have to show for my year in Bologna was "a *di-plOH-ma*, sweetheart"—that long "O" making it sound like a certificate for winning points at a boardwalk arcade. She told her friends that her younger daughter had decided to take a temporary (at least I *hope* it's temporary!) "leave of absence." When I explained my decision to Raffaella, she said, "Okay," and then asked what I was planning for dinner. Salva said, "Oh! We have a showgirl!" He pronounced it *show-gEErl*.

I spent the summer working on audition pieces, and came back to Italy in the fall ready to find out where the Italian productions were and to try to get cast. Little did I know that though I was in the land of Dante's *Divina Commedia*, the comedy of Italian theater wasn't always so divine.

--- ✦ ---

My first audition in Italy was for the Neapolitan director Tonino Reale's musical version of *The Picture of Dorian Gray* at the spectacular baroque Teatro Bellini in central Naples. I brought my "I Could Have Danced All Night" sheet music and the text of a Blanche Dubois monologue from A *Streetcar Named Desire* in Italian. I was nervous, and looked anxiously for the waiting room, expecting to commiserate with other water bottle–nursing actors dressed in black. What I found instead was a hot eighteenth-century salon that stank of BO and powder. The communal stage fright of the scantily clad *velina* types was palpable.

There was a lot of exposed flesh and thick Pan-Cake makeup. I should keep my eyes down, I thought, so they don't land inadvertently on cleavage or thongs. I sat down and opened my *Un tram che si chiama Desiderio* text to keep busy.

"*Che cos'è? Che fai?*" An absurdly beautiful adolescent girl was leaning over my script. Her boobs were touching my forearm! She wanted to know what I had brought. What play is that? Why are you doing it? Can I hear you do it? You need a little more eyeliner. I have some, you want to borrow it?

Minding one's own business was not part of the deal. I told her about myself, that this was my first audition in Italy. When I mentioned that I was American, a great big *oooooooohhhh* rose up in a wave from the girls. They were wide-eyed and even silent for a moment, until a blonde in spike heels said, *"Vabbò, io me ne vaco a casa!"* They all laughed. An American's here? Maybe I should just go home.

Fortunately, the director had made the same assumptions about American talent that the girl had. As I was singing the very first "I could have daaaanced . . ." he interrupted me to say that I was cast. God bless Italy! I was emotionally prepared for "Don't call us, we'll call you," even *"No, grazie."* And here I was cast without even a callback, and without bringing out Italian Blanche. Kindness of strangers, indeed.

I stayed in Benedetta's old room while the play was in rehearsal. After Benedetta and Mauro's Positano wedding, the newlyweds had moved into an apartment on the first floor of the building where Salva and his parents lived. Some friends warned that living in the same building as parents and in-laws was a recipe for disaster, but others congratulated Benedetta and Mauro on their luck at having a *mamma* just two floors down. Lasagna could be sent up in the elevator. Shirts could be ironed free of charge. When children came, the *nonni*, or grandparents, would be babysitters in residence. An intercom was built in to save on phone bills, for the daily Mamma, do you have an onion? Or, Can I substitute *provola* for *scamorza* cheese in my stuffed peppers?

Raffaella was busy. She now fed not two children but four

twentysomethings. When Benedetta asked her mother for lasagna, Raffaella would bake it (remembering to leave out the
sausage—Mauro didn't like pork) and then buzz her daughter to
say, "It's in the elevator." So as not to intrude on Benedetta and
her new husband, she would not bring the lasagna herself, but
would put the hot pan on the floor of the elevator (oh, how that
smell would linger! A *ragù* cooked for hours, tiny fried meatballs hidden in the layers of pasta . . .) and push the button of
the floor where her daughter lived. Benedetta would walk out of
her apartment to find the elevator doors opening, opening to
the smell and the sight of that aluminum-foiled labor of love
inside the little lift.

One morning, about a month into rehearsals, I was running
out the door of the Avallones' to grab a taxi for the theater, when
Raffaella told me that she had made a *pizza di scarola* for my
snack. I had to go, I was already late, I told her, to no avail. Raffaella had to make sure that the focaccia-like pizza was properly
packaged. The director could wait.

By the time I made it out the door, I was majorly, unjustifi-
ably tardy. In addition, all of downtown was in gridlock. As I sat
in the taxi, watching the meter ticking away, I asked the driver
if there was a strike or a demonstration. Yes, he told me, it was
the demonstration of illegal aliens, and it would block traffic the
entire morning. Policemen were escorting the African, Bangladeshi, and Southeast Asian demonstrators in an attempt to keep
some kind of order. I wondered: but if they are illegal . . . and
these are cops . . .

The demonstration would not be a viable excuse—I was
now disastrously tardy. I had been late for rehearsal once before,
a matter of about fifteen minutes, and had expected to discreetly
join the rest of the cast, score in hand and causing not a ripple

(maybe just mouthing *Scusa!*). Instead, the director screamed, *"Chi sei!"* Who are you? as soon as I entered the room.

It confused me. Did he really not know who I was? Granted, I was not the lead. Nor was I an important supporting character. But we had been rehearsing the musical for almost a month, six days a week, and there were only about eighteen members of the cast. So I would have liked to think that the director, Tonino Reale, knew who I was. He had cast me, after all.

Many international theater professionals have not heard of the Neapolitan director Tonino Reale. He is an actor/director/narcissistic tyrant who bears a striking resemblance, physically and temperamentally, to Rumpelstiltskin. He has been known to jump onstage during performances, whisper "You suck" to the lead, and play the role for what remains of the show. He is usually wearing a black T-shirt printed with nonsense English phrases like GOING STRONG UNIVERSITY. When he sings, a sort of hoarse, screaming sound that disregards notes and rhythm, he totally blows out his voice (which is already suffering from the pack of cigarettes he smokes each day). For curtain call, he likes to keep coming back onstage for applause until all of the audience has left. Sometimes as many as seven times. Needless to say, he has not been nominated for any Italian Tonys.

That's why I was more than a little tense in the taxi on the way to the Teatro Bellini. I had some idea how the ogre would react to my being thirty minutes late. When I arrived, I braced myself for the worst. I entered the theater and found the actors doing some blocking on the stage while Tonino surfed the Internet on his laptop in one of the ornate boxes that had been reserved for royalty two centuries ago.

Maybe he wouldn't see me! Hope! I ran onstage and tried to blend in with the other members of the cast.

"Americana!" he screeched. The sound of his voice was not tempered by all the red velvet. But, looking on the bright side, at least this time he remembered who I was.

"Multa!"

A fine? For being late? But just a few days before, the director had failed to show up! Twenty people waited for him all day long! And he never even explained his absence when he came to rehearsal the next day.

So it went that I had to pay a twenty-euro fine for my tardiness. But at least I was saved the humiliation of being the object of a ten-minute tirade. On another occasion, the director, instead of suggesting that I move a few feet stage left, screamed, "Girl with the nineteenth-century ass! Move over! You're blocking the people I *really* want to see!"

I learned the hard way that stage actors in Italy have a tough lot. Very little money. Exhausting tours. School matinees where high schoolers throw food onstage and shout "Take it off!" and teachers stand up every few minutes to shout *"Basta!"* This, compounded with Tonino Reale's howling onstage and off (and his regular groping of the actresses) persuaded me to take my wobbly soprano voice, bizarre accent, and nineteenth-century ass to a dubbing studio.

If an actor in Italy is not interested in being on a reality show, perhaps his or her most promising (read: most lucrative and stable) future is in the world of dubbing. All foreign films in Italy are dubbed into Italian. "Subtitles cause headaches," Italians often say. And so each big American star is dubbed by one Italian voice. The voice of Tom Cruise is a friend of mine and a phenomenal actor. Sylvester Stallone is dubbed by a fat character actor famous throughout the country. The Italian public is very attached to these voices, particularly the voices of stars like Cruise, Tom Hanks, and Sharon Stone. There was an uproar when Tom Cruise's dubber was replaced in one of his films because of a contract disagreement. My friend Roberto, the Italian Cruise, was *tranquillo*, however. "They will rehire me. I am Tom."

Italians are so attached to the stars' Italian voices that they can be greatly disturbed when they hear the Americans' real voices. "The voice of *our* Robert De Niro is so much better than yours," someone told me recently, apparently not concerned about the fact that the English-language version is the man's real voice. But I agree that some performances are greatly enhanced by dubbing. Not the Fonz, and most definitely not Meryl Streep, but Jean-Claude Van Damme, for example, and Keanu Reeves.

Good dubbing is an art form. Not only do you need to understand the character and "find" the voice, like any good actor, but you need to pay close attention to "synch"—the ability to start speaking the second the actor opens his mouth, take breaths when he or she does, and keep the rhythm so that you finish the line exactly when the actor does. Dubbing successfully depends of course on having a translation, or rather an adaptation, that works. But it also takes talent and skill.

I started to get calls from studios in Rome to dub in English. Since Italian dubbing studios are some of the best in the world (and cheapest to use—you could pay dubbers and technicians under the table), we would get all kinds of work: Chinese martial arts films, Philippine horror movies, Brazilian cartoons. Basically anything that was headed for distribution in English-speaking countries, or that needed an English version on DVD. I immediately fell in love with cartoon dubbing. I could go crazy with my voice without having to worry about following the mouth of the actor onscreen. Although a dubbing director might suggest that I could let my British woodchuck get in touch with her anger, or that my melancholy marshmallow could incorporate a touch of bitterness, I generally was not told "you suck." That was important for someone as *permalosa* as me.

So I was happy when I got a call for a turn (three hours in a dubbing studio) for the English version of *Snow White and Her Seven Dwarves*. I hopped on a train for Rome excitedly. Snow White! My voice would be perfect. I should have paid more attention to the possessive pronoun in the title, though.

I soon realized that this Snow White was not a cartoon. The film was intended, in fact, for a very adult audience. The director came into the studio, fitted me with my headphones, and put a chair behind me. "In case you start hyperventilating," he told me.

Hyperventilating, in fact, is the greatest risk in porn dubbing. Fortunately for the dubber, the director can usually use the heavy breathing in the film's original language. But every once in a while, along comes an *"O Dio!"* or some such cry. The dubber has to record an "Oh God!" and all the cries and breaths surrounding it. I'm telling you, it's exhausting.

Snow White's director listened behind the glass division, looking bored and sleepy. He'd watched these scenes thousands of times, having already dubbed the dwarves into English, Spanish, Portuguese, and Chinese. He stopped me mid-wail, and with a tone of voice that I'm used to now with Italian directors, told me that I sounded like I was tired and in pain. Bianca Neve (Snow White) isn't in pain, why should I be? Relax and enjoy it, *Americana*.

A Manicure Before Mass

"Before we go, Ketrin, could you cut my fingernails? It will only take a minute." We were walking out the door, late for the service. The baptism of Benedetta's newborn son, Emilio, was to begin at ten o'clock, and it was now 9:55. The organization was difficult because there were so many of us: Benedetta and her husband, Nino and Raffaella, Salvatore and myself, Zio Toto (owner of the aforementioned fingernails), and Benedetta's Sri Lankan nanny and housekeeper, who was the only one sitting in the car downstairs ready to go. "*Mi raccomando!*" Raffaella had announced that morning, meaning I trust you all will listen to me. "Don't be late. We must leave the house no later than nine-thirty!"

I was in Naples on break from tour. I had been cast in the Italian production of Andrew Lloyd Webber's *Jesus Christ Superstar*, and had been traveling for months with a group of thirty dancers and singers throughout Italy. We hopped from city to city, baroque opera house to baroque opera house, seedy hotel to seedy hotel. When there were breaks, I would come to Naples and stay with the Avallones. Salva had a few more exams left, and I awaited his graduation eagerly. It was time to begin our life together as grown-ups. It was time to stop sleeping together in a room with stuffed Garfield toys.

On the day of Emilio's baptism (my hair done, toenails painted, and ever the punctual American), I searched the apartment at 9:30 for any sign of life. I found it in the kitchen, where Raffaella was, believe it or not, grilling squash. And talking on the phone. With curlers in her hair.

"Raffaella, *basta*. Enough. We have to go." I was beginning to behave like a *mamma* myself, even with the older generation.

"*Ah sì! Sì! Sì!*" She hung up the phone and turned off the stove. Before scurrying off to get dressed, though, she had to tell me something. "Ketrin, when you're grilling squash, remember that it's always better to—"

"*Basta*. We're late."

"You're right, you're right." And she was off to her walk-in closet, a Never Never Land that would become the favorite place of her four grandchildren. Rosary beads hang next to bright pink and purple belts, alongside a crucifix on the wall. There are five- and six-hundred-euro Valentino suits, luscious furs, and enough rhinestones and beads to make an adolescent girl flip out.

I would have preferred to hang out in Raffaella's glittery closet, but Zio Toto was summoning me to the guest bathroom for his manicure. I knew about Zio Toto's missing hand but honestly had never thought about how he managed to trim the nails on his other hand. And I don't think it ever would have occurred to me had he not asked me to do it at 9:55 on the day of Emilio's baptism.

Why me? Why now?

"Come on! Here are the scissors!" he was telling me. He was sitting on the closed toilet, so I balanced my butt on the bidet and got to work. The nails were very tough, very yellow, and very long. The job was not easy. And it didn't help that I had a nervous fluttering in my stomach because of our lateness. This was a rite of passage, a sacrament! For Protestants as well as Catholics. And we were going to sail in during the Apostles' Creed. Father Giampietro, complete with spurs, was probably already beginning the mass at Santo Strato. My hands were shaking.

Zio Toto was humming, relaxed, oblivious. "Ketrin!" Salva was calling me from the other room. "I'm coming! I'm coming! Just a minute!" I yelled. Somehow I managed to finish the job, leaving little yellow pieces of Zio Toto's nails littering the floor, and flew down the steps of the palazzo to where the others were waiting. I was anxious and annoyed and bitter. And then I saw my nephew.

He was already in the car, in his mother's arms (car seat? no car seat?), wearing a long white baptismal robe. Proud tears sprang to my eyes. It had been less than a year before that Salva had called me in Milan (where we were performing *Superstar*) to tell me, *"Zia! Sarai una zia!"* I hadn't understood. An aunt? I was an aunt? What was he saying?

"Capito, Showgeerl? Benedetta è incinta!"

Benedetta was pregnant and I had a new title in the family: *Zia*. I was confused. Salva and I weren't married, so how could I be an aunt? Was something expected of me? Salva was so excited to tell me my new title, though—repeating *Zia Ketrin, Zia Ketrin*—that I didn't tell him what I was thinking: Congratulations to Benedetta, but I don't have anything to do with it. I'm not even a blood relative, I'm just the little brother's girlfriend.

The feel of Emilio's tiny black head against my chest exactly nine minutes after he was born changed all that. Since Benedetta's husband was a cardiologist, she got a private room in the hospital. The room was filled with about ten people when mother and son were rolled in immediately after the C-section. The baby was still crusty and blood-streaked; Benedetta looked pale and nauseous. Raffaella was opening a bottle of champagne and fumbling with fifteen plastic cups. She left the job to one of her sisters when she saw her daughter and grandson. She strode over to grab the baby out of Benedetta's arms and lift him for all to see. "*Ma quanto è bello!*" How gorgeous he is!

I thought, There's no easing into this, Emilio. You've had your nine months of peace and quiet and personal space. Now, as they say in Neapolitan, "*T'è scetà!*" Gotta wake yourself up.

I was about to slip out to visit a bathroom (if nobody else washed their hands or used disinfectant, at least *I* would) when the baby was literally passed to me like a football. These women of Salva's family had handled newborns and knew something about it. I had never held a baby in my arms, let alone one that still had his plastic ID bracelet on and umbilical cord attached. But there was no time to protest, the fuzzy black head was resting against my chest and everyone was talking about something else. I was a kinswoman, and my body was forced to grasp that concept immediately even as my brain needed a little more time.

And so it was, packed in the car going to mass, that I transformed from a punctual priss to a gushing, emotional mess of a *zia*. Toto, apparently satisfied with his manicure, came out to find that there was no space for him in the car. "*Che problema c'è?*" He grinned. He had his motorbike. Raising his plastic hand, he called out, "See you in church!"

A Home for Good

The tour of *Jesus Christ Superstar* led to a tour of *Evita*, which led to small roles in Italian sitcoms. At dubbing studios, I was called to lend my voice to heroines in low-budget Filipino horror movies, or to neurotic badgers in Brazilian cartoons. There was work, but none of it was in Naples.

As I got ready to go onstage in Mantova, or Cremona, trying desperately to find a pocket of oxygen in a dressing room that was a haze of cigarette smoke, I would call Salva in Naples. The whole family was gathered for risotto and *arrosto* to celebrate Santa Benedetta, or San Salvatore. Or it was Nino and Raffaella's wedding anniversary, and they had gotten fresh *gamberi* for the linguine. It was Emilio's first birthday, and I should have tried that *caprese* cake! The family gathered, and I was missed.

How much longer, I wondered, until I can come home for good?

"How many years do couples usually date in Naples before getting married?" I asked Salva on the phone one evening, trying to sound like I was performing a sociological survey. He had only one exam left to complete his university degree, and I wondered where we stood.

Well, Salva told me, his cousin Giorgio had been with his girlfriend for fourteen years. Another friend was going on sixteen years, with no engagement on the horizon. Hard to tell.

"*Comunque, più di dieci,*" he decided. More than ten years for sure.

"That is a decade. Of dating."

"The reason is economic," Salva explained. Italian *ragazzi* don't earn enough to rent their own place. (He didn't mention mothers, or lasagna.) You can't get married if you're still economically dependent on your parents, after all.

It was time to tell him about my family's history, and the money that my grandparents had set aside for their grandchildren, in the form of a trust. This was difficult, since there is no Italian translation for the term. Italian children who inherit wealth usually get it in the form of apartments or land or jobs. When their parents die, they get whatever they get directly. Taxes? *Eeeeeeh*, on the exhale—you don't pay them during life, you don't pay them after death.

"I have a trust fund." (To trust is good, not to trust is better: *Fidarsi è bene, non fidarsi è meglio!*) I tried to explain. "It's this American thing where we skip generations." My translation made it sound like all Americans like to hop over their kids on principle. "It isn't my parents' money, it was set up by my grandparents."

"Why? They didn't trust your parents?"

It was a conversation going nowhere. The truth was, I had no vocabulary to translate terms like *estate tax* or *loopholes*. In reality, I didn't even know what they meant.

I was very confused about money as a child. I knew that we had an extravagant house, and that we took a lot of nice vacations. But my parents reminded me often that we weren't as rich as other people thought we were. Our family had never actually *owned* Wilson. My grandfather was just a shareholder when it was sold and it wasn't sold for much and I should just laugh when my classmates in elementary school asked me for a free tennis racket. When my family socialized with the Marriotts and Firestones, my mother always commented that "these people are just in a different *league*, precious." And she was right, they were in a different league if you were going to compare the rich with the superrich. But my mother pushed the point so much that my sister and I believed that we were one step away from food stamps.

So I realized only embarrassingly late that the trusts in the hands of family bankers, the studying of tax loopholes, the bizarre generation skipping—all meant that we had money in our names. My father's grandfather, the industrial magnate, left him trusts. My grandfather, in turn, left me trusts. But these trusts, my mother believed, were not meant to be spent. "They exist to avoid estate tax," she would tell me when I asked what a trust was. Interest could be skimmed off for emergencies, but the phrase *tapping into capital* was akin to *shooting up heroin*.

For Bonnie Wilson, money that you don't earn shouldn't really be yours. Rags to riches is a heroic story to be told. It is the American dream, Calvinism exemplified! Riches to doing just fine—not so much. Better to pretend you're poor.

The trusts that I inherited were enough to allow me to buy an apartment in Italy, and Salva and I could establish ourselves as an independent couple. I explained this to him, but he seemed strangely uninterested in the matter.

"*Ho capito, ho capito.*" Oh, I get it, is what he said. After a pause he added, "Why don't you buy new sneakers? The ones you have are all worn down," and that was the end of it.

Inheriting money from your grandparents was a quirky American way of passing money down, he seemed to think, but there was nothing momentous about it. Salva came from a family that had had money, and had lost money, and were doing fine. He would graduate from law school, and find work. He would never be dependent on me or anyone else. As his parents had taught him, *Fidarsi è bene, non fidarsi è meglio.*

'O Purpo

"*Facciamo la strada o le scale?*" Raffaella asked. Do you want to use the road or the steps? We were in Positano, carrying beach bags stuffed with towels, thick sandwiches, peaches, bottles of water, sunscreen, a change of clothes—a load of stuff—down to the beach. The Avallones have a house high on the cliff overlooking the water, and to get to the small pebbly beach there are exactly . . . I don't know how many steps. A lot. Salva, when he was little, would count the steps every day of his two-month summer vacation in Positano, and every day he would come out with a different number.

Salva would run down these steps barefoot, with no parental chaperone, at the age of seven. He would stop on the way down to the beach only to buy a chocolate *cannolo*; on the way up, a lemon granita made with those Amalfi coast lemons as big as a human head. The little granita cart that is strategically positioned at the Piazza dei Mulini made enough lire in the summer months to support three Positano families all year long.

The road, meanwhile, is winding, narrow, and petrifying, whether you are on foot or in a vehicle. In Italy, hairpin turns present no reason for cars, buses, or motorbikes to slow down. The use of brakes is limited to the moments when two wide vehicles meet head-on (the tiny roads on the Amalfi coast are mostly two-way). It is not uncommon to see the Interno Positano bus reversing and then scraping up against the cliff to leave space for the Montepertuso bus to pass. The clown-nose honking of horns echoes frequently through Positano. When you are walking down to the beach and vehicles whiz by, or two buses have a honking tête-à-tête, you have to hop to safety either by jumping onto and clinging to the cliff or by ducking into one of the chic jewelry shops carved into the rock.

Road or steps? *"Le scale,"* I tell Raffaella. Definitely the steps.

As Salvatore's callused little soccer feet ran down these steps thirty years ago, his mother's pedicured feet never stopped moving around the kitchen of their villa. She would bake all sorts of delicacies to bring down to the beach for lunch: *polpette al sugo, frittate, peperoni saltati.* "It was simple," she told me when I suggested that food shopping, cooking, cleaning, and generally managing small children in hot, vertical Positano must have been exhausting for her as a young mother. She was on her own most of the time, as Nino, like most of the other fathers, stayed in Naples and joined his family for weekends and August. "We just ate sandwiches for lunch." Well, yes, but the sandwiches weren't peanut butter and jelly—they were sandwiches filled with something she had *baked* that morning.

At the beach, the family rented umbrellas and lounge chairs close to their friends from Posillipo. There is a hierarchy to the positioning of the chairs: those closest to the water are the families who have been coming to Positano the longest and who spend all summer. Farther back are the families who don't have vacation homes, who come to Positano for only a few weeks.

The Avallones' umbrellas and chairs have always been in the first row, despite the fact that they would spend at least a month every summer away from Positano, at their apartment in Roccaraso. They were, and are, prominent in the preening Posillipino-Positanese posse.

My one-piece bathing suit and last-minute depilatory efforts did not, I realized as we neared their *ombrellone*, cut it. Raffaella was wearing a Pucci caftan, and somehow, even in early June, was already deeply, uniformly tanned. She moved from umbrella to umbrella (only in the first row; her friends were as linear as a chorus line), praising wraps and pinching grandchildren, while somehow negotiating the sharp pebbles along the beach in her high-heeled flip-flops. "*Conosci Ketrin?*" she asked. Do you know Katherine? The *americana* girlfriend of Salvatore was introduced as I struggled to stay upright. (How did one stand on rocks that felt to my bare feet like fiery shards of glass? My New Balance sneakers were up in the changing room.)

We had come to Positano to celebrate Salva's graduation from university. Raffaella and Nino were so proud: their son had graduated with top honors and was now Dr. Avallone. Hallelujah! He had done it. Six years of pulling teeth, of sweating bricks, of memorizing tomes, and now he was a free man. Free, I assumed, to marry me and move out of his parents' apartment. Everything else was immaterial.

But every time I uttered the word *marriage*, Salva would change the subject.

A Neapolitan expression that Nino taught me helped me to avoid a diplomatic coup d'état and dramatic breakup: '*O purpo s'ha dda cocere dinto a ll'acqua soia*. Literally translated: An octopus must be left to cook in its own juice. After boiling an octopus, apparently, you turn off the flame and leave it in its pot, where it continues to emit its own juices. You can write emails or pick up the kids from soccer practice while the big, slimy, puckering animal stews, because the longer the *polipo* steeps in its own dark pink liquid the better.

Nino taught me this expression that fateful weekend in Positano. When, on Sunday night, Salva hadn't popped any questions except of the "Do you like the stuffed calamari or the steamed *cozze* better?" sort, I confided in Nino and Raffaella. Salva was showering after our day at the beach, and I was sitting with my future parents-in-law on the terrace of their villa. The twinkling lights of Positano were reflected in the blackness of the sea below; the light breeze and smell of orange trees added to the aura of potential romance.

On the other side of the mountain we could see a religious procession, complete with a band playing music that resounded against the rocks. From the terrace they looked like the tiny figures of a Christmas *presepe*. With raised banners and statues of the Madonna, the Positano faithful slowly snaked their way around the winding roads. What a perfect setting to dispatch the parents, get on one knee, and present a ring! Any goddamned ring!

I came out with it: Why does Salva change the subject every time I bring up the idea of getting married? Is it because I'm American? Is it because he wants to stay single, living at home and eating magnificent dishes? "He's like an octopus," Nino replied. "He has to be left to cook in his own juice." Raffaella nodded in agreement. I was not to pressure him or add any external stimuli, but let him come to the decision on his own. Salvatore is a handsome guy, and I was attached to the image of him on one knee asking for my hand in marriage. Instead, I was presented with the image of a bubbling sea creature who, perfectly content for the time being to stew in the pot *by himself,* needed to cook for another five years or more.

Apparently the whole "Will you marry me?" scene with ring and candlelight is an American tradition. It took me a surprisingly long time to realize this, but at a certain point it came to me in a flash. People don't do that here! They just start planning for the wedding. I was waiting for the Easter Bunny! When I tell Italians that in the States, a proposal is often romantic like in the movies, they can't believe it. It cracks them up. We thought that was just another *americanata*, they say, a cheesy and dramatic exaggeration invented by Hollywood.

Having grown up in fast-paced, do-it-yourself North America, I realize that letting people and situations cook in their own juices is decidedly not my forte. (This is probably why my *ragù*, even after eighteen years in Italy, tastes nothing like that of my mother-in-law.) So, to leave Salva alone and trust him to come to a decision without my prodding was a challenge. I succeeded, I am proud to say, for exactly twenty-one hours after that conversation. I probably would have managed longer, except that I found myself, returning from Positano, in a position in which I thought that I was surely going to die.

My puckering *polipo* and I were returning to Naples in his tiny Fiat, on the narrow two-way coastal road. The view of the crystal-blue ocean five hundred feet below; the sea air coming in the open windows: it could have been an enjoyable and picturesque drive. Except that Salva was speeding like a madman around the curves and actually passing other cars. He would honk his horn. (The English verb Salva uses is *to horn*. As in, "I was just horning! The man is going too slow.") I thought this was the moment for our conversation, as it was probably my last.

"So are you going to ask me?" I yelled. We had trouble hearing each other for the wind.

"What?"

"To marry you!"

"Who? What?"

"Wedding! *Matrimonio!* Us!"

"*Okay!*"

"*Fine!*"

"*Fine!*"

The octopus was cooked.

Till Dessert Do Us Part

ecently, I overheard two Neapolitan ladies I had never seen before talking about "that wedding in America." Sitting by the swimming pool and gossiping, one said to the other, "Did you hear? All the friends of the bride wore *the same dress*! There was a *rehearsal*. And everyone got up from the table to dance, during dinner!"

I felt proud. Proud that in some way I helped a group of Neapolitans understand that one can party without pasta and live to tell the tale.

There is a word that you will not find in your Italian-English dictionary: *sfamarsi*. Like *sdrammatizzare*, *sfamarsi* uses that little *s* to turn a verb into its opposite. *Sfamarsi* is to dehunger oneself. I learned at my wedding to Salvatore that it is very difficult for Neapolitans to dehunger themselves without pasta.

No one will come if we get married in the United States, Salva had said. It's too far. It's too expensive. (He didn't say, how will we dehunger ourselves? That came later.) So we planned the wedding for mid-August, when all of Italy is on vacation anyway. My mother organized a four-day affair in Washington. Months before the event, Salva's Neapolitan friends and family got an invitation that looked like a book. It contained individual invitation cards for the rehearsal dinner, the ceremony, and the Sunday barbecue, as well as maps, pickup times, contact numbers, and dress codes. In Naples, they'd never seen anything so organized. They got their butts to the travel agency, bought tranquilizers for their fear of flying, and signed on. Forty of them.

The Neapolitans who arrived for the Wilson-Avallone wedding averaged three suitcases a head. After they finished their American tour (and learned a new word in English: *outlet*, pronounced *aauutlet*), that number rose to four. The women's sporty casual look was white and pastel oxford shirts with tight, tapered pants and ankle boots. Big rhinestone-studded sunglasses held back their perfectly styled hair. The men wore linen jackets and moccasins that were red or lilac. Most had a terracotta tan.

In the evening, necklines plunged and heels soared. The ladies' chiffon wraps seemed to match their husbands' silky-soft made-to-order suits. My aunt and uncle hosted a buffet dinner for out-of-town guests two nights before the wedding. "Katherine," my aunt whispered to me soon after the Neapolitans had stepped down from the bus in their stilettos and Maglis and partaken of the buffet, "*there's nothing left to eat.*" The caterers had brought huge platters of baby lamb chops, sautéed vegetables, cheese wheels. "*They've already eaten everything.*"

What had happened? These were not bingers, and no one was obese. Benedetta later explained to me that the Avallones and their friends had dehungered themselves in the only way possible. "We were just trying to *sfamarci*. We don't know how to do it without pasta, *voi americani come fate?*" How do you Americans do it? How do you satisfy yourselves in this Land Without Pasta?

When it came to determining the menu for our wedding reception, Salva and I decided that rather than serving pasta that would surely not taste like the *primi* Italians were used to, it would be better to stick to typical American dishes. Actually, "Salva and I decided" is perhaps a simplification. Our conversations about the day of the wedding went something like this:

ME: Shrimp, crab cakes, prime rib. It'll be fine. So, after the first dance, my father will . . .
HIM: And the shrimp cocktail will be followed by . . . ?
ME: Give the toast.
HIM: Toast?
ME: We need to decide the music for the first dance.
HIM: We're having toast?
ME: *Steak!* Crab cakes and steak!
HIM: And the pasta course?
ME: I think the seating at our table should be . . .
HIM: And the pasta course?

He could not get over the fact that at our wedding there would be no pasta. On the most important day of his life, he would not eat pasta: this was extremely difficult to *mandare giù*, to send down or swallow. He and his compatriots would have to eat an entire cow and a school of fish to dehunger themselves. On top of that, they would have to focus their attention (at least part of the time) on something other than the food.

Italian weddings are about what you wear and what you eat. And what other people wear and what they eat. I have been to weddings in Naples where I have sat, masticating, for five straight hours. No dancing, no mingling. Conversation is limited to what is being served and what color sandals the mother of the bride is wearing (with some inevitable soccer discussion among the men).

"Hi, nice to meet you! Where are you from? What do you do?" I do not recommend this line of conversation at a wedding in Italy. I have tried it. Feeling like a bored overstuffed pig, I have ventured out into the taboo territory of putting questions to people I don't know. The response is usually "Here," and the job description is one or two words with the subtext, "I do it because I have to but count the minutes until my next vacation." That shuts me up and sends me back to examining the twelfth plate of food that has been set before me. Praise the food, dissect the consistency of the risotto, and you will find people interested in conversation at Italian weddings, I have discovered. At least that way you'll find something to do with your mouth other than chew.

———— ☀ ————

It is tradition in Naples for the mother of the groom to hand the bride her bouquet, ceremoniously. The photographer is there, ready to record the ritual. The bride and her future mother-in-law look in each other's eyes, faces glowing with respect and love. Other emotions are hidden for later: *Now you're the one who's going to have to make his* pasta con piselli, *grinding up the little pieces of onion! Ha!* Or, on the other side: *You'd better not even think of coming over to our place uninvited!* This is a moment of calm before the storm of daily life and grandchildren, and the photo of it is usually displayed in a silver picture frame in Neapolitan newlyweds' living rooms.

No one told me about this tradition. I had to figure it out for myself. Unfortunately, I figured it out after the photo op.

At the entrance of Washington's National Presbyterian Church, Salvatore and his Neapolitan groomsmen stood tall in white tie and tails, greeting the American guests in their best English. They looked gorgeous. I had explained to my future husband that in the States, tuxedos can be rented, and after his initial terror of powder blue and ruffles, he agreed to let my mother and me herd him and his six buddies to Bob's Tuxedo Junction a few days before the ceremony. The fact that we Americans had successfully costumed the Neapolitan men, and that their women kept saying that they were *elegantissimi! Elegantissimi!* was a great source of pride.

In the women's dressing room, my bridesmaids were adjusting their matching sleeveless sky-blue dresses and putting the finishing touches to their makeup. Benedetta's two sons (Claudio had been born after Emilio, and I was getting the hang of being a *zia*, falling deeply, hopelessly in love with both boys) were playing tag in their ivory silk ringbearer outfits. My sister was trying to fasten my grandmother's necklace around my neck. It had a minuscule silver clasp from around 1910 that was impossible to hook. My mother was in such a state of tension that at a certain point she just started doing laps around the perimeter of the room, managing to look stunning in her eggplant strapless gown despite her anxiety-induced dementia.

The photographer arrived, and told us he wanted to get some candid shots of the wedding preparations. That's when Raffaella came up to me with my bouquet. She was silent, and she was still, two things that seemed odd for my future mother-in-law. I said, "Oh, thanks!" and then laid it down on a coffee table so I could have my hands free to touch up my lipstick again. After a few minutes, she came up to me again with the bouquet. Again I said, "Oh, thanks!" and then gave it to my cousin to hold while I adjusted the netting under my gown.

Apparently, the third time she alerted the photographer. He snapped what is possibly my favorite picture of our whole wedding (followed closely by the one of Zio Toto doing the twist with a Waspy Massachusetts schoolteacher aunt). In it, Raffaella's two hands are holding mine and the bouquet. She is looking at me with acceptance, gratitude, and love. I am looking over my shoulder, mouth open, shouting something about a safety pin to a bridesmaid who was having an issue with her bra strap.

Maybe it was a good thing that I didn't know about the bouquet ritual. Oblivious to the significance of the moment, I unwittingly was the one to *sdrammatizzare*, and nobody's mascara ran before the ceremony.

Rome

If you asked somebody in one of the lands that Rome conquered two thousand years ago what the Romans were
like, you would probably hear that they were arrogant, aggressive know-it-alls who thought they were the shit. I asked Salva
why he didn't like Rome, and he said that Romans were arrogant, aggressive know-it-alls who thought they were the shit.
Center of the world, and all that (well, they were for an awfully
long time, I wanted to point out . . .). Plus, they don't know how
to cook.

Salva and I had moved to Rome in 2001 and rented a loft in
Trastevere. We didn't sit down with a bottle of wine and decide
our future; we didn't map out, as some couples do, the pros and
cons of staying in Naples or moving north. There was very little
free will in the matter, because we were literally shoved out by
my mother-in-law.

The Avallones owned two apartments on the first floor of
their building in Naples. One was Benedetta's, and the other
was destined for Salvatore and his wife. It was rented out when
Salva was finishing his studies, and I assumed that when we

were married we would move in. We were next in line for the lasagna in the elevator, after all. I'd even gotten the hang of the recipe advice via intercom! But Raffaella had other plans. My mother-in-law almost never speaks in dialect and is careful to use correct Italian when speaking with family members, but when she heard us talking about moving into the apartment in Naples, she used pure Neapolitan. *"Te nè 'a í,"* pronounced *tuh neh ayeee.* You gotta get outta here. Her middle three fingers pointed down and sliced the air, showing me that we needed to leave, and we needed to leave soon.

Wait, wasn't a Neapolitan *mammà* supposed to wring her hands and beg us to stay close by? Wasn't she worried that her grandchildren would be raised on processed food, without cuddles and the sea and the music of Napoli? No, she wasn't.

"Ketrin, there is no future here. Go to the U.S.! To Rome, Milan, northern Europe! Anywhere. Naples would be a waste for you. For me, *figurati che gioia!* It would be such a joy! But for your family it would be the end. *Niente, non c'è niente a Napoli.*" There is nothing in Naples. "I will bring you the food in my suitcase, wherever you go."

I was shocked. Salva's roots and the Avallones' love ran so deep that I'd assumed that if we ever suggested leaving, there would be resistance, a battle even. The opposite happened: the lady basically kicked us out. She was loving, but she was forceful.

When Salvatore and I talked about it, it was clear that the idea of leaving Naples didn't make him happy. But he would follow the plan. In true Neapolitan fashion, the man might be pampered, but in the end it was a woman who would decide.

Naïvely, I believed that the Eurostar line connecting Italy's most important cities (Milan, Bologna, Florence, Rome, Naples) was a longitudinal measuring stick in which culture got more southern in degrees. If people in Florence are more laid-back than in Milan, I figured, then they are very relaxed in Rome, and in Naples, life's a beach. If everyone plays by the rules in Milan, most do in Florence, a few do in Rome, and no one does in Naples.

What I didn't realize was that Italy is a young country. Unification didn't come until 1861, and for a thousand years before that what is now Italy was composed of city-states, each with its own language, culture, and identity. *Insomma*, Naples is not just a more southern version of Rome. It's an entirely different country altogether.

Salva got an internship at the Rome soccer team. He was in the marketing office, working with their sponsorship group. Salva's passion had always been sports. When he graduated from law school, I encouraged him to look for something in sports marketing. After all, the law stuff would come in handy sooner or later. But he left our apartment in the morning with the face of someone going to work in a sweatshop. *It's not my team, Katherine,* he explained to me when I wondered at his lack of enthusiasm. I would find him sitting in a chair near the window looking at the "view" of the building across from ours in Trastevere. He might as well have been uprooted and dumped in Detroit.

Raffaella advised me about what to cook. *Maybe we shouldn't have moved to Rome after all* was met with, "If you can't find *friarielli* greens at the market, Ketrin, try *broccoletti*." She knew that if her son ate what he loved, things would work themselves out. *He mutters under his breath how he can't stand Rome,* I would tell her. So? she answered. Let him mutter.

During the week, I spent my time reproducing Raffaella's recipes and keeping Salva away from the Romans. But every weekend and holiday, we were on the train for Naples.

San Gennaro

One such holiday was the feast of San Gennaro, the patron saint of Naples. "He ain't no second-class saint," a wizened man told me in the Duomo on the nineteenth of September when I went to witness the miracle of San Gennaro. Only a few weeks before, the government had issued a decree eliminating the holidays of patron saints. There are about twenty important saints' days throughout the year, and the government decided that they could be attached to celebrations on the Sunday before or after. The decree would mean that those delicious long weekends, or *ponti* (bridges), when Saints Peter and Paul fell on a Friday in Rome or Saint Ambrose fell on a Monday in Milan—or even when it fell on a Tuesday, the vacation bridge spreading over four days!—would disappear. Most Romans thought, Shucks, that would be a shame. Most Milanese thought, Too bad for us but it had to happen sooner or later.

Neapolitans went positively ballistic. Not because they would miss another day off work (although that would be bad enough—"Work makes you throw away your blood" is an oft-heard Neapolitan expression) but because whatever scandalous thing you do in Naples, whatever combinations of food you order, however you eat your pizza, *you do not under any circumstances mess with San Gennaro.*

The old man in the Duomo was a San Gennaro groupie. He came to the Duomo to witness the miracle every year, he told me, he wouldn't miss it for the world. The idea of taking San Gennaro's day away? "You can't just ask San Gennaro to liquefy his blood on Sunday the sixteenth because on Wednesday the nineteenth you have better things to do! *Ma stiamo scherzando!*" You've gotta be kidding.

The decree was a sacrilege, an offensive blow to Neapolitans and to their history and identity. Not to mention, my gentleman friend reminded me, that it would piss off San Gennaro himself, and then the trouble would really start. "San Gennaro loves us. He protects us. *Ci ama. Ci ama* . . ." He kept repeating "he loves us, he loves us," almost inaudibly.

Gennaro was the archbishop of Benevento (a city not far from Naples) in the fourth century, and was beheaded for his Christianity by the Roman emperor Diocletian. Legend has it that a woman collected an ampoule of his blood and conserved it as a relic to be worshipped. The blood solidified, or rather gooified. It is kept in an elaborate golden safe at the Duomo, an exquisite church hidden in the dense, old center of Naples. The blood did not, however, remain solid: two times almost every year for centuries (in May and in September) a miracle occurs—the blood in the vial liquefies.

On those rare occasions when the blood has stayed solid, disaster has struck the city of Naples—or so it seems to Neapolitans. They will point out that after San Gennaro's blood failed to liquefy in 1980, an earthquake struck Naples and killed nearly three thousand people. Another solid-blood year was 1528, when plague devastated the city. If the blood stays solid, Naples could be prey to any catastrophe from the eruption of Vesuvius to international terrorism.

So it is no wonder that women stay in the church the day and night before praying to San Gennaro to liquefy his blood and thus protect the city. These faithful *signore* don't take their eyes off the statue of the saint, which is displayed next to the altar. He has a pointy red hat, a red cape, and a pose that is serene and Buddha-like. He's kind of grimacing, though, and honestly looks a little pissed off.

The women flatter him. "*San Gennà, comme si bbello,*" how handsome you are! And "*Tu si 'o primmo santo nuosto,*" you are our first, our most important saint! (As the competition between the saints is ferocious, the women have to reassure him that he's their guy.)

We were packed like sardines in the side chapel of the Duomo, where the safe was located. In just a few minutes the mayor of Naples, with the archbishop, would open it with a special golden key to take out the vial of blood. When the vial was removed, there would be a procession into the narthex and we would all follow the blood, the priests, and the politicians to the main altar, where the blood would be placed next to the statue of the saint. Only then would we learn whether the blood had liquefied.

I had come to the ceremony alone. "I want to go with you to San Gennaro," I told Raffaella when she described the blood and screaming and magic that went on at the Duomo. "Oh, we don't go to San Gennaro," she told me. Then she continued to tell me how women weep and wail all night long to the saint.

They fall on the floor! They start screaming curse words at him if the blood doesn't liquefy—even the eighty-year-olds! They . . .

"Wait—you don't go?" I was surprised. Raffaella is devout, and she is Neapolitan. Yet she had never been to the Duomo on September 19 to witness the miracle? I couldn't figure out why. "Can I ask Zia Pia?" Raffaella's sister Pia is even more devout than she is. She regularly makes pilgrimages to Lourdes and Medjugorje with twenty of her friends. Recently I got a call from her as her tour bus was en route to the Medjugorje shrine. Earlier, I had asked her about her frittata and she wanted to make sure I had the recipe right. In mid-conversation I heard a booming voice amplified by the microphone on the bus. "Our Father, who art in Heaven . . ."

"Gotta go! It's the *Padrenostro*! Remember, one egg for every one hundred grams of spaghetti! And then throw an extra egg in at the end for good measure!" (One Lord's Prayer for every ten Hail Marys is the rosary ratio. Zia Pia probably throws in an extra *Padrenostro,* too—she's that kind of lady.)

Surely Zia Pia would be at the Duomo praying to the saint all night long, I figured. But when I asked her about the miracle, her sentences (like Raffaella's) started with, *"Si dice che"*—I've heard that . . . She'd never been, either.

I soon realized that it was a matter of class. San Gennaro is a saint of the *popolino*, the "little people," the working class. The Duomo is located in the poor inner city of Naples, and the ceremony itself is viewed by many middle- and upper-class Neapolitans as a hocus-pocus ritual that gets the ignorant *popolino* worked up.

That is how I, a Protestant, a rational anthropologist, ended up alone at the Duomo. I expected folklore. I expected voodoo. I didn't expect to be profoundly moved.

The tension in the side chapel grew. The ornate, frescoed chamber smelled of incense mixed with BO. I rested my arm on what I thought was a pedestal but soon realized was a lady's shelflike hip. We were that close. As we all waited for the muckety-mucks to arrive with their Alice in Wonderland golden key, there was silence. There was no wailing. There was no screaming. Even the man next to me had stopped murmuring, *"Ci ama."* There was only prayer.

Only prayer . . . until a cellphone started ringing. Its standard default ring signaled that the owner was of the older generation. It was in a purse wedged in the middle of the crowd, forgotten by the owner (whose mind was certainly on San Gennaro's blood). There were a few whispered, "It's yours!" "No! It's yours!" until one of the priests waiting next to the safe shot his finger to his lips and performed a hearty, loud *Ssssshhhhhh!* that involved his entire cassocked body.

When the mayor and archbishop arrived with the key, people started pushing and standing on their tippy-toes in a futile attempt to see whether the blood was liquid. *"Si vede?"* Can you see? they started asking each other. *"È liquido?"* Is it liquid? And then, "He's closing the safe! He has the blood!"

The man next to me had begun to cry quietly. He was wiping his nose. He saw me looking at him. *"Signurí, lloro 'o ssanno! Lloro sì e noi no!"* They already know! They know and we don't. It was almost unbearable that the priests knew whether the blood had liquefied and we would have to wait.

Thankfully we didn't have to wait for long. We followed the procession, led by the vial of blood (held in a golden reliquary high above the head of the bishop) to the altar where the statue of San Gennaro watched over the proceedings. The bishop positioned the reliquary near the altar—ceremoniously, calmly, God! he was taking forever!—and we tried to distinguish whether the black that we saw in the ampoule was liquid or solid. It was impossible to tell.

Then the bishop raised a white handkerchief, the symbol that the blood had liquefied.

At that precise moment, San Gennaro, with his red cape and pointy hat and pissed-off expression, became a rock star. He was the Beatles, he was Elvis, he was Madonna at Madison Square Garden. The crowd gave it up, cheering and clapping and crying. Outside, fireworks started popping. The bishop announced, bellowing over the crowd, that when he opened the safe, the blood was *already liquid*. "People of Naples!" he paused, waiting for the commotion to quiet down. "San Gennaro loves us! San Gennaro will protect us!" The crowd answered with shouts of *Evviva San Gennaro!* Long live San Gennaro! Then he repeated, "*Cari Napoletani*, dear people of Naples, the blood was *already liquid*."

My gentleman friend shook his head in amazement and gratitude. "*Era già sciolto*," it was already liquid. His subtext was: Despite my hard life, despite the fact that I'm unemployed and my son has gotten in with the *camorra*, despite this, *I am loved*. I am so loved that it was already liquid. And there I was worried and lacking in faith!

The blood, in its magnificent orbed scepter, was carried by the bishop down the aisle, lined today by a red carpet. The pushing became ridiculous. I touched (I think) boobs, thighs, elbows, wispy old-man hair, sweaty underarms. And I was touched in ways that probably would be considered molestation in some countries. But what everybody wanted to touch was the blood.

Again, we would have to wait. After mass, the bishop announced that the relic would be available for kissing between four and six that afternoon. Only those hours. (So it's pointless to get your hopes and puckers up before that!) He also announced that someone had lost a set of keys—he would keep them at the altar after the service.

There was one last, explosive *Evviva San Gennaro!*, followed by applause, before everyone left the Duomo, exhausted but renewed. Confident of the protection and love of that little Buddha with his pointy hat.

Wall-to-Wall Carpeting

Raffaella visited us often in Rome. We decided to look for a bigger apartment—Salva's internship had become a job in sports marketing, and he had made some Neapolitan friends in Rome and wasn't grumbling so much about the Romans. We were planning (read: I was chomping at the bit) to start a family. Raffaella helped us find and remodel a new place near the Colosseum.

From the time I was a little girl, I imagined that my home as a grown-up would have wall-to-wall carpeting. I didn't have a specific mental image of where my home would be, whether it would be a house or an apartment, in the city or in the country, in the United States or abroad. But I knew that when it was my turn to decide for myself, there would be no talk of area rugs or parquet. My family's and my bare feet would sink into soft, thick, creamy carpets in our home.

My parents' house in Bethesda, Maryland, is not cozy. The living areas (called "the sitting room" and "the craft room" by a team of designers in the eighties, no TV room or actual *living* room for us) look a little like Louis XIV met up with Liberace and went to a Sotheby's auction. The walls are painted to look like marble. Statues of whirling dervishes stand on gilt pedestals. There are small, valuable Persian rugs on the wood floors.

My childhood longing for wall-to-wall carpeting bespoke a desire for us to be a "normal" suburban family, and a need for comfort, quiet, and peace. I could hang out barefoot and in PJs on a carpet. Loud voices would be absorbed, not echoed. One day, when I was big, I would cuddle with a golden retriever or a child of my own on my carpet (in some soft pastel color) without being eyed by a nineteenth-century nude lady in a painting.

"*Amore*, there is bug inside," Salva told me gently, when he understood that the wall-to-wall carpeting issue was close to my heart. He was trying to talk me out of it with sensitivity, using English instead of Italian, since he knew it was a touchy subject. What he meant was that wall-to-wall carpeting was not hygienic, particularly in Italy, where there is so much dust in the stone buildings.

"Do you mean dust mites? What, dust mites can't live in area rugs? Or you just want to get freezing marble so if we have children they'll be forced to wear ski socks in the apartment and probably crack their heads on the travertine?"

"*Shh, shhh.* There now."

I had known the battle was coming. I had never seen wall-to-wall carpeting in Italy. I didn't know whether it was a matter of aesthetics, or the fact that marble is inexpensive, or the reality of the "bug inside." Whatever the reason, people looked at me like I was nuts when I said the word *moquette* (there's not even an Italian word for it! They had to use the French word! Where had I ended up?).

There were so many decisions to be made. How big to make the *salotto*, or living room? Will the dining room be a room of *rappresentanza*, for formal entertaining? Should the kitchen be small and compact, or American with Formica and room to play? These questions brought to a head the central one: What kind of people are we, American or Neapolitan?

Since Salva was working, it was Raffaella who jumped on the train and accompanied me to the architects, the carpenter, the upholstery guy, the marble cutter. These artisans, after they understood that the apartment was mine, would explain to me the advantages of this or that molding, this or that kind of wood for the paneling. Then Raffaella would take over. Of course they need a separate room and bathroom for their live-in nanny (but the apartment is small! And we didn't even have children yet!). Of course they prefer a small kitchen, because it's easier to cook well in a small kitchen (but I'm uncoordinated and will burn myself!). Of course the curtains must have brass rods with curlicues and the door handles must have silk tassels tied on them (but if we have kids?). The countertops near the stove should be travertine, though it's a shame that you can't put lemon or anything hot on them. Can't spill on them, in fact. *Ma sono bellissimi!*

What did I want for my home? What kind of wife and mother would I be? I hadn't figured it out yet. I listened to Raffaella's advice and nodded and said, "I'll talk it over with Salva" until Raffaella offhandedly said these words: "Oh, and I meant to tell you, when Nino worked at the hotel he had a client who sold beautiful Persian area rugs. We have a bunch of them in the basement. The colors are gorgeous—deep red, midnight-blue . . ."

When I get riled up, you can tell from my upper lip. It starts to quiver. It's where I hold my tension. Not in my stomach, or my shoulders. My lip started to tremble, but Raffaella didn't notice. She was talking about the carpenter and the kitchen cupboards. Finally, when she said, "off-white trim," I burst into tears.

"*No! Non ce la faccio più!*" I can't take it anymore. And I stormed off.

I canceled all my appointments with Raffaella for the next week. Oh, I have to meet a friend on Tuesday. Wednesday I have a dubbing turn . . . that lasts all day. No need to come to Rome, thank you very much. I snapped at Salva and didn't answer Raffaella's calls. I wanted this home to be mine, bug inside or not.

By the time we got to the bug-in-the-rug conversation, Salva was handling me with kid gloves, because he could see how upset I was. He folded me in his arms when I started to cry, blubbering and letting it all out. "But I want a playroom, *amore*, I want to spill on my counters! I don't want to *rappresentare* with our dining room! I don't want a lady from the Philippines living in a closet! I don't want tassels on the doors. I want air-conditioning everywhere! *I want the bug inside!*"

"Have you told my mother these things, Ketrin?"

"Not exactly."

"She wants to help us. She won't be offended if you say what you want. She's not *permalosa*."

"But when we talk about choices for the apartment she says things like *si fa*—this is what's done. Like it's the only way to do things here. She's the expert."

"*She* decides for her home and *you* decide for ours. That is what's done here."

I loved him a lot.

I answered Raffaella's call on my cellphone the next day. My end of the conversation was tense and fake. Hers was relaxed. She'd heard of an acupuncturist that she wanted to get

Nino to; the stuffed zucchini she had made for a lunch the day before had turned out exquisite. Surprisingly, she didn't mention the architect or the carpenter or any of the arrangements. "Ketrin, my friend Paola wants to meet you. She said Saturday afternoon we can stop by for a coffee, what do you say?"

Salva and I were going to Naples for the weekend, but I didn't feel like accompanying her to the *salotto* of one of her chic friends. I didn't want to listen to her tell her friends about "our" decisions regarding shower stalls and shelves. But I felt guilty saying no after I'd been avoiding her for a week. And I had been working up a monologue in which I described how although I found the doorknob rosettes she had chosen lovely, I wanted first to make sure that there was air-conditioning, everywhere.

Paola Martone lived on the top floor of an apartment building overlooking the Bay of Naples. Raffaella and I squeezed into the tiny elevator, the sweet smell of her perfume enveloping us. She pushed a stray hair from my forehead. "You'll *love* her apartment," she told me. Oh, would I? I was irritated. I wanted to get this over with and go home.

A blond, curvy lady with enormous collagen-filled lips opened the door. *"Raffffffa!"* she cooed, as my mother-in-law hugged her with a *"Paoliiiiina!"*

That's when I looked down to see the lady's elegant beige Magli heels resting on thick, royal-blue wall-to-wall carpeting. I understood why we were here.

"Paoliii, thanks so much for having us, honey. I wanted to show Ketrin what's possible with wall-to-wall carpeting. Yours is the most beautiful in Naples."

Autospurgo

S oon after we moved into our new apartment, I learned that there was no surer way to provoke a fight with my husband than to throw the wrong thing down the sink, the bidet, the shower drain, or the toilet. We, along with most young couples who redo their homes in Italy (with even more likelihood if there is a foreigner in the mix), have major plumbing problems.

The ancient Romans figured out how to flush toilets, and imported water from miles away for their sinks and elaborate fountains. This was over two thousand years ago, when the rest of the world was using buckets and digging holes in the dirt. But that expertise didn't trickle down to contemporary Italian plumbers. It seems that the basic rule for Roman toilets is: the longer ago the system was put in, the better it works.

While Raffaella and I picked out curtain rods and searched high and low for synthetic countertops that would stand the test of my acidic American salad dressing, our plumber was screwing up big-time. He decided to put one tiny drain, which would service the whole apartment, in the corner opposite the kitchen and bathrooms, far away from the fixtures.

Along with the wall-to-wall carpeting and air-conditioning, a disposal in the kitchen was one of my longings. The Avallones had never seen one. I explained how convenient it would be, especially given this country's garbage collection difficulties. Our plumber installed one, but did not communicate three important facts: 1) that disposals are illegal in many parts of Italy, 2) that ours could never be used because the tubes for the plumbing in our apartment were too small, and 3) that he had rigged our pipes and our drains in a such a way that nothing could ever go down the kitchen sink but water.

Salva had a sense that the disposal (*tritarifiuti* in Italian—chop up the trash) was a recipe for disaster. "Let's not use it, Ketrin, okay?" Oh, I thought, he's just a traditional Neapolitan man who is wary of technology. Especially newfangled appliances in the kitchen. His mother still has clay pots, for Christ's sake! I will introduce them all to the wonders of the microwave! I will usher them into the twenty-first century in our high-tech American kitchen! These were my thoughts as I stuffed the contents of a two-pound bag of *erbette*, spinach-like greens, down our new disposal.

The *erbette* had gone bad. I had bought them and forgotten about them, which is something that you just don't do in Italy. Nobody was home, and I wanted to eliminate all traces of them. I wanted to mince them to oblivion. They never existed, I told myself as I turned on the disposal. The green mass went down okay, it was only a minute or so after the procedure began that I saw green goo start to slime up from the bubbling drain.

Salva and I were Lucy and Ricky Ricardo that evening when he got home. "*Amore?* There are plumbing problems."

"*Perchè hai quella roba verde dappertutto?*" Why are you covered with green slime, dear?

Physically speaking, the locus of anger in many American men is their chest. It is a puffed-up chest, a *who-do-you-think-you're-messing-with* chest. The arms are still, the head up, and the torso rotates from side to side. It is a torso that is looking around to see who else might be trying to fuck with it. *Bring it on.* American men often become larger in their anger, more horizontal and more intimidating. Salvatore, meanwhile, like many Neopolitans, gets angry with his legs close together and his feet in first position. His heels touching and toes splayed outward, he moves vertically. There was a Neapolitan toy sold after the war, when people would invent anything to make a few lire, called *scicchegnacco int'a butteglia.* It was a marble suspended in a bottle that would go up and down when children shook it. It is this image that best conveys Salva's up-and-down anger, his long, lean body expressing its *furia.*

I know that it's not healthy or psychologically enlightened to engage in name-calling. I know that would be the first thing that we would learn in an anger management seminar. But have the leaders of those seminars ever had to call the *autospurgo* at 3:00 A.M., after six hours of wiping and plunging and dumping? (Collins translates it as a "gully sucker." My not-so-technical translation would be "a man who comes, sucks, and pumps.") On that night of the green slime, we were not managing our anger in any sort of enlightened way.

"*Ma quanto sei scema!*" (How stupid you are! His hand hits his forehead at a forty-five-degree angle in the Neapolitan gesture meaning there's nothing inside your head, your brains are gone.)

"*Sei uno stronzo.*" (You're an asshole. No hand gestures, but boy, is my upper lip quivering.)

"*Pigliati una camomilla.*" (Have a chamomile tea, but no, it's not the kind suggestion that I might benefit from the calming effects of an herbal tea. The translation might be something along the lines of get a grip on yourself. His hand is doing the motion of lifting a cup of tea.)

"Vaffanculo." (Fuck you.)

"Stai dando i numeri!" (Literally, you're giving the numbers. His hand hits his forehead perpendicularly, which means that I've gone from being just stupid to being out of my mind.)

"The numbers" in Naples refers to the centuries-old *tombola*, a game similar to bingo. Each number from one to ninety is associated with a person, an object, a concept, or an event. So, for example, the number 61 is hunting and 51 is a garden or yard. If I dream of hunting for a mouse outside, I might be advised to play the number 61, 51, and 11 for mouse at the lottery the next day. I must consult an expert (usually an old wizened Neapolitan grandmother who has "the gift") who can interpret the numbers.

When must I play the numbers? Either when I have a strange dream or when something completely out of the ordinary occurs. For example, several years ago I had my wallet stolen in Rome the day after my sister had her wallet stolen in New York and the day before my mother had her wallet stolen in Washington. Now, either word had gotten around the globe about the Wilson ladies' absentmindedness, or something supernatural was up. My father-in-law called me immediately when we realized the "coincidence."

"I've found someone who is *bravissima*, an expert at interpreting your numbers," he told me. "You're going to play them, aren't you?"

I didn't, in fact, play them, but learned that my number would have been 79, 70, and 52 (79 for thief, 70 for a tall building, New York, 52 for *la mamma*).

Benedetta, at one point during her teenage years, was dating a guy named Luca who was unstable and had abandonment issues (his nickname was 'o *pazzo* or Luke the Crazyman). When my sister-in-law decided to break up with him, he threatened suicide, calling out from the top of the rocky promontory of Posillipo where he lived that he loved her and would throw himself into the Bay of Naples below if she didn't take him back. In the crowd that soon gathered around him, there were of course people trying to dissuade him from jumping. But there were others who, in hushed tones among themselves, whispered, "*Sta dando i numeri*"—he's giving the numbers. It was an event that was out of the ordinary, and smart Neapolitans knew they had to find a soothsayer in the crowd to interpret the numbers so they could play the lottery. There was even, Salva tells me, one man calling to passersby on the road, "Ladies and gentlemen, there's a crazy man about to jump. Come and find out the numbers!"

So, back to our fight. According to my husband, I am so out of my mind that I'm "giving the numbers," and according to me, he is quite simply being an asshole. I remember with nostalgia the days when we were first dating and I didn't understand Italian and he didn't understand English. What wonderful discussions we had! How we saw eye-to-eye on everything! It was idyllic. As I learned more Italian and he learned more English, though, our communication became more complicated.

I realize now that the real difficulties began when we mastered the subjunctive and the conditional. When you are limited to the present indicative of verbs, you are inevitably drawn to the present: to needs, to wants, to likes and dislikes. *I need to pee. I like ice cream, do you?* What you say is necessary and true, and that makes for great relationships. Just look at the simple beauty of second-grade friendships as evidence.

Unfortunately, though, if you know how to use the subjunctive and the conditional, the relationship changes. You start thinking, and then saying, *If you hadn't insisted on the disposal, we wouldn't have stayed up cleaning pipes* and *I wish you weren't such an asshole.* Life is no longer in the here and now but is being compared to some ideal in your brain. Gone are the days of *I'm hungry* and *Do you want to cook* erbette? It is now *I wish we had hired a different plumber* and *There wouldn't be any green slime if you hadn't said we needed to eat more vegetables.* Your life and the person you love are measuring up (or *not* measuring up) to the ideals that you've created with your fancy old verb forms.

I suppose I must be grateful that, despite the complicated nuances of our language of litigation, in the language of making up, nothing is lost in translation. I threw a balled-up Kleenex at him as a peace offering. He grabbed me in his arms and said, "*Ma quanto mi fai arrabbiare!*" You get me so darned mad! We admitted to each other that neither of us liked *erbette*—they were nothing compared to the *scarole* sautéed with olives that you find in Naples.

"Promise me that you won't use the *tritarifiuti*? Ever again?"

I promised him. It has stayed under our sink, unused, ever since.

Pasta alla Genovese

After our frequent plumbing rows, there were frequent occasions of making up. In the summer of 2004 I found out that we were pregnant with our first child.

I learned that what a Neapolitan mother eats during her pregnancy is very, very important. I'm not talking extra protein, or cutting out caffeine and sushi. I'm talking cravings. If the lady doesn't satisfy her cravings, the baby will pay. Things can get ugly.

"I really have a *voglia* (craving) for *rigatoni alla Genovese*," I told Raffaella sometime during my fourth month. I didn't realize at the time how important this comment would be, that it would set a great ball rolling. In Naples, if a pregnant woman has a craving that is not satisfied, her baby will be born with a *voglia*, or a mark. Usually this mark is a skin discoloration in the form of the object of her craving: a strawberry, for example, or a little cup of coffee. In the case of *pasta alla Genovese*, the birthmark might come in the form of a great big onion tattoo.

Despite its name, *la Genovese*, the sauce has nothing to do with the Ligurian city. Various theories have been offered to explain why this typically Neapolitan dish is called the dish from Genoa (one is that the Neapolitan cook who invented it was nicknamed *'o Genovese*), but nobody knows for sure. The fact is that you cannot find this recipe anywhere in Italy except Naples.

It is a kind of *ragù*, in the sense that the sauce is cooked with meat, but it is characterized by the kilos of Montoro onions that are sautéed to give it flavor.

Raffaella immediately dispatched Nino to the market to buy the onions, and bought her train ticket to Rome. Her grandson would not risk being born an onion face.

I was shamelessly spoiled, but honestly didn't feel guilty about it. I deserved to have my cravings satisfied; I deserved to see the schedules of my husband's entire family governed by my every whim. I deserved to be spoon-fed onion *ragù*, and lie on the couch watching bikini-clad starlets dance. I deserved all of this not simply because I was pregnant, but because the rest of my time was spent at the painful, exhausting, humiliating *centro di analisi*.

The folder that contained the results of the lab tests was so thick you could almost call it a binder. The receptionist at the diagnostic center handed it to me, closed with a sticker for privacy, and I had the same feeling as when I was little and it was time to see my report card. Let's see how I've done, or rather how my blood and urine have done. Do I eat right? Is my lifestyle healthy? I can't wait to see!

My excitement turned to disappointment and confusion when I opened the folder to find that my lymphocytes were at 1,800 per microliter of blood and my cytokines were at 1.4. What did that mean? I leafed through the folder to find very ambiguous graphs that had disturbingly sharp peaks and cavernous lows . . . my C-reactive proteins were doing some pretty funky stuff. Did I have something serious? To find out, I had to make an appointment at another office on another day in another area of the city. This center did not diagnose, it only took your blood, urine, and stool samples, then ran the necessary tests.

When I went the first time to have my blood taken, I was unprepared. I had had breakfast, and blood is taken only on an empty stomach. So I was told to go home and come back the next day. When I showed up hungry and cranky the next morning, the receptionist asked where my pee was.

I really did not know how to answer, the matter being complicated by the fact that I did not know the word for bladder. So I repeated the question: *Dov'è l'urina?* The ball had been deftly bounced back into her court. *"Non l'ha portata?"* You didn't bring it? Now, whether it's linguistic, or because of my *permalosità* (oversensitivity), I tend to interpret questions formed in the negative about what I've *not* done as accusations. They're really not, particularly in Italian. They are simply factual. "Did this lady before me with the accent not bring her own pee?" the receptionist was asking.

It proved to be a problem. Once again I was sent home, this time with instructions to buy a little plastic pee cup at the pharmacy and to come the next day with my pee. But not any old pee, only the *first pee* of the morning. The purest pee. This kind of pee is best for the tests, apparently. Don't be coming in with any of that watered-down stuff, the *centro di analisi* clarified, we want the yellowest, smelliest pee you got.

This was all logistically problematic given the fact that I had to drive in Roman traffic the next morning with my plastic pee cup, without having had any sort of coffee or breakfast. Where was I to put the pee? The cup had a lid, yes, but it was flimsy. Aha! A lightbulb turned on in my brain. I didn't have to hold it in my hand or balance it on the seat next to me. I could put it in the little coffee cup holder! It fit snugly, and I was off.

Tutto a posto, or everything in its place, everything going well, until a kamikaze *motorino* swerved in front of me and I had to slam on the brakes. I need not delve into the details of where my pure pee ended up, but my next stop was the car wash, not the *centro di analisi*. When I returned to the center, I did so on foot, carrying my deep yellow pee cup very carefully by hand.

I really wanted to find out from those little old ladies how they did it: I now noticed that everyone who entered the *centro di analisi* was discreetly carrying their pee. A veritable bring-your-own-pee party! At my doctor's office in Maryland, there is a sterile bathroom where you put your pee in a cubbyhole. From there, it mysteriously disappears—you don't have to hand it off, or even write your name on it. It's a totally anonymous procedure.

I struck up a conversation with a grandmother next to me, pointing to the plastic cup in her hand and saying, *"Difficile, no?"* "No!" she answered. "It's more difficult with the feces." What were they going to make me do next?

Mercifully, the feces examination was reserved for Salvatore. To be present at our son's birth, he had to be tested for salmonella. He was given a little transparent gelato cup and a plastic spoon and told to bring his sample to the *centro di analisi*. Now it was bring your own poo.

"Ketrin? Mi porti un giornale?" His request for a newspaper was the first coherent communication that emerged from behind our locked bathroom door the next morning. Salva had been in there muttering and cursing for the better part of an hour (the Virgin Mary had been called all sorts of unkind things

in Neapolitan dialect). The atmosphere was tense. I was confronted with the choice of giving my husband the *Gazzetta dello Sport* or the *International Herald Tribune*. Was the newspaper to help him relax enough to relieve himself or to be implemented in another way?

I was taking too long.

"Ketrin!"

"Ma per . . . leggere?" If it was to be read, then I should definitely go with the pink *Gazzetta* with the picture of the star soccer player Buffon jumping for a miraculous save against Milan.

"No! Macché leggere?" Not to read! What are you thinking?

And so I handed him the *Tribune*.

Our bathroom was plastered with the advertising supplement of the newspaper—really, there are so many reasons to visit Vietnam!—when Salva emerged. He'd been stabbing at turds for an awfully long time, poor guy. In his triumphant hand was the little plastic cup, on which he wrote his name with Magic Marker: SALVATORE AVALLONE. He was ready for show-and-tell at the *centro di analisi*.

"Ecco." Here it is, he told the receptionist later, and placed his poo proudly on the counter.

Recently my father told me that he had to send a stool sample to a lab in suburban Maryland. I was interested to find out how that worked in America. As in Italy, a little plastic ice cream spoon was provided, but it blew my mind when he told me that he *sent it away in the mail.* You mean you took your little transparent cup to the post office? No, he told me, he put the little anonymous prestamped package in the door slot!

"Now, that's what I call a great country, where you can send your shit out anonymously into the world without carrying it anywhere!" I was about to break into "The Star-Spangled Banner" when my father told me the addendum: the sticker with the lab's address had come off and his poo was returned to sender.

Vestiti

After Salvatore and I had survived the *centro di analisi*, there was nothing that could rock our confidence as new parents. That is, until we tried to figure out how to clothe our newborn.

The following are comments Raffaella has made to family members who are not properly dressed:

"Nino, mi sembri un sacco di patate." Nino, you look like a sack of potatoes.

"Amore mio, mi sembri figlio di nessuno." Sweetheart, you look like the child of no one.

"Che sei? Uno scaricatore di porto?" What are you, a dockworker?

Family members are subject to these comments if their shirts are untucked, if there is lint on their sweaters, or if one of their pant legs is hitched in a sock. If they have a stain, or a collar that has not been ironed to perfection, they might get a simple "Don't worry, there's time to change before we go."

I am off-limits—I do not receive these comments. This may be because I am a daughter-in-law. It may be because everyone knows I'm *permalosa*. I think, though, that it has more to do with the fact that Raffaella first met me in fleece: there was nothing but room for improvement. There was nowhere to go but up from my bingeing, intellectual feminist look of 1996.

I get a proud smile if I wear something that matches. I get a *come sei carina!* You look great! if I so much as put a belt around my jeans. That beautiful freedom, however, that license that I hope lasts until I enter an Italian nursing home, does not carry over to my children.

When I was eight months pregnant with my son, the private clinic where I was to give birth gave me a list of clothes to bring with me for the newborn. There were articles of clothing that I'd never heard of before: *bodino, ghettina, tutina.* They all ended in *-ino* or *-ina*, which meant they were little and cute, but what were they?

If this wasn't enough to send my hormone-assaulted brain into a spin, the clinic specified the required type of fabric. So my fetus and I set out to find a *ghettina di lana leggera* (light wool leggings) and other outfits that would compose his first foray into the world of Italian fashion.

My plan was to hand the list to the lady in the store with my credit card and be done with it.

The shopkeeper was around sixty, a beautiful, gravelly-voiced grandmother. I was done for. Approximately two hours and hundreds of euros later, my fetus and I emerged, sweaty and agitated. The *signora* had regaled me with questions. Which kind of cotton do you prefer? Lace at the collar or on the sleeves? Oh, she was full of questions. But somehow I couldn't get up the nerve to ask mine. I had only two, and they were fundamental at that point in time.

Which is cheaper? And, where is the bathroom?

Later, I handed my completed assignment over to Raffaella.

She put her glasses on to examine the list and to feel the tiny garments. She was Giorgio Armani before a *Vogue* photo shoot. She was a Hollywood image consultant. She described the workmanship of each minuscule article, saying things like "cross-stitch embroidery" and "cream and sky-blue appliqué." I tried to figure out if these descriptions meant the clothes passed the test. I did not want to visit the exacting, gravelly-voiced grandmother at the baby store again.

My son was not yet at term and his look was already being scrutinized. He would have to be stylish and elegant as soon as he saw the light of day. Weren't they going to give him a couple of months to get into the swing of things? Couldn't he be given a few weeks of leeway on account of his American, sweatpant-wearing mother?

"*Hmmmm* . . ." Raffaella would have to think about it, work on it, match some of these things with items she had bought. But it looked like my job was over. Hallelujah.

"You know, in the U.S., we usually buy baby clothes that can go in the washing machine," I ventured, finding renewed confidence in my ninth month.

"Are you serious? They get ruined that way! What about the satin lock-down stitch?"

I didn't mention that we also tend not to spend two hundred bucks on a wardrobe that would last less than a month, and that was destined to be covered with milk and vomit. It was pointless. I didn't want my son to get the *figlio di nessuno*, the "no one's kid" label, as soon as he was born, so I let Nonna Raffaella handle my newborn's wardrobe. After all, I figured, who cares what they dress him in? I had enough on my mind.

So it's ironic that what I remember most vividly about the birth of my first child is a tiny cardigan of merino wool. When the nurse brought Anthony in, an hour after our C-section (I do not believe that the disproportionately high percentage of cesareans in Italy has nothing to do with aesthetics. The mommy looks better, the baby looks better. The mommy can get her hair done and hands manicured the morning of the birth; the baby's head is a perfect orb. I mean, natural delivery? *Per favore!*), he was wearing a pinstripe lambswool sweater. It was cerulean and cream, and must have been chosen by Nonna Raffaella and approved by a panel of nurses. His hair had been combed to the side, a dab of cologne had been applied behind his ear.

My first thoughts were: What if he doesn't like me? What if I have bad breath? What does my hair look like? Can somebody please get me a *mirror* in here?

I was ready for fatigue, depression, joy. I wasn't ready for an eighth-grade crush. No one prepared me for the butterflies in my stomach, the dry mouth, the sweaty hands. Oh Lord, help me. For the second time in my life I was falling for an Italian man.

"Mamma!" Raffaella came into the room and used a term that nearly paralyzed me with its weight of responsibility. All those *m*'s spoke of lasagna made by hand, ironing shirts for a thirty-year-old, and a love that was *totale*. She saw my face, she saw Anthony in my arms looking for my breast, and she knew that it was time to *sdrammatizzare*. "Did you see the pullover? It's so elegant!" Yes, he was elegant, and the sweater was a jewel. Let's focus on the lamb's wool.

But where was Salvatore?

"He's splashing some water on his face. [Read: bawling for joy in the men's room.] Tomorrow I'm thinking that Anthony would look dashing in the white silk romper suit. What do you say?"

"I totally agree."

Extracomunitari

The women of Salva's family assumed that I would hand over my baby—the piece of my heart, as they say in Naples—to someone from the Philippines, Ukraine, Sri Lanka, or Brazil. It was assumed that this lady would be not too attractive, not too expensive, and would live in a corner of our apartment and have Sundays off.

Things that were not taken into consideration were: carpet time, take-out dinners, sweatsuits with vomit stains on them. The concept, *insomma*, that mothering would be my job.

Immigrants from Sri Lanka are dirty, and *The great thing about Filipina domestic workers is that they stay out of your way*, or *Brazilians are too pretty to be live-in babysitters* are all comments I heard from Italian mothers. Mothers who otherwise seemed to be kind, sensitive people dismissed whole continents because *fanno schifo*, they're gross. I, too, was an *extracomunitaria*, I reminded them. No, Ketrin, Americans don't count! *Extracomunitari* are people from North Africa, from Asia, from poor areas of Ukraine . . . people who don't look like us and who work for us.

Oh, and by the way, Ketrin, why don't you have one?

When Emilio was born, Benedetta had hired a lady named Marieli from Sri Lanka. At the same time, Raffaella and Nino hired her cousin, a young man with a Yankees baseball cap named Mitzi. (Nunzia the working-class Neapolitan had retired—Mitzi helped with the cooking as well as the "heavy cleanings." He was young, strong, and knew how to fix appliances.) Both Raffaella and Benedetta would complain, however, that "they"—referring to Marieli and Mitzi—have no idea what hygiene is (they don't even bidet!); that "they" are clueless when it comes to packaging leftovers. "Look," Benedetta told me one day, holding out a plate of sausages and *ragù*. It was covered with cellophane, but the edges were coming loose. "Marieli did this. This apparently is how they package things in Sri Lanka. *Limitate, sono limitate.*" They are mentally deficient. (Note to self: When in Benedetta's or Raffaella's home, get rid of leftovers and pretend you ate them. Do not try to wrap.) She obviously considered me an Italian *signora*, a lady of the house, who had nothing in common with these *extracomunitari* domestic workers.

But she was wrong. I have the same work permit issues as these women. I am far away from my home like these women. I don't know how to get Italian plastic wrap to stick around the edges of a bowl, just like these women. And I don't bidet. Sure, there are huge differences. I have a lot more resources and a lot less courage than these women. But on a human level, when I hear Neapolitan *signore* complaining about their domestic workers, how they *just don't get it*, I feel like they are talking about me.

How could people feel this way about "the help" and then hand their babies over to them? I wondered.

So I resisted. I became a stay-at-home mom, American-style. I was sleep-deprived and overweight (no bingeing, just eating what I wanted when I wanted it). I wore no makeup, didn't fix my hair. For me, these were the consequences of being a full-time mother with a baby. In a way, I was proud to look so bad: my scrunchies and sneakers were badges of honor, showing the sacrifices that I made for my "work" as parent. I don't sit around pampering myself, my crusty velour pantsuits said, I take this mothering thing *seriously*. I suffer for it.

For the Italian women in my life, my appearance was the start of a slippery slope that would end with unwaxed legs and microwaved dinners. "*Sta diventando una scema appriess'ai bambini,*" I heard a friend describe another mother whose nanny had left and who was reduced to wearing sweats at the park like me. She's becoming demented being around the kid so much.

They were not just worried about what I looked like, they were worried about my mental health.

When Anthony was about one and a half, I got a call from Zia Pia. "Ketrin, have you thought about the babysitter idea? You need it. You're with that boy way too much. *È troppo legato a te.*" He was too attached to me? But he wasn't even two! Pia's children lived at home until they were thirty! I got riled up. I interpreted her comments as an attack, a judgment on my mothering style. What I didn't understand was that she was not saying I was a bad mother, or that Anthony would suffer. She was saying that I needed to take care of myself. She was thinking of me.

Inexpensive child care is a mixed blessing. In southern Italy, you can hire a live-in nanny for a month at the same rate you would probably pay a New York babysitter for a day at Central Park. It made it *very* hard for me to say no thanks, I like my vomit stains. I like eating from a can, and asking Salva to pick up pizza five times a week. It's *so* good for my child. After all, he gets to be with me, on a carpet!

So I agreed to have someone come in during the day. No serving lunch at the table, or massaging necks, just some cooking and cleaning and taking care of Anthony while I went to get a cappuccino. Of course, he would *never* want to be with her. He would put up with it and count the minutes until I got home. I would help him understand that Mommy needed a little time for herself, too.

One of Anthony's first English expressions was "When de Jackie come?" He would waddle over to the door and sit there, waiting. Another early expression was "Mamma leave now, okay?" Jackie would race him to the park, tell him about climbing to the top of the volcano near Lake Taal in the Philippines when she was a little girl, pretend she was a goalkeeper of the Series A soccer league.

I, meanwhile, learned how the vacuum cleaner worked. I found a fantastic lemony anticalcium spray for cleaning the toilets. I had a blast. I didn't need to get a cappuccino or go to the beauty parlor. I simply needed to do *anything* that did not involve interacting with a two-year-old brain. I had judged my friend who said that you can become demented being around a kid so much, but I started to realize that she could be right. Admittedly, my excitement about getting the crud out of the bathroom tiles was a little disturbing.

For the first time since my English classes in Naples, I decided to go back to teaching.

Act the Food

I strongly believe that acting is the best way to learn another language, to really learn to speak it. Everyone has to create a new persona when they learn a language that is not their own. So, I told Italian friends who wanted to learn English, instead of spending all your time studying grammar, try some dialogues and improvisation exercises. Create a character. The language will get inside you, emotionally and viscerally. You will free yourself of the little judge in your mind who says things like, "Wow, you really sound stupid! Are you *sure* that's the third person singular of that verb?"

An acting school located in a tiny black-box theater near the Colosseum hired me to teach a course for Italians called Acting in English. About ten actors in their twenties and thirties came for the first class. They didn't feel confident speaking English— they'd studied it in school but couldn't seem to *sbloccarsi*, or unblock, themselves with the language. Be an animal in English! I told them. Get pissed off at this other actor who has just stolen your girlfriend! Invent a joke and make us all laugh! Do whatever's necessary to free yourself and go for it.

At the end of the course, I told my students, we would work on dialogues from *Pulp Fiction* and *Death of a Salesman*.

To help my Italian actors find their characters' truth (and focus on something other than their linguistic limits), I introduced some improvisations to tap into their emotional memory. To try to get them to remember the feeling of their first kiss, their rage in an argument with a family member. A moment of joy with a friend. Surprisingly, I got almost nothing from them. Or rather, what I got was fake, demonstrated, showy. I tried to get them to talk (in English, I know it's not easy) about their relationships with their mothers. Rather than tears and depth of feeling, I got "My mother is a little rigid" or "We are different in character, my mother and I." Voices were level, faces were inexpressive. Were these really *Italians*? Talking about their *mamme*? These were people who, when describing the traffic they had encountered coming to class, were as dramatic as Jim Carrey in *Batman*.

Part of the difficulty was cultural. While an American actor will dissect and analyze his parents, an Italian will protect them. There is, still, a certain respect for family. Young Americans often bond by dumping on their parents: Italian *ragazzi* most definitely don't. There are no who-has-the-most-dysfunctional-family competitions.

But the problem was more complicated. I didn't want the actors simply to air their dirty laundry in class, I wanted them to feel and then express with emotional intensity in English. I mulled this over as I walked home from school. Then the light-bulb suddenly appeared above my head. Duh! What was I, a dunce? How long had I been living in Italy? How was it that I kept forgetting that the answer was always in the food?

I put away the Stanislavski and Uta Hagen acting texts for the next class. I told the students that we were going to skip the sense memory exercises, I had to ask their advice on something. I wanted to try out some new recipes for my husband—we'd had a tough period with the baby not sleeping and had been fighting a lot. I wanted to cook something special for him. Can you each describe your favorite dish? If you remember, tell me about the person who makes it for you and how they do it. I need to learn.

The first actor was from Salerno, just south of Naples. He described his grandmother's ravioli. He showed us how her fingers pinched off the little balls of ricotta and *spinaci* and folded the dough in pockets. "In *this* way," he specified, making a perfect *th* sound, tongue between the teeth and all! His eyes were full of tears; he didn't need to tell us that his *nonna* had passed away.

Barbara from Turin showed us how her mother cut the vegetables for the *bagna cauda* stew, and again we knew without being told that Barbara loved and hated her with a passion. She told us that her *mamma* cut everything in *ssstrips* (good—not ztrips! I had been working with them for ages on *s* plus a consonant! *Ssssnow,* not *zznow. Seven snakes slept in the snow!*). They lived the emotions honestly through food; they remembered through recipes. They spoke in English, with almost no accent.

Toward the end of our course, when we began to work on dialogues from movies and plays, those actors had so much to think about. The character's truth, their own truth, those big fat American *a*'s that felt so weird in their mouths! But my job as a teacher/director was easy. When they got lost in their brains, when they stopped being honest and started to fake it, I knew how to direct them. Michele, ravioli. Chiara, *pasta alla Genovese.* Barbara, *bagna cauda.* Tap into that and you will give us a performance that is nothing less than inspired.

Cotoletta alla Milanese

When Anthony was two and a half, Salva and I decided it would be a good idea to enroll our son in nursery school. Actually, Salva thought it was a great idea, and I felt like I was dispatching him to a forced-labor camp. Anthony had become a *mammone*, a southern Italian mama's boy, and it was 100 percent my fault.

Before I gave birth to an Italian boy, I had passed judgment quickly and cheerfully on all the mama's boys in Italy. Actually, I had passed judgment on the mothers. After all, the problem with Italian men is really Italian mothers, isn't it? You will never hear blame being placed on an Italian thirty-year-old who still lives at home and has a special "Me and You" telephone contract so he can call his *mamma* free of charge to tell her to put the pasta on, he's coming home from work. That's the *mamma*'s fault, of course! Why does she let him do it? Why does she put the water on to boil?

Before having an Italian son, I thought it was because these Italian women didn't know better. They cooked for and pampered their boys because they obviously hadn't read any books with titles like: *Helping Your Toddler Thrive* or *The Childhood Handbook* or *The No's That Help Them Grow* or *Boundaries and Love*. I mean, would it really be so hard to order some parenting books and make life a lot better for these young men and their future wives?

I was quite sure that my son would never become a *mammone*. I had read the books. Plus, I was American: food would not be the expression of my love. My love as a mother would be expressed by teaching, by guiding, by enriching. By reading! By practicing letters! Mother to son, brain to brain. The bodies and tummies of my son and me would be separated by some good old healthy Anglo-Saxon distance.

That was my thinking before having Anthony. Before hearing his first "*Mammmmmmà*," already the intimate Neapolitan dialect for Mommy; before seeing his little hand twisting his finger in his cheek (in the Italian gesture meaning *delicious*) after nursing from my breast. Um, can I return that *Independence and Boundaries with Your Toddler* book and get my money back?

So I confess that I am *guilty*. Guilty of aggravating Italy's problems—if things follow the *mammone* template, my son will not be part of a flexible and mobile workforce, but will hang out in his boyhood room with soccer trophies and Garfield stickers into his thirties. There will never be an empty nest. (Ah, the laughs I have gotten from my Neapolitan friends when I translate that expression! What do the mothers and fathers do when the kids go off to university so young? they ask. *Si guardono in faccia?* They stare at each other's faces?)

I was trained in my *mammone*-raising not only by my mother-in-law but by the nuns at Santa Chiara nursery school. When I would go to pick up Anthony, the elderly nun at the door, Suor Alfonsina, would tell us how the day went before letting us into the garden to collect our little ones. The conversations went something like this:

"Hello, I'm Anthony's mother. How was he today?" (Read: Did he hit/kick/spit/injure/offend, reflecting horribly on me as a parent and his environment at home?)

"Anthony, Anthony . . . *ah, sì!* He finished most of his pasta but ate none of the *cotoletta*. Does he not like veal cutlets?" She was worried. What *was* the situation at home?

"No . . . I mean yes! We're working on that. At home. And . . . did he play with the other kids?"

"Play?" Suor Alfonsina must have extra patience with this American mother who asks well-intentioned but totally irrelevant questions. "Well, I'm sure he did. And tomorrow maybe we'll start with the meat." She turned to another mother. "*Mamma di Emanuele?* He was such a good boy! He finished all of the pasta with lentils!"

The *mamma* was proud. She beamed.

The menu of the week at the Santa Chiara nursery school was posted next to Jesus on the cross. The fact that conversation at pickup time was relegated to "Leonardo ate all of his tortellini but left some of his meat" and "Does Enrico have a problem with fruit?" made me wonder how these nuns remembered such details. And why did they care?

Anthony had major separation issues when I first began taking him to nursery school (okay, fine! I had major separation issues too. The *mammone* thing implicated both of us). He was so miserable in the mornings that he would vomit almost every day before we left home. I tried to talk to the other mothers about our problem. I learned the Italian terms for *letting go* and *separation anxiety.* I got a lot of advice. They cared, and they shared. One said lay off milk in the morning. Another said it was a problem of acidity—was I giving him orange juice? They discussed among themselves whether it might have been my tendency to give him too much cereal in the morning. Finally a grandmother came up to me and put her two cents in.

"Dear, I went through exactly the same thing with my son, for years. I know what you're going through." I was starting to feel relieved, looking into her wrinkled face. I was talking to someone who really understood my predicament, and her time-tested advice about mothering with boundaries and love was going to be wise and true. "I'll tell you the secret," she whispered, "*no* breakfast at all! He'll have nothing to puke up!"

I accepted this advice with genuine gratitude, even though, as a woman raised in a culture of psychoanalysis, it offered me no solution to my problem. I knew that for the grandmother this was not something trivial. A *nonna*, after all, telling you *not* to feed your child was a rare event. She too had suffered, and she had found her answer.

When kindergarten began, Salvatore and I set up a meeting with Suor Alfonsina to talk to her about Anthony and his behavior. He was misbehaving big-time at home—challenging Salva and me, refusing to take time-outs, jumping on the furniture, you name it. I wanted Suor Alfonsina to help us understand what was going on at school and maybe give us a few pointers. I was working on the veal cutlet issue; she could give me a hand with the discipline thing.

We were flabbergasted to hear that Anthony was an angel at school. She used the words *obedient, social, sensitive,* and—get this!—*caring*. Anthony Avallone? Were we talking about the same kid? Brown hair? Wears a Naples soccer jersey twenty-eight days a month? After verifying that we were in fact talking about Anthony, I expressed my contentment that at least when he was out of the house he knew how to behave. Better that way, I later told Salvatore.

"What, are you crazy?" my husband replied. "It would be much better if he behaved himself at home and misbehaved at school! Then someone *else* would have to deal with his tantrums, not us!"

I, as an American, felt that our son's behavior outside the home was a positive indicator that in the future our son would perform, socially and professionally . . . and then I realized that for a Neapolitan, your behavior *inside* the home is the real indicator of your character. Not in the workplace, not in school. Sure, it's nice to look good when you leave your home, and make a *bella figura*. But in terms of your identity, the most important thing is who you are with your parents, with your children, with your cousins. The important thing is how you behave with the people who *really* matter.

Pants on Fire

As soon as Anthony learned to walk, he joined in the free-for-all to open Nonna's suitcase and dive into the *pizzette* and *mozzarelline* she brought when she came to Rome. Anthony and Raffaella loved each other with a passion. Raffaella spoon-fed him, cuddled him, played with him.

She also lied to him, regularly. I was ready to embrace a whole lot about the Avallones' Neapolitan parenting style, but when it came to telling the truth, my American cultural conditioning ran deep.

One of Anthony's favorite games as a toddler was Memory. Because I have never liked to make life simple for myself, I gave my son a Memory game of horses that included about thirty pairs—all of which looked almost exactly alike.

Raffaella and Nino were visiting, and it was Anthony's bedtime. He wanted to play Memory with his *nonna*. I told Raffaella it would take too long, to which she replied that I should distract Anthony in the kitchen and she would try to memorize the position of the cards so she could win quickly. "I'm good at cheating," she explained. "We'll be fast."

"What's Nonna doing?" Anthony asked me. Raffaella, sitting on the living room floor in a Fendi suit, was memorizing the stallions as quickly as she could.

"She's setting up Memory, sweetheart," I told him. I was complicit in the cheating. The child would take drugs and lie about it as soon as he hit puberty.

"Siamo pronti!" Let's start! She was excited about the game. Not surprisingly, she racked up pairs quickly, peeking at the cards whenever my son looked away. It was a challenge, and she was having a blast. Anthony was suspicious. Every once in a while he said, "Nonna! You peeked!"

"What are you talking about? *Quando mai!*" she laughed. But never!

I expressed my reservations later to Raffaella, saying that it might be a good idea to teach Anthony that it's better not to cheat. It's better not to lie.

"But didn't you want a quick game of Memory?" she answered, confused. "Who knew where those damn stallions were? And now he's sleeping soundly!"

"I understand," I tried to be diplomatic, "but in the long run . . . cheating at Memory could mean cheating at school—"

"What does school have to do with it?"

And at that point I remembered Salvatore's reaction when I was in graduate school and complained about a difficult exam. His response would be, "Wasn't there someone who had studied sitting near you?" His law exams were all oral, but little slips of paper and huddled desks were common when there was a written exam in Naples.

"We can't do that. We don't do that."

"You could save yourself a whole lot of trouble. You Americans, why is it that you are always making life so difficult for yourselves?"

In Naples, people do not lie. They re-create, artistically and playfully, their own truth. It is normal to tell untruths, creative reconstructions of reality. These untruths are told with great calm and finesse. They are told not only to dupe or deceive but also to protect, out of love for the person being misled.

In a culture where the truth is like a game, relationships often focus on trying to *svelare*, or take the veil off, a friend's version of the truth. This is done with very little drama, and almost no condemnation or judgment. So what if a person just invented and described an imaginary experience? He could be, using the vulgar vernacular, a *cazzaro*, or a person who tells *cazzate*, meaning lies. In Naples the expression would be *spara cazzate*: he shoots off the lies.

"That's fascinating that Alessio went to India for a month!" I say to Salva.

"Oh, Alessio's a *cazzaro*," he'll reply, not all that interested whether his friend lied or not.

But the friendship sails along smoothly, despite Alessio's tendency to shoot off lies. Nobody's pants are on fire or anything drastic like that. As an American, I immediately take this tendency to the next level. I assume that if he lies to you about a vacation, he'll lie to you about important things. Where's the trust in that friendship? Just like Clinton: If he cheated his wife, he'll cheat the country, right? If he lied under oath about sex, he's capable of any sort of deception.

But in Naples, that is not the line of thinking. What does sex have to do with politics? It's totally irrelevant. What does a lie about a vacation have to do with what kind of friend he is?

Disturbed, I continued to try to talk it through with Raffaella. How about Pinocchio? I asked my mother-in-law. Wasn't the moral of Italy's most famous fairy tale that one should never tell a lie?

"Oh, that Pinocchio story," she began, and I understood immediately that Pinocchio was not Neapolitan but northern, and thus foreign. "I guess it can be useful to teach children not to lie to their parents. But Pulcinella . . ."

She went on to describe animatedly how Pulcinella, the Neapolitan clown from the commedia dell'arte, lies regularly and gets caught only because he isn't smart about it. Now *that's* an important lesson for a kid.

I heard a revealing conversation take place between my mother-in-law and my son, the evening of a dinner party and bridge tournament at the Avallones' apartment. About forty people were to arrive in a few hours. The new Sri Lankan housekeeper Mitzi was frying zucchini to make *zucchine alla scapece*, a marinated zucchini, mint, and garlic dish. He had already set up the card tables in the living room, and had collaborated with Raffaella on the other nine dishes that were going to be served when the players took their ten o'clock break.

Raffaella wanted to get Anthony to sleep before the guests arrived. The only way was to tell him that nothing was happening later.

"Nonna, are you having a party tonight? Are people coming over?"

"*Ma no! Che dici?* No, of course not. What on earth are you talking about?"

"I saw the card tables in the living room. . . ."

"Oh, those! I set them up for next week when your grandfather is going to have a meeting with his friends."

"Meeting? Nonna! That's not the truth!" He was smiling,

and adorable. He was thrilled that he'd won the little truth game. She started laughing and enveloped him in a hug.

"Amore mio! Quanto sei scetàto!" My love, you are awake!

Kissing and tickling him, Raffaella was so very proud that Anthony had called her out on her lie. Her grandson wasn't no kid sleeping with his mama's titty in his mouth. He was being raised well.

Anthony accepted the Find the Truth game as just that, a game. He knew that he could play it with his Neapolitan grandmother, aunt, and cousins. But if I was around, his little eyes made contact with mine as if to say, Mommy, I'm going to ask you later what the real answer is. As he grew, Anthony enjoyed the game less and less, and sought out the truth more and more. He knew where to look.

After all, this wasn't a game his American mommy knew how to play.

Eggplant Parmesan

enedetta and Mauro's marriage was on the rocks. Salvatore noticed that Benedetta was buying her groceries at the discount supermarket: that's how he knew.

At the beginning of their marriage, love was expressed through both Benedetta's and Raffaella's cooking. It was a mother-daughter team. Raffaella had prepared her daughter well—Benedetta knew that peas were to be cooked in May, that eggplants were not to be canned when she was menstruating. (One day I tried to help Raffaella pack her boiled eggplants in jars, and she asked me, "Do you have the *ciclo*?" I didn't have the cycle, but wanted to know why it mattered. "They say the eggplants will become acidic," Raffaella explained, "because hormones are transmitted through your hands. Better not to take the risk.")

A weekly menu was established based on what was fresh that moment, which vegetables were particularly good in the countryside around Naples that year. (Neapolitan women have found it genuinely funny that I cook sausage in the summer or asparagus in the fall. She must come from a place where they grow asparagus in September! This is considered akin to wearing ski boots in July.)

As her relationship with Mauro deteriorated, so did Benedetta's cooking. She no longer asked Raffaella to make her specialty casseroles. All she asked her mother to do was to cook for her two boys—don't worry about Mauro! He can eat anything, it doesn't matter. Benedetta's dishes were *arrangiati,* meaning put together with no care. She was cooking without love.

Was this the woman who had made *tagliolini* casseroles for her husband, taking special care to use the cheeses that Mauro preferred? Who went across town to get the ricotta that was the freshest? The woman who based her (and her mother's) cooking on "how Mauro likes it"?

When Salvatore saw the plastic bags from Tuodì supermarket, he confronted his sister and asked her what was going on.

Benedetta had fallen out of love with Mauro. "He doesn't do anything here. He's never even changed a diaper! He's a *peso* [a burden]." That word, *peso,* which literally means a weight, was the same word that I'd heard other Neapolitan women use for their husbands. "Things are so much easier without him" was another sentence that I had heard before.

I told Benedetta that I was surprised. In the early years of their marriage, she would often say what a caring and helpful partner Mauro was. Her response now was an *"Eeeeh"* on the exhale—what are you gonna do? That was before children. "You know? He's never even given the boys a bath! He doesn't know how to screw in a lightbulb, or fold a shirt. I mean, come *on.*"

My sister-in-law did something that would have been impossible in Naples in the past: she left her husband. (Well, I shouldn't say left, since it was she who kept the apartment and the kids and the lasagna in the elevator.) Salvatore tried to mediate. He understood his sister and the problems she had with Mauro, and at the same time felt for his forty-five-year-old brother-in-law who had to move back in with his mother. (Live on his own? That option wasn't even considered. Mauro didn't know how to fry an egg! How would he survive?)

Is there any chance that he could get custody? I asked Salva. In Italy, no. The mother has to be a drug addict or a prostitute, and even then, she usually gets custody of the children. "*La mamma è sempre la mamma*" is an expression that you hear all the time: Mama will always be Mama, there's no one like Mama. The subtext being that Papa is a nice addendum, but never a substitute.

It seemed to me that Salvatore was an objective mediator. He had the necessary emotional distance. He wasn't blinded by anger and showed respect and consideration for all involved. That is, until the Day of the Eggplant Parmesan.

The whole family had gathered for Sunday lunch. Benedetta's two boys played with their little cousin Anthony; Raffaella cooked and served. Salva, Nino, Benedetta, and I sat at the table and consumed. No one mentioned Mauro. Benedetta seemed to be happy—she had even started dating a man she worked with. She'd been separated from Mauro for a few months, but it would be years before they could officially divorce. (In the best-case scenario, when a husband and wife are consensual, an Italian couple can apply for a divorce after three years of separation. If not, it can take closer to a decade. This was the case for Benedetta and Mauro.)

Tutto a posto, everything in its place. In a new place, granted, but in place. There was peace and children's laughter and magnificent food.

Benedetta's new flame lived a short drive away, by himself. If I had been raised in Naples, I probably would have thought,

It's Sunday, and Benedetta's new boyfriend is alone! What's the poor guy going to have for lunch? but it didn't occur to me. After we had eaten the pasta with beans, the sautéed *friarielli* greens, huge milky balls of mozzarella, and the most divine eggplant Parmesan Raffaella had ever baked, Benedetta got up and asked her mother for a plastic plate.

"What are you doing?" Salva asked her as she cut a hunk of the deep purple *parmigiana* and positioned it on the plate.

"Can you give me some plastic wrap, Mom?" she said.

Salva stood up menacingly. "What are you doing?"

Benedetta was wrapping the cellophane around the plate. Once, twice . . .

"*Who is that for?*"

Salva knew that his sister was planning to take their mother's *parmigiana* out of their home. She was going to put it on the passenger seat of her little Fiat and take it to the apartment of her new partner. She had fallen in love and this was the way she expressed it.

But Salva saw it as a betrayal. His mother had dried the eggplants in the sun for two days. She had then fried them in strips. Raffaella had even used the tomatoes that she canned herself. All this to satisfy the appetite of his sister's lover? Suddenly that dark purple *parmigiana* was so sexual. Salvatore never spoke of honor, or of family, or used any words that a Neapolitan brother would have used just one generation ago. But he lost his *shit* over that eggplant Parmesan.

My husband's knees bounced and his hands flew. Benedetta cried and screamed and used expressions in Neapolitan dialect that I didn't understand. I swept Emilio, Claudio, and Anthony off to the bedroom, where I taught them rock, paper, scissors in English. When I heard silence at last, I came back to the kitchen to find the plastic plate with the *parmigiana* snapped in two and the floor splattered with blood-red tomato sauce. Everyone else had stormed off and Raffaella was alone with that heartbreaking mess. How could I help?

Raffaella put on her magic yellow kitchen gloves ("When I put these on I'm more efficient," she told me once. "Without gloves I don't even know where to start!"). She picked up the chunks and wiped the oil away with newspapers. Then she started mopping. She was a cleaning machine.

I felt sick with pity for this mother who for forty years had stirred and fried and baked her love for her daughter, and for the last ten had learned to do the same for a son-in-law. Suddenly she had to unlove him at the drop of a hat. She had to not care anymore what he ate and start learning instead how Benedetta's new partner liked his *pasta e fagioli*, whether he preferred his Easter *pastiera* cake with or without candied fruit.

After wringing out the dishrags, my mother-in-law looked me in the eye and I saw her concern. There was no Neapolitan tradition that told her where the *parmigiana* was to end up in a broken and blended family. Her Catholic church didn't give instructions on how to uproot someone from her heart, someone who with great effort she had taught herself to love.

But I had misinterpreted Raffaella's concern. "*Tesoro*," Honey, she said, and grabbed my hand, "did you want another piece of that before it went on the floor?"

Jealousy

"What do you have to do with it?" Raffaella asked me, genuinely baffled.

The problem was Anthony's jealousy. My son had turned into an eighteenth-century southern Italian, sword-brandishing, jilted lover. One of the things I appreciated about my husband was that he didn't have the possessive love that so many Neapolitan men have for their women. The *You're not wearing that, are you?* to short skirts or plunging necklines. The *When you go out, we go out together.* It exists, still. Although Salva is passionate and chivalrous, he has never had any macho possessiveness. I always credited his mother for having raised him to respect women's independence.

But apparently, mothers have nothing to do with it. The character trait jealousy—just like *permalosità*, shyness, aggression, you name it—is something you inherit from your relatives just as you would blue eyes or curly hair.

"*Zio Renato era geloso,*" Raffaella informed me. Apparently Anthony had gotten the trait from an uncle on his grandmother's side who was known for his possessive jealousy.

I was pregnant with a girl, and Anthony was on fire with rage. He spent his time glaring at me as if he had caught me in flagrante with a nemesis. It made no difference how I played with him or doted on him or spoon-fed him his favorite dishes: he was ready to pull out the saber and sing a Puccini aria before putting an end to it all.

Anthony and I had been spending a lot of time together at the park of the Domus Aurea—Nero's golden palace, on the Oppian Hill above the Colosseum. While the Italian mothers chatted about what they were preparing for lunch, I loaded my pudgy love on my back and pretended I was a racehorse at the Kentucky Derby. Faster, faster, *here's* the starting gate, Mommy! Not there. *Here!* I neighed, very loudly. Everyone thought I was insane. I was having more fun than I'd ever had in my whole life.

The doctor told me when I was pregnant that it was probably better not to reenact the Preakness at the park with my son.

"We can play with Legos!" I told Anthony. "And pick-up sticks!" He wasn't interested. "Horsey wasn't fun, Mommy," he told me. "No fun. Never."

I neighed. I thought we'd had something good.

He didn't want to go to the park with me anymore. He didn't want to *see* me. Although he'd been potty-trained for a while, he pooed in the middle of our living room, and said, "Mommy, something in *salotto*. Clean it up."

I asked Raffaella for advice. Where had I gone wrong? It must have been the way I'd handled it. I shouldn't have told him . . . I should have waited . . . I shouldn't have . . .

That's when she asked, "What have you got to do with it?"

As an American mother, I assume that every negative behavioral trait that my children have can be traced back to me. Specifically, to what I did or didn't do. This is absolutely unheard of for a Neapolitan. What a strange Anglo-Saxon cocktail of omnipotence and narcissism! Sure, *la mamma è sempre la mamma* and all that, but what can you do if your kid inherits Aunt Mary's rudeness?

I was off the hook. When we went to Naples for the weekend and Anthony had a tantrum, I was spared the *Katherine really should handle the situation better*. At most, Zia Pia or Raffaella would murmur *Good thing the jealousy gene skipped over Salvatore!* or *Yup, that's Zio Renato's jealousy there. Remember the time he camped out near his girlfriend's apartment?*

The period of my daughter's gestation and birth was a haze of tantrums, rage, and exhaustion. There were enormous amounts of caffeine and a lot of shouting. Anthony fumed; Salva and I fought. There was no Mozart played for the fetus. The books would say that didn't bode well for having a healthy, happy baby.

Luckily, my little girl inherited not only the name but the character of her *nonna*.

One of the most miraculous things about a newborn is her hands. I'm sure that little Lella's hands were tiny pink gems. At some point they probably rested, inert, on an embroidered sheet in her bassinet. But I have no memory of them. Because I have no recollection of Lella's hands ever being still.

It seems that from the time she was born, my daughter's hands were showing me how to do things. They were blending the blush on my cheeks (*dis no look right*), defending herself from her brother (*me hold up fist like dis*), braiding her best friend's hair. *This is the best way to cut potatoes, Mommy!* (Where'd you learn that?)—and the little fingers would fly, showing me the width of the strips.

When I told her, "I know it's hard for you when Anthony . . ." she waited patiently for me to finish, stroking my arm as if to reassure me that what I had to say was important. Then, it was: "Okay, *me* talk now. Remember, Mommy, it's always better to . . ." and there were the hands, showing me how to tie shoe-laces, or fold wrapping paper.

At school, she cheerfully organized playdates for the other kids. "Simona wanted to go over to Francesco's house. I made sure they worked it out and told him what she likes for snack." *Li ho sistemati,* I set them up. With a great big smile, the girl got people where they needed to be, doing what they needed to be doing. She made sure her mommy looked decent, put her brother in his place, and learned how to make her grandmother's tomato sauce by the age of six.

Che problema c'è?

Air-Con

In the early years of Anthony's and Raffaella junior's lives, my priorities as a mother were to raise children who were:

caring
principled
intelligent
accomplished
entertaining
disciplined
bilingual

Salvatore's priorities as a father were to raise children who were:

well fed
warm
dry
fans of Napoli and not of Roma soccer team

If Salva was fixated over these priorities for Anthony, the birth of a defenseless baby girl took his fixations to the extreme.

During the first summer of little Raffaella's life, Salva's fathering was dependent on two all-important remote controls, each kept in a separate pocket of his velour dressing gown. The television remote was used every five minutes to check on the ranking of Napoli in the Italian seasonal tournament. The other remote regulated our air-conditioning units, or as Italians call them, our "splits."

We have remote-controlled wall units in all rooms of our apartment, and they are usually (even in the worst heat of the summer) turned off. This is not because air-conditioning per se is hazardous to your health (although it is! Don't you know that?) but because the splits create drafts that cause, among other things, the common cold, neck cricks, and bronchitis. In the worst-case scenario (among the very young and very old), they can provoke pneumonia and paralysis. "Drafts" can be translated as *correnti*, a word Italians pronounce with a menacing rolled *r*.

Hence the importance of my husband's vigilant control of the splits. Who is responsible for regulating the air-conditioning at my house in Washington? I have been asked by my in-laws. Who has the holster for the sacred remote? My mother, who is *freddolosa* (always cold) or my father, who is *caloroso* (would downhill ski in his Speedos)? No one? With central air, we just set the temperature and forget about it. It astonishes them that day and night, morning and afternoon, there's *no regulating*.

When Raffaella junior was tiny, I would strap her into her high chair far away from her roaming, raging brother. No matter the room, Sal Quick-at-the-Draw would find her. He would find his daughter—buckled in, immobile, defenseless—regulate the vents with his remote, and exit. It would happen in a nanosecond. We would not hear the sound of footsteps, nor would we get a glimpse of him in his loungewear. Sal's presence was heralded by the *beep-beep-beep* of the remote control. *Beep-beep-beep*, another child rescued from a *corrente*, and he'd be gone.

Recent sightings of Quick Draw Sal have revealed that, even in summer, he dresses in layers. The Italian expression is *a cipolla*, like an onion. His loungewear begins with a white short-sleeved undershirt. Then come the pajamas—long-sleeved gray pajamas printed with little white curly-tailed cats interspersed with fluffy clouds. The legs of the pajamas are tucked into his very long navy-blue knee socks, so that no chilly air will come up his pajama legs. The undershirt and pajama top are tucked into the pants tightly so that, once again, no air will make its way to his belly. As a general rule, air is not to touch exposed flesh unless one is at the beach in Sardinia and it is 101 degrees. Salvatore's dressing gown, worn over his pajamas, is soft velour and is tied (tightly) around the waist.

Bedroom slippers are often mismatched in our household. In Italy, and in Naples in particular, bare feet are not to touch floors, even in the summer. When I wake up in the Avallones' apartment, I find slippers already on my feet before I put them down on the parquet. Some concerned kinswoman does not want me catching a cold, and everyone knows that I, as an American, have been known to walk around the apartment barefoot and sometimes even with wet hair. Salvatore, careful not to touch the floor, dons the slippers closest to the bed when he wakes up in the morning. There have been times when one of those slippers is pink, has feathers, and is mine.

In Naples, most sicknesses can be directly traced to one of three culprits: the aforementioned drafts or *correnti*; a moment when a person has *preso freddo*, gotten a chill; or, worst of all, *preso umido*, has taken humidity into their bones. For me, much of the difficulty of raising small children in this country comes down to the fact that I, as an American, do not recognize these dangers. I take my children out when it's fifty degrees and not raining. I know enough to keep them bundled in hats, scarves, and gloves, with no inch of bare skin showing. But if it's humid, or if all of a sudden it starts to get windy, I do not grab them and sprint to the nearest shelter.

Once, when Anthony got a cold, I overheard some Neapolitan family members talking about how I had taken him out on Wednesday. Yes, Wednesday! The day of that humidity! They tried their best to understand. "Maybe in Washington, where she grew up, the climate is so dry that they don't know what humidity is!"

Since the possibility of humidity and the risk of getting a chill loom large during winter, you can only imagine the stress of an outing with children when it rains. If it rains, children should stay at home, and adults should go out only if absolutely necessary.

If anyone has any negative preconceptions about Italians and their organizational abilities, they should watch a family with small children getting out of their car when it's raining— a family that has made the decision to venture out in the *tempesta*. In our family, Salva briefs me on how the tag team is to proceed with the umbrellas as we're about to arrive at our destination. "I will drive up to the front door. You should have the small umbrella in your pocket. I will open the big umbrella and accompany you with Lella in your arms into the building. Leave her inside and give me the small umbrella. I'll give you the big umbrella. Go get Anthony from the car and I'll go and park the car with the small umbrella."

The whole relay proceeds without a glitch. It is fast, it is efficient but also highly stressful. The fear that the kids might get wet is so real and so intense that I forget that the drops that are falling from the sky are only water.

I've come to realize that the number of sweaters and ski jackets that my husband puts on members of his family is in direct proportion to the love that he feels for us. If I manage to leave the apartment in winter without his accosting me, pinning me down, and zipping up my ski jacket, it means that he is angry with me. Let her go out with no jacket in March. To hell with her! Let her dig her own grave.

When it comes to the children, the smaller and more vulnerable they are, the more sweaters they get. As babies, Anthony and Raffaella were often hot and sweaty and fussy. It drove me crazy to see Salva pile on the layers, so, as soon as he was out of sight, I would strip them down. This was complicated, though, because they were small and uncooperative and confused by the continual costume changes. In a moment of particular tension on this front, my sister (an accomplished seamstress and costumer) told me that she thought our marriage could be saved and the harmony in our family restored if she just got rid of our zippers and buttons and Velcroed us all.

The reason I tend to get angry and a little bitter is that it's hard enough to have kids who are sick, without being accused of provoking it. My rational brain tells me that colds are viruses, and they get passed from person to person. I don't mention that to people in Naples, though. One way to find yourself friendless and ignored in Italy is to start a sentence with "Studies show" or "Scientists have found."

So I've decided to go with the flow, avoid *umidità* and *correnti*, and bring along my CVS disinfectant so that all the bases are covered.

Total Hunger

In ancient times, rich Romans would go to the seaside near Naples for the summer. It made sense. It still does. Without the ocean, Rome gets hotter than Naples in the summertime, and when you can't turn on the air-conditioning splits, and you're breast-feeding, and you're not allowed to sweat . . . the only option is to pack the kids up like *signore* have been doing for thousands of years and go to the beach. Or, if you happen to be American, to a swimming pool.

Salva finds my preference for swimming pools (no fiery rocks, or sand in crevices, or seaweed—the reasons are endless) immoral. Preferring a swimming pool to the ocean is akin to preferring frozen pizza to a fresh one right out of the oven. But I was hot and sleep-deprived and nursing and my husband knew what was good for him.

He called his friend from high school, Enrico, and told him we were coming with the kids for lunch and a swim.

Enrico had grown up in a *basso* in the dense center of Naples. The *bassi* are the street-level apartments that house extended families in the Spanish Quarter. "What adorable little restaurants!" I gushed to Salvatore the day he stripped me of jewelry, wallet, watch, and cellphone and took me on a tour of the Quartieri. I saw little tables propped up in alleyways, just outside of kitchens with lace curtains. The smell of peppers frying made me drool. "Do you think they're open?"

"What restaurants? Those are people's homes, and if you stand there salivating any longer they'll invite you to lunch."

Motorbikes whizzed by, missing us by millimeters. Salva, despite the fact that this was not his hood, could tell me which young guys on the bikes were thieves and which were undercover plainclothes cops. ("You can tell, that's all," he explained when I wondered how he could distinguish them.) Neither category wore the obligatory helmet.

"*Enrico abitava qui,*" he told me, pointing to an alley strung with laundry. He had a friend who lived here? I was surprised. "Who *used* to live here," he clarified.

Enrico had grown up heading soccer balls against the graffitied stone walls of his *basso,* but now lived in Bacoli, a suburb full of single-family villas. It's where many stars of the Naples soccer team (most are South American or eastern European) have chosen to live. In Bacoli there is space, there are pools. Gone is the stench of garbage and the constant buzz of motorbikes. Even robberies are high-class affairs: they are not *scippi* (pickpocketing and purse snatching) like in the Spanish Quarter, but full-fledged team efforts with drills and other power tools, performed by "expert" thieves. (A psychologist friend in Naples told me that one of her patients proudly noted that her husband was a *mariuolo di case,* a house thief, rather than a simple pickpocket. There is a major difference in terms of job profile.)

Enrico and his family made their money in clothing stores. They are *commercianti*, store owners, a term that is used by the Neapolitan bourgeoisie with not a little prejudice. Store owners who have been economically successful are considered nouveaux riches, but the term's Neapolitan translation, *cafoni arrichiti*, doesn't need to be uttered—it's enough to say *commerciante*. The Cardones have worked hard and moved up in the world. They have sacrificed, skipped afternoon naps, brought lunches from home to their stores (which don't even close! Some of the first stores in Naples not to close even for lunch!).

We arrived at the Cardones' villa in Bacoli just before noon on a scorching Saturday in July. The cameras on their high-tech alarm system ("Best ten thousand euros I ever spent," Enrico told us, and Salva later explained that a telltale sign of *commercianti* is that they speak in numbers, never afraid to tell you exactly how much something cost) blinked blue as the electric gate buzzed open. It was a slow curtain opening for Enrico's mother, who greeted us center stage in a tiny sequined bikini holding a one-year-old grandchild on her hip.

"*Salvató! Viene ccà!*" she called in a voice that was not of the gravelly grandma variety but a high, hysterical trumpet. Her voice told me she didn't smoke; her body told me she had other vices. She held the arm that wasn't supporting the baby out to hug Salva, and he disappeared for a moment into her 250-pound, dark-skinned embrace. She wore Ray Charles sunglasses and sported a platinum-blond bob. The sequins were under severe garment duress.

"This is Ketrin," Salvatore told her. When she didn't move

her head but just reached her hand out to pinch my chin, looking for me with her bloated fingers, I realized that if she was not totally blind she was close to it. *"Che nome è? Kay-tree?"* What kind of name is that? "Salvató, where did you go to pick this chick up?" They both laughed and I joined in. Kay-tree! Go figure!

She led us to the pool where her daughter-in-law Giada sat on a deck chair reading the riot act to her three-year-old child. Giada and Enrico had three daughters under the age of six. The girls, dressed in Ralph Lauren, Tommy Hilfiger, and Lacoste, were all blond and scowling. ("See that little horse, American flag, and crocodile? Five hundred euros a month," Enrico told us later. "That's Giada's clothing allowance for the girls.")

Giada had told her daughters that they could not go in the swimming pool today. There was a little wind; Ludovica had had a cough last Tuesday. This is never going to work, I thought. They're being asked to spend all afternoon moving between their grandmother's hip, deck chairs, and a lunch table? Listening to grown-ups talk and gazing at the crystal-blue water? When it's ninety-six degrees?

Little Raffaella was already splashing her feet in the water and Anthony was doing cannonballs. I was not going to veto that. It was ninety-six degrees.

Enrico's oldest daughter started to whine, and Giada shouted, "No is *no!*"

Before I knew what was happening, Giada had smacked her daughter across the face with speed and efficiency. Were my children and I responsible for child abuse? Giada saw my concern. "What, you never hit your kids?" The exact words that she used in Neapolitan dialect were: *"Nu' ll'abbuffe maie 'e mazzate?"* Whop them upside the head, I think would be the most accurate translation.

In Naples, it's still common in schools for teachers to strike kids with rulers, or spank them. When I taught English to a group of preschoolers, the director of the school told me on the first day that if things got out of hand I shouldn't hesitate to hit them. Not hard, of course. Just to get them to listen to you.

But I had never seen skill like this woman's: bam bam! Front of the hand! Back of the hand! Before I knew it the girl was sitting immobile next to her mother and Giada was talking to her mother-in-law about the state of the stuffed peppers.

Giada doesn't call her mother-in-law Mrs. Cardone or Angelica. She uses the term that Neapolitan daughters-in-law are meant to use: *Mammà*. With the accent on the final *a*, it is down-home dialect for the Italian *mamma* (accent on the first *a*) and thus even more intimate. If *Mamma* is Mom, *Mammà* is Mommy.

Since Enrico and Giada live with his extended family, the two women spend all their time together. While their husbands man the stores, Giada and Mammà plan, buy the ingredients for, and cook the three meals that are nothing short of feasts at the Cardone household. (Cleaning is done by a uniformed, thin Brazilian maid. To see the women of the house all overweight and the help skinny seems a throwback to the last century.) Breakfast consists of homemade cakes and *crostate*, or fruit pies, and lunch and dinner include a *primo*, or pasta course, a *secondo* that is meat or fish, and at least two labor-intensive vegetables. Because the gentlemen do not come all the way back to the villa for lunch, the team of wives package up their husbands' lunches for them to take to work.

In Naples, packaging food is an art form. Newspapers, rubber bands, Styrofoam, freezer bags, soft rags, string, and twine are used. Temperature and distance to be traveled are taken into consideration, and obstacles such as customs regulations in a foreign country or the length of a transatlantic flight are seen as exciting challenges. A friend who is an Alitalia flight attendant told me that Neapolitans can always be recognized by the packages of food that they hold close on board a plane. They often refuse to put them in the overhead compartments—after all, who knows what the exact temperature is up there?

The last time I flew back to Washington, D.C., at Christmas, Zia Pia called me a few days before the flight. "We've figured out a way!" she told me. A way to do what? "To get the octopus to your father!" Aunt Pia knew that my father loves *insalata di polipo* and damned if she wasn't going to get it to him. In my already packed suitcase. Her plan involved nestling the slimy creature in the underwear compartment of my pull-along. Bubble wrap and rags would do the trick. What if it starts to drip? I asked her.

"*Eehhh* [on the exhale] . . . *che vuoi fa'?*" she answered. What can you do? These are just the risks one has to take.

Because the Cardone gentlemen's fried eggplant, roast veal, and baked pasta casseroles only have to travel across town, Giada and her *mammà*'s packaging job is simple. All they need is some old *Mattino* newspapers, Tupperware, and heavy-duty rubber bands.

Mr. Cardone appeared from inside the house wearing a Speedo. He was tall and thin, with lots of white hair and skin the color of dark clay. He introduced himself, sat down, and lit up a cigarette.

"*Giada, vedi nu poco i peperoni a Mammà.*" Angelica too had lowered herself onto one of the deck chairs and wanted Giada to check the stuffed peppers in the oven, which smelled like the Quartieri Spagnoli, where the family had its origins. Her sentences, whether she was commanding, cuddling, or cursing, always ended by underlining the relationship she had with her listener. Her words brought her family members back to her broad brown bosom. To her daughter-in-law, Can you check the peppers for Mammà? To her niece, Oh, how beautiful you are to your aunt! To her granddaughter, Baby girl, wipe your nose for Nonna.

"*Kay-tree, viene ccà.*" She motioned me over. I wasn't part of the family, so her sentence didn't end with Mammà, Nonna, or Zia. American with the weird name, come here.

Angelica had focused on the fact that I was from the United States. Although I know absolutely nothing about medicine, I am often considered a medical expert simply because I am American. People ask me about new procedures that are being performed in the States, and which American doctor is the expert of which disorder. So many Italians have blind faith that in the land of miracles any condition can be cured, as long as you have money to pay. I assumed that Angelica was going to inquire about new laser technology for her eye problem, but no.

"In America, they've gotta have a pill that you can take to make you lose weight. Can you ask around for me, honey? I'm ready to pay."

Angelica's hunger is described by her skinny whip of a husband as *totale*. An all-consuming, black hole of an appetite. Her smile and sequins glittered as Carmine described an incident from the early years of their courtship, when Angelica climbed over a neighbor's spiked fence at 3:00 A.M. to get a *cornetto Algida*, a chocolate ice-cream dessert ("I knew what I was getting into," he told us). Later in life, unable to drive because of her eyesight, Angelica made her son, at the age of fifteen and with no driver's license, drive her two hundred miles to a sandwich joint in the mountains of central Italy ("*Tenevo na famma 'e pazze*"—I had myself a crazy hunger—"and I'd heard it was the best"). After undergoing an operation on her hands, she developed the skill of eating pasta with her elbows (and actually gained weight! she told us proudly).

I listened and laughed, my sweaty thighs sticking to the plastic deck chair. I was hungry, too. Angelica and I both knew just how much it sucks to feel fat and hungry. And hot. But once again in Naples, my hunger, my readiness to dig into the steaming stuffed peppers that Giada brought from the kitchen (barking at the little blond toddlers that got in her way, "*Ué, te vuó spustà?*"—Hey you! Git, why don't ya?) didn't feel pathological. It felt human.

As I sat next to this smiling woman with an overwhelming hunger, I thought about the days when I would put away three boxes of Oreos. I imagined Salva bragging about it someday to friends who came for lunch.

"So," she asked me, "do you Americans have this pill that will let me eat what I want and not be fat?"

In Naples, a hunger like Angelica's is not seen as pathological or as a disorder but, like the love she has for her children and grandchildren, quite simply *totale*. So I didn't tell her about Prozac or appetite suppressants. I simply informed my hostess that even in the land of medical miracles, that is a condition for which we have yet to find the cure.

Peanut Butter

In Neapolitan culture, foods that could potentially damage children's health include crackers, ketchup, hot dogs, cold milk, anything in a can, anything that has ever been frozen, and anything that has ever been in a microwave. Oh, and anything that comes from a supermarket. Fish must be consumed regularly. But not *pesce di allevamento*, farm-raised fish—only fish from the ocean. And which ocean matters: there's a difference between Adriatic and Mediterranean sole, for example. Fish from the Mediterranean is almost always superior.

Nino, who had rarely interfered in our decisions as parents, called once a week to find out whether little Raffaella had had her fish, and which fish. I threw little George Washington out the window and started lying through my teeth.

We lived in Rome, for God's sake. Salva was at work all day. No one would find out that I gave my kids Cheerios and crackers! I refused to spend my time boiling vegetables for hours, when I was sure that those vegetables were the wrong vegetables, and when I was sure that my kids would ball them in their little fists and hand them back to me. Wasn't it better to sing "Ten Little Monkeys Jumping on a Bed" and tap-dance to it?

The problem arose when we visited Naples and Anthony got to the point of expressing himself well in Italian. Much to my dismay, he often told the truth. It must have been my fault. What was I thinking, telling him all that garbage about the cherry tree? I should have read up on that smart Neapolitan Pulcinella clown who lies and gets away with it!

"Mommy opens these cans with . . . how do you say *baked beans* in Italian? I like them but Lella doesn't so she just eats crackers. Can I have some more *ragù*, Nonna?"

"Sweetheart," I would tell him later, "you don't always have to tell Nonna everything, you know."

"Are baked beans a secret?"

"No, sweetheart. The beans are fine. It's the *can* that's a secret! *Cans* are always secret! And bottles! Or jars! Ketchup, mayonnaise . . ."

"And peanut butter?"

"What are you talking about?"

"That you eat on the couch when Papi isn't looking."

"*Sssshhhhhh!*"

How did he know about that?

My best friend is a woman from Connecticut named Katrina who moved to Italy around the time I did. Fresh out of Smith, she started out in 1998 wearing scrunchies in her hair and respectable Banana Republic tops, and soon found herself dating testosterone-driven Italian boys with too many hands in too many places. Now, seventeen years later, we call each other with life-altering dilemmas like this one: in the absence of chocolate chips and double-acting baking powder, is it possible to bake chocolate chip cookies and, if so, will they have the consistency of cobblestones?

Like me, Katrina is an adult woman with a family, a career, and an advanced degree who is forced to eat peanut butter in hiding. We call each other at the precise, delicious moment that we sit down on the couch with crackers, Diet Coke, and a jar of Skippy. We have to do it when our husbands are out of town; ours is a clandestine crunch. We've analyzed Italians' aversion to peanut butter, and have realized that it's not just the consistency (*O mio Dio!* It sticks to the roof of your mouth!); it's not just the fact that it comes from the United States (Do you know what they put in food there?), but is primarily classist.

It's not that Italians consider people who eat peanut butter low-class. It's the peanuts themselves that are low-class. Katrina's husband, Gianluca, who is not only Italian but also works in the food industry, explained to me that certain nuts are *nobile*, others aren't. The most noble, or aristocratic, nuts are apparently pistachios. Walnuts are also pretty hoity-toity, followed by hazelnuts and cashews. The most *cafone*, or low-class, are— you guessed it!—peanuts. To have a wife who not only eats hick nuts but eats them in processed, American form, on the *couch*, is a kind of disgrace.

Anthony had found me out. *Non vi preoccupate*, don't worry, I planned to tell my father-in-law if word got out, I may have a problem, but your grandchildren are safe from the processed hick nuts.

I couldn't say the same about sandwiches.

'A Marenna

"Fishing is not just about catching fish. It's about stillness, becoming one with nature. Breathing the ocean air. Hearing the lapping of the waves. It's about the process, not just the result. And if and when fish are caught, we are going to throw them back." Nobody was interrupting me. I was having an environmentalist, humanitarian field day. After all, this was an invaluable opportunity to teach my son a lesson! I was an American mother who would not see her children plundering, taking from the world! Who would not see her son brag about numbers, swaggering back to his preschool to tell how many fish he caught and how long they were! I would not have a little Mussolini triumphant in Ethiopia!

Nonna Raffaella waited patiently for me to stop.

Anthony totally ignored me, focused as he was on helping his father get the bait, a slippery little shrimp head, stuck on the hook.

It was early spring of 2009, and we were in Naples for the weekend. We had come down the steep steps to Marechiaro, a breathtaking corner of the rocky coastline. A restaurant down the shore had advised us where the fish were biting. Far from the discharge of garbage, the water was crystal-blue and we had each found a flat part of rock for our buttocks. The sun was shining, the kids were excited, and I was brimming with life lessons.

I was also in a particularly good mood because that day, for the first time ever, my children would eat sandwiches for lunch in broad daylight. In front of their grandmother. I had insisted on this, much to the confused dismay of Nonna. I wanted everyone involved to understand that the world would continue turning if we didn't schlep home to make pasta with vegetables or pork roast. It was a gorgeous day: we could get sandwiches and stay out at lunchtime.

Lessons and sandwiches! I was positively euphoric.

We had stopped at a little *salumeria* before starting down the steps to the water. The old man behind the counter with dirt (or maybe oil? basil?) under his fingernails was patient with all of our questions: "Anthony, do you want tuna? What kind of bread?" and "Will Lella eat *prosciutto crudo*?" and "Katherine, do you want to do half and half with peppers and *fior di latte*?" The *salumiere* waited, he advised which cheese would be best with the fried eggplants, and he said no when I asked for ricotta with zucchini. (Those two *non sposano bene*, they do not marry well. In fact, they fight big-time, he told me.) We were in his shop for the better part of an hour.

A note on sandwiches in Naples. In dialect, a serious sandwich is called a *marenna*, which sounds like the word for snack, *merenda*. This I think is indicative of how a sandwich is considered: it is not a legitimate meal. *Marenne* are eaten at construction sites and at soccer stadiums. Substituting a *marenna* for a real *pranzo* with first course, second course, vegetables, and fruit is one of the sacrifices that Neapolitan workmen make for their jobs and that Napoli fans make for their team.

When Salva was in middle and high school, the Napoli team had its heyday. Thanks to the "golden feet" of Diego Maradona, Naples crushed every other team in the Series A league, including the historically strongest teams of the North—Juventus, Inter, and Milan. Maradona led the Napoli team to win the national championship twice, after sixty years of northern victories. (Diego Maradona is an unofficial patron saint of the city. Devoted fans still light candles and lay fresh flowers at an altar dedicated to him in downtown Naples. He's fortunately kicked his cocaine habit and coaches in the Middle East.)

On Sundays during Napoli's glory days, Neapolitan *ragazzi* who didn't have tickets for the 2:30 game would get up at dawn and risk life and limb to climb the gates and sneak inside the San Paolo stadium.

Salva and his friends had tickets, and would bring their sandwiches to the stadium. That is, all his friends except Gino. Gino waited to hear the results at home, because he could not bring himself to eat a sandwich.

Recently, my family and I traveled to Munich to watch the Naples soccer team play Bayern Munich. There were thousands of Napoli fans, some of whom we met on our Alitalia flight to Germany. After takeoff, we could smell fried peppers. The expertly packaged *marenne* had been opened—and it was 8:00 A.M.! I decided to ask one of the young men about his sandwich. "*Signó*," he began. (Oh God, I'm old! These guys don't think twice about giving me the formal *signora*.) "*Siamo in trasferta. Chisto è 'a marenna*." It's an away game, ma'am. This here's our sandwich.

They were well-mannered *ragazzi*. I went back to my seat

with half of one of the most succulent sandwiches I'd ever tasted. I had protested: "No, thank you." "Really, I just had my cappuccino." "Come on, you'll want it for the game." None of my comments registered. I shouldn't have even tried. It was clear that I had no choice but to share the *marenna*.

"Papi, when are the fish gonna come?" Anthony had been holding the rod and staying still for a good twenty minutes. He wanted to catch a fish, and he wanted to catch one *now*. There you go, Salva! Now you can talk to him about the process, about patience. . . . But instead, it was: *"Adesso, amore. Lo sento!"* Now, my love. I feel it in the air!

Nonna Lella was sending text messages on her cellphone. Ever the multitasker, she was also playing peekaboo with little Lella and offering words of encouragement to Anthony and Salva. "Of course you're going to catch some! And I'm going to fry them tonight!" she offered cheerfully. I had stopped spurting my philosophical advice, and was starting to realize that I too would be extremely frustrated and pissed off if we didn't catch anything.

"I'm going to the bathroom! Be right back." Nonna Lella took off for the restaurant that was down the rocky beach. When she came back, Anthony and Salva still had not caught anything and we were all hot, hungry, and frustrated. Nonna told Anthony that she had seen a crab behind that rock over there—see if you can catch it, *amore*! At which point she produced from her Louis Vuitton handbag a plastic bag of dead fish and a small pasta strainer.

"The crab was crawling right over there! It can't have gone too far. . . ." She distracted him with her words as her hands flew. The plastic bag disappeared and she dumped three of the fish into the strainer and lowered it into the water. She was ready. *"Anthony! Vieni!"* Come! Look!

There was amazement in my son's face as he pulled up the pasta strainer. Nonna Lella grabbed it from him immediately so he wouldn't see that the fish were dead. "Three of them! You got three of them! And they're at least ten centimeters long! *Amore, sei bravissimo!"* Watch out, Ethiopia.

We looked in to see that they were not only dead but headless.

Nonna had gone to the kitchen of the restaurant and asked the chef if he could give her some fish for her *creatura*, her little grandchild. "He's fishing, and will be so disappointed if he doesn't catch anything. . . . How about those?"

"Ma'am, I've already taken the heads off. Was just about to fry them—"

"They're fine! Oh, and while you're at it, do you have a net or something so it will look like the boy 'caught' them himself?"

Che problema c'è?

"This is a very rare kind of fish. It's called the headless haddock," Nonna was explaining to Anthony when he asked why the fish he had caught had no heads. "They're so hard to catch. And they are delicious. Tonight, *frittura di pesce*! Now it's time for our *marenne*."

Throw them back? The process not the result? Patience in life? She had even invented the name of the fish! So much for lessons. Now at least we had the sandwiches for consolation.

I opened the bag and thought, Damn, we should have made labels so we knew whose sandwich was whose without having to open them all up. *Vediamo*, let's see. I pulled the first one out and saw something scribbled in ink on the brown paper packaging. *Entoni?* What did that mean? I got out the next one: *Nonna*.

Then *Papi Salva. Piccola Lella.* When I got to the big oily luscious monster at the bottom I saw *Mami Ketrin.*

While we conversed in the shop, the man had focused on
and remembered each of our names and, of course, our relationships. The sandwich man didn't just write Salva, or Ketrin,
but included the *papi* and *mami.* These *marenne,* the first sandwiches of my children's lives, were made specifically, personally,
lovingly, for each of us. The sun was still shining, and we had
caught a rare, delicious species of headless haddock with a pasta
strainer. Lessons or no lessons, things could have been a lot
worse.

Raffaella Junior

Nonna Raffaella had three grandsons, whom she tried to dress in lace well into elementary school. When a granddaughter was born, Raffaella's costuming instinct went ballistic. For as long as Nonna Raffaella could get away with it, little Raffaella wore things that were gorgeous, scratchy, expensive, and couldn't go in the washing machine.

And then my little Neapolitan American girl *s'è scetàta*, as they say in dialect. She woke herself up.

As a child, I knew one thing as a deep, unshakeable truth, and it was that my mother was beautiful and that she knew how to dress. I also knew that only dumb, lazy rich people shopped at places like Neiman Marcus and Lord & Taylor (we certainly couldn't afford to shop there, my mother convinced us, and wouldn't have, even if we could!).

Women who were smart shopped at one store, and one store only: Loehmann's.

We learned math by calculating the Loehmann's Red Dot

Sales prices for Mommy. She would ask us, "What is the 'compare at' price?" (Read: How much did your smart mommy save?) Anna and I learned addition, subtraction, and percentages at Loehmann's. We learned that you *can* get a Ralph Lauren evening gown for the National Symphony Ball for $13.99 and look fabulous in it. If you're smart.

We also learned about death and mortality at Loehmann's, when we saw an elderly lady collapse under a pile of clothes that she was going to try on in the dressing room of the Rockville, Maryland, store in 1984. "Girls," our mother told us, "that's probably how your mama's gonna go."

Unfortunately (and tragically for my mother), Loehmann's did not have children's clothes. So when it came time for Bonnie to bring clothes from the States to her granddaughter, my mother brought cheap, comfortable clothes from other discount stores. She waited with anticipation for her granddaughter's rite of passage: the day when she could take little Raffaella to the Loehmann's dressing room to find the bargains beyond all bargains. In the meantime, there would be no lace collars or subdued pastels. There would be $2.99 T.J.Maxx leopard skin leggings and Marshall's $6.99 (compare at $19.99!) fluorescent off-the-shoulder sweatshirts.

Little Raffaella ate them up. *These* were clothes.

My mother-in-law despaired. When we went to Naples, she would lay out pink cashmere wraps and dresses with frills on little Raffaella's bed as a "surprise." Silently, when no one was looking, little Raffaella would fold them neatly and replace them on her grandmother's bed.

"*Raffa, amore, hai visto il regalo di Nonna?*" Sweetheart, did you see Nonna's gift on your bed? Raffaella would ask over lunch, her smile concealing how important the outfit was to her.

My daughter would ignore the question and ask for some

more *pasta al forno*. "*È buonissima, Nonna!* It's the best *pasta al forno* that you've ever made."

She would *not* be wearing the frills.

I didn't get in the way. I was proud of her. My girl could negotiate her two worlds, her two identities, with *naturalezza*. She could appreciate the divine dishes that her *nonna* prepared but say no thanks to embroidery and lace.

When Nonna Raffaella finally gave up, little Raffaella was almost seven. My mother-in-law came to Rome with a shoe box in one last-ditch effort to save her grandchild. "*Le scarpe, Ketrin, solo le scarpe,*" she whispered to me, on the verge of tears. The shoes, just the shoes. Give me that, at least.

They were patent leather Mary Janes. There was no chance. Once again, I stayed out of it, leaving the two Raffaellas in my daughter's room to hash it out. I heard a few words through the door, though. "*Amore, hai visto come stai meglio? Come sei elegante? È tutta un'altra cosa!*" Love, can't you see how much better you look? How elegant they are? You look like a different person!"

And then my daughter. Trying to make her grandmother understand, patiently explaining an obvious truth. "Nonna, don't you see? I can run *so* much faster in these sneakers! And if they get dirty it's no big deal. Bonnie got them seventy percent off at Target."

Lasagne

Of there were a New Testament play in Neapolitan, I imagine Nonna Raffaella in two possible roles. One is the female lead, the Virgin Mary, and the other is a man who is not named, who is simply called a friend.

First, Maria. Her most important line is one word, and one of my favorite expressions in Italian. *Eccomi.* Here I am. But even simpler than "Here I am," because it is just one word, fluid vowels flowing into consonants. *eh-ko-me:* one word that sums up her approach to life. When the Archangel Gabriel came to give Mary the Son-of-God-in-Your-Tummy announcement, Mary's response was *Eccomi.* It was not *"What the **?!"* or *"Actually, I'm not even married"* or *"When were you thinking, 'cause I was planning on finishing my degree?"* It was a very simple *Eccomi.*

This is the expression that Nonna Raffaella uses when someone asks her for help, for time, or for lasagna. "Raffaella? Salva is really down and stressed about work. Can you make him a *sartù di riso*?" *Eccomi!* "Raffaella? I'm worn out by the kids. Can you take them for a few days so I can rest?" *Eccomi!* No questions asked or emotional price tag attached. Here I am.

The other role for Raffaella would be the man who figured out a way to get his paralyzed friend into the crowded house where Jesus was performing miracles. The tiny house was packed and there was a multitude outside the door, trying to make it in. A crowd of the crippled, the sick, the desperate. The friend cut a hole in the roof, and with some helpers lowered the paralyzed man down to where Jesus was preaching.

Che problema c'è? I imagine Raffaella saying to her friend paralyzed on a mat. I'll get you in. Who needs a door?

I imagine her cheerfully studying the logistics of the house and finding the right instruments. I imagine her calling three friends (all Neapolitan women, all in Pucci caftans) to help her cut a hole in the roof. I imagine them lowering their friend down to Jesus, not even seeing Him themselves. Lowering their friend through the roof and making it home in time to prepare lunch for the family.

<hr />

Last summer Raffaella invited some of her blond, Botoxed friends to Positano for a girls' beach week. No men allowed. "And Nino?" I asked her. Her husband is past eighty now, and depends on her for everything. "*L'ho sistemato,*" she answered— I set him up. "Mitzi will take care of cooking, and I've organized a gin rummy playdate for him every afternoon. *Ketrin? Ci vuole.*" Katherine? I need it. I need to take care of myself, too.

Five *signore* packed their sparkly fuchsia bikinis in Louis Vuitton suitcases and headed to Positano to join Lella for beach week. During the day, they sunbathed and read magazines. In the evenings they played cards until 3:00 A.M. And the food? "Sometimes, Ketrin, you don't feel like cooking."

Raffaella had Mitzi cook platters of risotto, *insalata caprese*, and *babà* cakes in Naples. She had trained him well, and the dishes tasted almost like hers. It sounded like she was coming close to trusting him. How did he get the stuff to Positano, though? Mitzi doesn't drive, and Raffaella certainly couldn't bring it several days in advance!

A hole in the roof big enough for a paralyzed man? The delivery of a feast on the beach of Positano? Why not?

Sri Lankan Mitzi with his New York Yankees baseball cap arrived from Naples on the *aliscafo*, the motorboat that crosses the bay. Raffaella, in her flowing beach cover-up, met the boat at the pier flanked by three of her cohorts, and examined the trays of food to be sure that Mitzi had cooked them to her satisfaction. "Make sure Nino is dressed properly for the gin rummy game at four," she reminded Mitzi after thanking him for his delivery. She bought him a croissant and a glass of cold milk on the pier before sending him back to Naples on the next *aliscafo*.

When beach week was over, and Nino went to pick up his wife at the port of Naples, he found her radiant and rejuvenated. Stepping down off the *aliscafo* with her posse, all talking at once, she rushed up to Nino, kissed him, and caressed his cheek. Her giddiness was like an adolescent's, not that of a sixty-five-year-old *signora*. She was ready to go home and embrace domestic life just as she embraced her beach week with the girls. When Nino sulked a little bit, miffed that she had left him for a week and that she had such fun without him, she asked what she could prepare him for dinner.

"*Lasagne*," he replied. Elaborate, time-consuming, his favorite dish. Mitzi, after all, doesn't make it just the way she does. And Raffaella's response to her husband of forty years was one word: *Eccomi*.

Salad

I make really good salad dressing. It's in my blood. My grandfather, the southern preacher of Italian origins, was known for his salads. When his church, in Hinton, West Virginia, hosted potluck dinners, the congregation would not expect my grandmother to bake a casserole. She didn't melt marshmallows over sweet potatoes or baste a pot roast. She bought the lettuce, picked the tomatoes, got out the great big wooden bowl, and left Reverend Salango to it.

I can't say how much oil, vinegar, salt and pepper, or garlic he used or my mother uses or I use. Impossible to quantify the amount of feta cheese or onion; impossible to describe in words how we do it. Which is a sign, I learned in Naples, that we know how to do it really, really well. Salads are in our DNA.

It was in my Americanized kitchen in Rome that I first made a salad for Raffaella. She had opened her magical suitcase, with eggplant Parmesan, mozzarella, lasagna, and *pizzette* from Naples. The kids and Salva dug into the suitcase, and I asked Raffaella what *she* wanted for lunch. She'd been up since 6:00 A.M. baking, buying the freshest mozzarella, and had just arrived on the Eurostar train. "*Solo insalata*," she said. Thanks, Ketrin, just a salad.

I got to work. Without thinking, measuring, or judging, I made the salad that I know how to make. I told Raffaella that she had to sit down and eat, the kids could wait. I served her.

"*Ketrin, è fantastica!*" This is the best salad I've ever tasted, she said. I'm having a lunch for the ladies next Friday—could you teach me how to make it? Is there more? Could you make some more?

I reached for a jar to fill with my salad dressing. As I squeezed the garlic and poured the vinegar, I heard the kids and Salva in the living room, laughing and fighting over the contents of the suitcase. Papi, I get the mozzarella! That's mine! Lella, those *pizzette* are for us, too!

There's enough to go around, I called out to my children. Nobody's going hungry.

I screwed the lid on the jar of salad dressing and wrapped it in cellophane. Then I rolled a sheet of newspaper around it and fitted on some rubber bands to keep the packaging in place. It was ready: Raffaella could take it with her on the train back to Naples.

Please appreciate the numbers that are included in the following recipes. They weren't easy to get. As Raffaella plopped and poured, stirred, and talked, I called Mitzi surreptitiously in from his living room rug cleaning to ask how much oil was in the pot, or how much that piece of mozzarella weighed. I had to use the stopwatch function on my iPhone to know how long the meat had been frying. It was better to do this unbeknownst to Raffaella: running numbers by her resulted in a confused, pained look on her face. It was enough to take the Joy out of Cooking.

Ragù

(Serves 6 to 8)

1 small yellow onion, diced

½ cup extra-virgin olive oil

¾ pound *gallinella di maiale*,* divided in three quarter-pound,
2-inch cubes

¾ pound veal shank, divided in three quarter-pound, 2-inch
cubes

2 pork ribs (about ¾ pound together), split lengthwise in
2-inch pieces

1 glass red wine

2¼ tablespoons tomato paste

Six 15-ounce cans of the purest peeled tomatoes you can find
(Check ingredients! See below!)

Salt to taste

A few leaves of basil

1½ pounds rigatoni

A handful of large-grain salt (sea salt, for example)
for boiling pasta

1 cup grated Parmesan

Fresh bread

**Gallinella di maiale* is Neapolitan dialect for the meaty muscle from the lower part
of the pig's thigh. (I come from the *We use every part of the pig but the squeal!* Wilson

My mother-in-law knows you're busy (*"Chiste hanno 'a fa, non tengono tiempo,"* she says. These people don't have time, Ketrin, they've got things to do), so here's the three-hour *ragù* recipe rather than the twelve-hour one. She also knows you'd prefer olive oil to lard, and that you probably don't have a pot that's made of hardened clay. So here's what you need and here's what she'll give you: a recipe for "rushed" *ragù*.

First, put an apron on, and don't think of removing it until you've turned off the stove. When the *ragù* starts to spit, it takes no prisoners. Get a pot that is not only wide but tall. (The height is important when the sauce spatters—Raffaella is worried about your kitchen as well as your clothes.) Dice the onion and put it in the pot with the olive oil.

Non ti ho detto di accendere ancora. She hasn't told you to turn on the flame yet, so keep your pants on. Position all the chunks of meat on top of the oil and onion, and scrunch them in tight with your fingers. Shanks and hocks, pigs and cows—all down there together, at the bottom of the cool pot.

Now it's time to turn on a medium-low flame. *Si deve imbiondire la cipolla,* the onion has to become blond, and the meat has to *rosolare,* pinken. You can put away dishes, or wash a pan in the meantime. You'll be tempted, like me, to keep walking over to the pot to make sure something bad doesn't happen. But you've got to leave it alone. It's like raising kids. They're always there, in your mind, but you don't have to hover over them. Don't be a helicopter parent to your *ragù.*

Move the chunks of meat around every once in a while with your wooden spoon so they don't stick to the bottom of the pot. After 8 or 9 minutes, turn the pieces over. The meat is re-

family but have no idea what this is called in English. Boned pork foreleg, possibly?) Talk to your butcher. The important thing is that it is fleshy and divided in three quarter-pound, 2-inch cubes.

leasing water, and will continue to do so for about 20 minutes. As long as there is water in the pot, it's too early to add the wine. You know there is water because of all the brown bubbles. (I thought that was oil boiling, but no, it's water. Oil doesn't boil. *What, do you fry blindfolded, Ketrin?*)

When the meat is a dark crusty brown, the onion looks a little burned, and there are fewer bubbles, turn up the heat to high. Pour a few drops of dark red wine on each chunk of meat, like you are performing a baptism. (*Nel nome del Padre, del Figlio, e dello Spirito Santo.*) Enjoy the sound it makes. After a minute or two, repeat until you have poured the whole glass of wine.

Continue to scrape the sides and bottom of the pot regularly. The chunks of meat should slide around more easily now, and the sides should look like you are never in a million years going to get this pot clean.

In the pools of dark purply-brown liquid in between the pieces of meat, drop half-teaspoon dollops of tomato paste. After plopping in each dollop, *stemperatelo*, mash it with the back of your wooden spoon. The paste should become one with the liquid in the pot. (You've been at this for around 45 minutes now, but don't despair! The *avviamento* of the *ragù* — setting it on its way — is almost completed. The time is coming when you're going to send this *ragù* off to college.)

A word on the tomatoes that you are about to pour in. The six cans of peeled tomatoes sitting on the counter ready to be ground up would ideally have been canned by you, during hot summer days, with your womenfolk. Since they probably haven't, you must trust the brand you have chosen. The ingredients should say: TOMATOES. *Basta*. Okay, salt we can let slide. But if it says anything else . . . Raffaella will teach you how to can your own. Oregano? Garlic? Preservatives? *Scordatelo*. Forget about it.

With an immersion blender, grind up three cans of the tomatoes you've chosen and add them to the pot. Continue to scrape the bottom and sides of the pan. After a few minutes, grind up the other three cans and add them to the now red *ragù*.

Turn the flame down as low as it will go—*piano piano piano piano!*—gently gently softly softly!—and cover the pot. Now you can get back to your busy life. (But remember, don't take off your apron, because in about an hour, your *ragù* is going to start spitting up a storm.) The sound that until now has been a frying *zzzzsssssssshhhhhhh* now should become a very mellow *bloop . . . bloop . . . bloop*, which Raffaella calls *purpullià*. (I thought the verb was *pippiare*, but I've heard *pappulià*, *pippulià . . .* apparently there are as many Neapolitan terms for the slow boiling of *ragù* as Eskimos' terms for snow.)

Check on your *ragù* every half hour or so. Take the cover off the pot, and wipe away the water on the underside of the lid that has accumulated from the steam. Add salt and the basil leaves. Stir the *ragù*, and make sure it doesn't stick to the sides and bottom of the pot. Admire how it is becoming denser, darker, and more *arraggià*—Neapolitan dialect for angry, but meaning tense and dense. A spitfire.

Cover the pot again. After hour two, you can take out all the pieces of meat except the ribs: leave them in until the end. When the *ragù* has been cooking for three hours total, turn off the flame. Boil rigatoni in salted water (use coarse sea salt for the pasta water, never table salt!) and after straining, dump the pasta into the pot of deep red *ragù*. Sprinkle grated Parmesan and serve with fresh bread to sop up the *ragù*. The pieces of meat can be served *after* all the pasta has been consumed, never together.

Ecco fatto: all done. Now you can take off your apron.

Insalata di Polipo

(Serves 6 to 8)

> One 2-pound octopus
> ¼ cup chopped parsley, extra for garnish
> ½ cup extra-virgin olive oil
> 1 clove of garlic, cut in quarters
> Salt to taste
> ¼ cup lemon juice, extra lemon slices for garnish

Raffaella starts her preparation of the octopus with this warning: You must make sure your *polipo* is *verace*. *Verace* means
authentic—an octopus that is a real Neapolitan, and not some
impostor from the Indian Ocean. You may trust your fishmonger; for all Raffaella knows, he may have been the best man in
your wedding. But still, my mother-in-law asks you to double-
check that he has sold you an octopus that is *verace*: a real, fresh,
just-yesterday-he-was-clinging-to-a-cave-in-Marechiaro octopus.

The way you do this is to look for a "double crown" of suction cups on each tentacle. Two parallel rows of suckers, or
you've been had. If he's the real thing, get out your meat hammer and cutting board and go to town. Pound the octopus as
hard as you can on the cutting board with a meat tenderizer.

Crush his squishy, slimy brains out. Then, in a calmer mode, put him under running water and caress his body, gently pulling off any little black filaments.

Turn his slippery head sac inside out with your fingers (*Peekaboo!* Raffaella sings with a sly smile), and take out all the gloop. Dig your fingers deep under the head to remove the *polipo*'s hard "beak."

In a large pot, boil water with the cork from a wine bottle. Hold the octopus by the head above the pot and dip its tentacles three times in the boiling water. Check out the octopus's curly new hairdo. Put the whole animal in, turn down the flame, and cover. You must maintain a *bollo dolce*, a gentle boil, meaning that the water continues to boil without spilling over the sides. To do this, Raffaella poises her wooden spoon between the lid and the edge of the pot.

Cook the octopus for 20 minutes. The water will become a dark pink, like rosé wine. (This piping-hot pink octopus water used to be drunk with salt and pepper on January 5, the night before Epiphany, in downtown Naples. It was served with the end of the octopus's tentacle, or *'a ranfetella*, floating in the cup, and it really warms you up, apparently. If someone gives you an espresso that isn't strong enough and you want to tell them it's too watery, you can say, "Hey, this octopus water is missing its tentacle!")

Turn the flame off, and let the octopus stay in the water until it cools. This can take a long time, so if you want to speed things up and the weather's chilly, take the pot outside. When it has cooled, take the octopus out and snip it into ½-inch pieces with scissors. Cut the parsley leaves (again, with scissors is the easiest way) and mix them with the octopus, olive oil, garlic, and salt. Let the *insalata* sit for at least one hour at room temperature. Add the lemon juice before serving, and garnish with slices of lemon and parsley leaves.

PS: Raffaella is worried about the fishy smell of your kitchen, your cookware, and your fingers. She hopes, for your own good and that of everyone in your family, that you've turned on the ventilator. For the bowls and your hands, smush damp, used coffee grounds around the pots with your fingertips before washing them with dish soap.

Parmigiana di Melanzane

(Serves 6 to 8)

  4 pounds eggplants (see below for physical requirements)
  Two 15-ounce cans of Italian peeled, whole tomatoes
  10 basil leaves
  1 clove garlic
  Salt to taste
  2 cups peanut oil
  1 cup grated Parmesan cheese
  1 cup *fior di latte* or other soft mozzarella-like cheese,
    cut in cubes a little smaller than dice

Your eggplants must be long, skinny, hard, and so dark they're almost black. *Insomma*, like a tall, fit Italian woman after a summer on the beach in Positano. Eggplants with the least pulp and seeds (found in summer and early fall) make the best *parmigiana*, Raffaella says. The ones you find in winter tend to be fleshy and moist inside and need to be dried out for at least a day. Otherwise all their white flesh will absorb the frying oil and you'll get a greasy *parmigiana*. One of the worst insults you can lay on someone's *parmigiana* in Naples is that it's greasy.

Cut the stems off your eggplants, and use a carrot peeler to take two long strips of skin off each of them, from opposite lengthwise sides. Then cut them (again, lengthwise) in slices ½ centimeter thick (1/10 of an inch). Each slice will be framed by some skin, but no slice will have an entirely purple side. Place the slices of eggplant on an unlined cookie sheet and set them out to dry. (Letting them sunbathe on your roof or balcony is ideal, but if that's not possible, lay them around the house. Warn family members not to knock them over, Raffaella reminds you.)

To get rid of the moisture in the eggplants, let them perspire for as long as possible. When you take them off the tray to fry them, you'll notice wet patches on the tray where they've been lying. This is good: it means they'll fry quickly and lightly, without absorbing oil.

Before frying the eggplant slices, begin your tomato sauce. With an immersion blender, grind up the contents of the cans of tomatoes (remember, the ingredients should say: TOMATOES, *e basta*) and put them in a pot with a few of the basil leaves and one smushed garlic clove. (*Gli dai un pugno in testa, e si toglie la camicia*, Raffaella says: Punch it on the head and its shirt will come off.) Cover the pot and cook on low for about 20 minutes. (After 10 minutes, take the lid off or wedge your wooden spoon between the rim of the pot and the lid. We don't want watery sauce.) Add salt to taste.

As the sauce simmers away, turn back to your bathing beauties. Line a tray with paper towels, to receive the slices of eggplant after they've been fried. Heat up your peanut oil so that it's hot enough to make the pieces sizzle but not so hot that they smoke. (Try the sizzle test with the edge of one piece before sliding them all in. If the piece bubbles, the oil is ready.) Now ease the slices in for their hot bath. Put in enough pieces to cover the surface of the oil, but not so many that they're crowded on top of each other. (Think of vacationers on the beaches of the Amalfi coast in mid-August. People are touching each other, but it would be uncool to get on top of anyone.) Flip them after about a minute, and then take them out when you see that they are becoming light brown. (This should happen pretty quickly if they've sweated properly beforehand.) Use a skimmer to take the slices out, and hold them over the pan to let the excess oil drain off before positioning the eggplant on the paper towels. Cover the slices with more paper towels to absorb the oil (Repeat: *My* parmigiana *will not be greasy!*). Make sure the oil is still hot enough for the next batch—if not, pump up the fire. After frying the next round of slices, position them on top of their predecessors, separated by paper towels. Repeat the process until you've fried all the eggplant. Preheat the oven to 375 degrees.

Now assemble the layers of the *parmigiana* in an 8-by-8-inch casserole dish. Start by putting a few spoonfuls of tomato sauce on the bottom of the dish and smoothing it into a red carpet with the back of your wooden spoon. Then arrange the first layer of eggplant slices (slightly shriveled and brown now, as if they've spent too much time at a tanning salon) side by side across the bottom of the dish. Spread another layer of tomato sauce on top of the eggplant, and sprinkle a few spoonfuls of Parmesan cheese evenly across it. Tear some basil leaves with your fingers (never touch basil with a knife, because it alters the taste! *Mi raccomando!*), and drop the torn leaves to the north, south, east, and west. Then distribute about a third of the *fior di latte* cubes.

The next layer of eggplant slices should be placed crosswise to the one before, so that the *parmigiana* is easier to cut. Continue with the same pattern—eggplant slices (each layer running crosswise to the one before), sauce, Parmesan, basil, and *fior di latte*.

Stop the pattern after the Parmesan. The top of the *parmigiana* should be Parmesan-dotted red, with only a vague hint of the brown treasures inside. Bake at 375 degrees for about 25 minutes, or until you see a crust forming on the top. Serve at room temperature.

If your *parmigiana* turns out greasy or is swimming in oil, please don't mention to anyone where you got the recipe.

Sartù di Riso

(Serves 6 to 8)

RAGÙ

1 small yellow onion, diced

½ cup extra-virgin olive oil

2¼ pounds of meat (boned pork foreleg, veal shank, pork ribs.
See recipe for *ragù*, page 268) in 2-inch cubes

1 glass red wine

2¼ tablespoons tomato paste

Six 15-ounce cans of peeled, whole tomatoes

Salt to taste

A few leaves of basil

MEATBALLS

2 cups day-old bread (the soft inner part of a loaf works best)

¾ pound ground beef

1 egg

Salt

⅓ cup Parmesan cheese

About 2 cups peanut oil

SARTÙ FILLING

5 eggs

3 tablespoons extra-virgin olive oil

2 small (¼ pound each) fresh pork sausages

½ white onion

One 15-ounce can cooked peas or 1½ cups frozen peas

Salt to taste

1 pound arborio rice

Butter for casserole dish

1½ cups grated Parmesan cheese

2 cups *fior di latte* or other soft mozzarella-like cheese,
    cut in cubes a little smaller than dice

4–6 leaves of basil

The *sartù di riso* isn't hard, Raffaella reassures you, it just takes organization and assembly. (And a big table, I would add. And an efficient, empty dishwasher. And a well-developed capacity for multitasking. And a few other things . . .) The various elements can be cooked ahead of time, frozen, and defrosted if need be. It's particularly helpful if you've already made the *ragù* and the baby meatballs.

(Heads up! Have *ragù* at the ready and make the baby meatballs first! Raffaella says, *che problema c'è* if you haven't prepared these beforehand. But I would argue that there is a *problema*.)

Prepare the *ragù* if you haven't yet (see page 268).

For the meatballs: Take off your rings. In a bowl, soak the day-old bread in 4 cups water. Smush together the ground beef, egg, salt, and Parmesan. Squeeze the bread to release as much water as possible, add it to the meat mixture with your greasy, sticky hands, and work it together like dough. Then roll out little marble-sized balls. Put the peanut oil in a tall pot or deep fryer and heat it over a high flame. As the oil heats up to its sizzling temperature, line a tray with paper towels. Fry the little balls for a few minutes or until they become light brown (they should float around in the oil, bubbling away. Don't skimp on the oil and don't crowd the meatballs). Remove them with a skimmer, and place them on the paper towels. Like anything small and fried, they are at risk of being stolen by hungry, roaming family members. Keep your wooden spoon at the ready: these *polpettine* are destined for your *sartù*.

For the *sartù* and to assemble: Boil 3 of the eggs in a pot of water for 10 minutes, and while they are cooking, put 1 tablespoon of the olive oil in a small skillet with 1 cup water. Cut the ends off the sausages and poke holes in them with a fork. Put them in the oily water, cover the skillet, and cook over a medium flame. The water will boil off and the sausages will brown. This will take 10 to 15 minutes.

When the eggs are done, place them in a bowl of ice water for a few minutes so you can shell them more easily. Take the sausages off the fire, cut them into 1-centimeter (quite thin) rounds, and set them aside in a bowl. Dice the onion, and in another skillet, heat the remaining 2 tablespoons of olive oil. Sauté the onion over a low-medium flame until it starts to brown. If you're using canned peas, drain them first and then put them in the skillet with the onions; frozen peas can be thrown in still frozen. Cover the pan and let the peas and onions cook for 5 minutes (10 to 15 if you're using frozen peas). Put the pea mixture in a bowl, then form an assembly line with the *ragù*, Parmesan, peas, sausage rounds, meatballs, *fior di latte*, and basil. Shell the eggs, cut them in quarters, and put them next to the sausage rounds and cooked peas on the assembly line.

In a tall pot, bring to boil 34 ounces (1 liter) of water mixed with two ladles of *ragù* and some salt. Put your rice into the orangey-red boiling water and stir. Take out a few ladles of the liquid and put them in another small pot on the stove. (The rice should absorb all the water like a risotto, but if it gets too dry, this hot broth will be useful. Ten or twelve more burners on your stovetop and a sous-chef would also be useful at this point.) Cover the pot of rice. Make sure you maintain the *bollo dolce*—the gentle boil that keeps on boiling!—and stir regularly. Turn off the fire 2 minutes before the advised cooking time of your rice, so that it's not crunchy hard but al dente. If the rice is cooked too much, your *sartù* will become a *papocchia*, or pigs' mush. (*Per carità!* Lord help us.) Let it cool.

Preheat the oven to 400 degrees. In a large bowl, beat the remaining 2 eggs with a fork, add a pinch of salt, and set aside. Using a piece of paper towel, spread butter over the bottom and sides of a deep casserole dish (Raffaella's is 3 inches tall, 9 by 13 inches across) to make a *velo di burro*, a veil of butter. Plop a ladle of *ragù* on the bottom of the pan and spread it out with the back of your wooden spoon. Make sure your rice is cool, then stir it into the beaten eggs. (If the rice isn't cool enough, you'll inadvertently scramble the eggs. Please. These eggs are what holds the *sartù* together—Raffaella says *unite* the *sartù*—important eggs, for heaven's sake.) Now stir into the rice pot one ladle of *ragù*, 2 spoonfuls of grated Parmesan cheese, a third of the sausage rounds, a third of the meatballs, a third of the peas, and a third of the *fior di latte*.

Put down a 1-inch-thick layer of *sartù* on the *ragù*-lined bottom of the pan and level it out with the back of your spoon. Spread out another layer of *ragù* on top: your rice needs to be *ben salsato*, or sauced up, Raffaella says, otherwise it will stop in your throat. Not pretty. Distribute a few more spoonfuls of Parmesan, a third of the peas, sausage rounds, meatballs, cubes of *fior di latte*, and a few torn-up leaves of basil. Start again with another layer of rice.

Now it's time to pretend you're the Easter Bunny and hide 6 of the hard-boiled-egg quarters in the middle of the casserole where nobody can find them. Don't tell anyone where you put them. Dig little holes if you need to. (Raffaella puts her glasses on for this hide-and-seek.) Repeat the pattern once more: rice, sauce, Parmesan, the last thirds of the peas, sausage, meatballs, *fior di latte*, and basil, and make the Easter egg hunt with the remaining hard-boiled-egg quarters. End with sauce and Parmesan. Bake at 400 degrees for 20 minutes or until the *sartù* forms a crust on top. Dollop some hot *ragù* on each slice before serving.

ACKNOWLEDGMENTS

It isn't easy when you're a *mamma* to let your baby go. You need people to hold your hand, put up with your craziness, and look at your little one, the piece of your heart, and say, "Hey, she's got a blob of something on her chin" that you hadn't noticed. Or "Don't you think it's time for a training bra?" You need loving, smart people to help her grow. It does take a village.

The village that has raised this book extends to both sides of the Atlantic. Without my agent, Anna Stein, the baby would be a pile of crumpled-up pages spat out by my wonky printer. She believed in it from the get-go and knew exactly what it needed, always. David Vine is a friend with a great big capital Quaker F for leading me to her. To the bicontinental guardian angels at Aitken Alexander, including Sally Riley, Nishta Hurry, Lesley Thorne, Alex Hoyt, and Clare Alexander: thank you for guiding me along the way.

At Random House, Andrea Walker is not only a brilliant editor but manages to be therapist and friend at the same time. She has been a true partner in raising the baby with *calma,* laughter, and peace of mind. Your little Tillie is blessed. Thanks also to Andy Ward for his help in the literary kitchen. And rather than thanking Susan Kamil in words for her passion and faith in this story, I'm going to help my mother-in-law get that *parmigiana di melanzane* to her office in New York (fresh, and at the right temperature!) so, hopefully, when we manage that, she'll be able to taste our gratitude.

Thank you to Ann Patty, who got me on course, and to John Thavis, who helped me stay there.

Early readers and friends Jordan Roth, Josh Conviser, Josephine Scorer, Dave Digilio, Massimiliano and Mireille Paolucci-Smit, Marco Maltauro, Alejandra Pero, Leo Kittay and Kim Dooley Kittay, Lynn Swanson, Heather Perrault, Silvia dell'Olio, Mercedes Roza, William Pratesi-Urquhart, Mike Rudolph, Laurie Kaye, Azar Burnham-Grubbs, Fee Huebner, and Doris Rametsteiner: *grazie, danke, bedankt*. I am so grateful for the atrium of Ambrit International School in Rome, and for the help and support of Paolo Isotta, Kris Dahl, Jennifer Gilmore, Renato de Falco, and of Ken, Vickie, and Alix Wilson.

Giovanni Vitale's rules of Neapolitan dialect (expertly compiled in his *Dialetto Napoletano: Manuale di scrittura e di dizione*) were an invaluable resource. *Grazie assai*.

The friendship of Kiersten Miller is a jewel at the center of my chaotic Roman life. At her Milk Bar, I've learned that when the going gets tough, the tough need to hang out for a little while with bighearted women from Naples and New York. Preferably over Ponzu.

Theo and Jim Yardley: Thank God you came to Rome. You are *maestri* of the craft and true friends.

Thanks to Monica Barden for her constant encouragement, generosity, and inclusiveness. Pia and Giuseppe Signori, Giorgio and Claudia: you have taught me the deepest meaning of family. And Antonio Mormone, I hope your spirit never wanes. The world needs it.

Katrina Smith and Gianluca Franzoni have come to the rescue often, and our friendship is a *punto di riferimento* that I cherish. The image of the two of you laughing together over the manuscript on your porch in Bologna was what I needed at just the right moment. Katrina, I hope we're smuggling Reese's Peanut Butter Cups into an Italian nursing home together one day.

Gracias infinitas to Irene Hernandez, my mentor from Madrid, who didn't say "I'm here for you," when on the verge of tears I suggested lighting a bonfire, holding hands, and throwing my manuscript in page by page. She said, Please! Will you stop being so *Neapolitan?*

Antonella Dugo is the grandmother of this book, and Andreas Giannakoulas its grandfather. You helped me to find and trust my voice, whether it was wobbly and off-key or full-bodied and right on pitch. Thanks also to my soul sister Jackie, for keeping me laughing no matter what. And for screaming at me, often, *Mommy! Write your book!*

To the Crossley family and especially my friend Tara, I am grateful every day that people of such faith have crossed my path. Thank you, Tara, for being an example of pressing on toward the goal, and running the race. And for reminding me always of what the prize really is.

To the whole Avallone family: My father-in-law asks me never to say thank you. Thank you assumes you're not family. So I won't say thank you, I'll say read the book. But I'll add that there are two people whose place in the story is infinitely smaller than their place in my heart: my nephew Claudio d'Albore and Nino himself. Thank you for loving me like a daughter.

And, finally, Salvatore, Anthony, and Raffaella: *Siete la mia vita.*

About the Type

THIS BOOK was set in Electra, a typeface designed for Linotype by renowned type designer W. A. Dwiggins (1880–1956). Electra is a fluid typeface, avoiding the contrasts of thick and thin strokes that are prevalent in most modern typefaces.

FLEET

To buy any of our books and to find out
more about Fleet, our authors and titles, as well
as events and book clubs, visit our website

www.littlebrown.co.uk

and follow us on Twitter

@FleetReads
@LittleBrownUK

To order any Fleet titles p & p free in the UK,
please contact our mail order supplier on:

+ 44 (0)1832 737525

Customers not based in the UK should contact
the same number for appropriate postage
and packing costs.